Northamptonshire County Council
Libraries and Information Service

Please return or renew this item by the last date shown.
You may renew items (unless they have been requested
by another customer) by telephoning, writing to or calling
in at any library.   100% recycled paper   *BKS 1 (5/95)*

GUESS MY STORY

The life and opinions of Keith Andrew, Cricketer

GUESS MY STORY

The life and opinions of
Keith Andrew, Cricketer

Stephen Chalke

with a foreword by
Micky Stewart

FAIRFIELD BOOKS

Fairfield Books
17 George's Road, Fairfield Park, Bath BA1 6EY
Tel 01225-335813

First published 2003

ISBN 0 9531196 8 8

Printed and bound in Great Britain by
Bookcraft Ltd, Midsomer Norton, Bath BA3 4BS

for

Joyce

who has done so much over the years
to make this a happy story

CONTENTS

	Foreword by Micky Stewart		8
1	A Good Memory		10
2	Guess My Story	*1954-1955*	18
3	Early Days at Northampton	*1953-1954*	31
4	A Lad in Lancashire	*1929-1952*	44
5	Looking for Replacements	*Northamptonshire*	60
6	Technical Development	*1953-1961*	69
7	Where is Wicket-Keeping Going?	*1955-1961*	86
8	Who, Me?	*1962-1963*	98
9	A Winning Formula	*1961-1965*	112
10	Let's Be More Imaginative	*Into the future*	134
11	A Month to Remember	*August 1965*	138
12	A Wonderful Adventure		163
13	Back to the Grass Roots	*1975-1994*	171
14	A Lucky Man		182
	Acknowledgements		184
	Index		186

FOREWORD

by Micky Stewart, O.B.E.

Keith and I first crossed paths during our days of National Service in the early 1950s when we were both stationed in the Aldershot area. I had come straight from school, and Keith's service had been deferred a couple of years or so whilst he completed an engineering qualification.

We played a lot of cricket together for representative teams – Aldershot Services, The Army and the Combined Services – and it was during this time that I first appreciated what an exceptionally talented wicket-keeper he was. He was not of the acrobatic technique of Godfrey Evans, England's keeper at the time, but his strong velvet-like hands, combined with quick anticipatory footwork, was the basis of his exceptionally consistent performances with the gloves.

In those days Keith could bat. Indeed we opened the innings together for Aldershot Services at times. He would like to be described as a deft stroke player with excellent placement rather than a hard hitter of the ball. I don't know what happened to his batting as his career progressed. He finished up hardly being able to hit the ball off the square, let alone to the boundary – but that's a trifle unkind, Keith!

He still tells the story of when he joined me in the middle, coming in as night-watchman against the 1963 West Indies team in the first Test at Old Trafford – of how he saw off the pace of Wes Hall and Charlie Griffith and the spin of Lance Gibbs and Gary Sobers. The facts are that we put on 38 runs and that he got a big nick off Sobers and was out for 15!

Although Keith was born a Lancashire lad in Oldham and used to tell me in those early days about his league cricket playing for Werneth, his first-class career was with Northants whom he eventually captained for many years. We competed against each other regularly with my playing for Surrey, and it was very obvious the respect he had gained both from the Northants team and the members and supporters.

It was similar respect he gained when taking over as Director of Coaching and then Chief Executive of the National Cricket Association in the final stages of his cricket career.

Keith was and still is a true cricket lover. He respected the traditional qualities of the game and always had the highest regard for those who played and worked voluntarily in what is called the Recreational Game – which is 99% of cricket in the U.K. He would fight his corner strongly with both the T.C.C.B. and the M.C.C. and never gave up an issue that he felt most strongly about. I know that surprised many round the table who had judged him on his quiet, calm image.

I will always know Keith Andrew as a lovely man, a real cricket man with a great sense of humour. An entertaining raconteur of stories of the personalities of cricket history – you would have to have at least half an hour to spare to

8

hear one of them – and as a magician of many tricks, a frustrated member of the Magic Circle.

It's been a pleasure and an honour to have been invited to write these few words but, Keith, if you had walked in 1957, when you nicked that one onto your pads, I would have had the world record of eight catches in an innings by myself, instead of sharing it on seven.

Micky Stewart
April 2003

Keith's reply

I thought it hit me just above the wrist, Micky, but on reflection, if I'd known that it was the world record, I'd have walked in any case – if only to get a celebratory drink from you at close of play.

Author's comment

Unfortunately, chaps, if Keith had walked, that would have left Harry Kelleher not out at the other end and he wouldn't have been 'caught Stewart'. So it would still have been only seven!

CHAPTER 1

A GOOD MEMORY

The wicket-keeper. Who is he?

He is the busiest man on the field. Each ball he goes down, watching with intense concentration as the bowler runs in, as the batsman prepares to play, as the ball comes off the pitch, even as the fielder runs into the deep and sends in his return. There is never a time when he is at the non-striker's end or catching his breath at fine leg. He is always concentrating.

He is the first one to notice that the bowler is growing tired, the first one to spot the technical flaws and the mental discomfort of the batsman, the only fielder who knows exactly how the ball is moving through the air and coming off the pitch. He is always at the centre of the game. Every movement comes under his watchful eye.

Yet who watches him? Who understands and can judge his movements? Who can explain the difference his skill makes to the fortunes of his team?

And with what confidence can we say who is our best keeper?

This is the story of a man reckoned by many to be one of the best wicket-keepers in the history of English cricket. Yet he played only twice for England, in Tests that were nine years apart.

Add that he was one of the most successful county captains of his generation, creating a winning side from a fairly unremarkable set of players, and that for twenty years he was a pivotal figure in the development of youth and recreational cricket, and his lack of recognition becomes hard to comprehend – until, of course, you meet him.

He has lived his life in the same style as he kept wicket, never drawing attention to himself.

*

I first met Keith Andrew in early 1998. I was interviewing cricketers of the 1960s for my book *Caught in the Memory*, and I asked Andrew Radd, devoted chronicler of Northamptonshire cricket, to recommend an old player from the county.

"Ideally I'd like somebody with a good memory, a nice turn of phrase, a sense of humour and some interesting opinions."

"Keith Andrew," he replied straightaway. "Definitely."

So, filled with expectation, I drove to Keith's village on the Bucks/Beds border, and we sat drinking coffee in the local hotel. I wanted to weave his memories around a particular match, and he chose a dramatic one at Cardiff in August 1965, when the unfancied Northants and Glamorgan sides were first and second in the championship table.

It was a special afternoon. We talked for three hours, and he introduced me to the wonderful mix of characters in the Northants dressing room that happy summer: the larger-than-life genius of Colin Milburn, the hypochondria of the gritty Brian Crump, the enigmatic persona of the ageing scorer Jack Mercer. "I'm amazed," he said, "at the things you've got me remembering." Then, as I packed up my tape recorder and papers, he beamed his appreciation. "You've given me a tonic today, talking about these people."

The sun had set by the time we went out into the car park. I gave him a copy of my first book, and he studied it with delight. He is the author of three books on cricket, on the skills of the game and its history, and his final remark rang in my ears for most of the journey home.

"I don't think I shall write another book now," he said, "but, if I did, I'd ask you to do it."

It was the best of interviews. We had found a wavelength and, even as he excavated the long-buried memories, his mind was spinning off intelligent observations on the game then and now. The chapter was easy to write and, when I sent it to a friend, whose critical opinion I always value, it came back with four words written across the top of the first page. 'What a lovely man!'

*

I do remember that summer of 1965. I was a seventeen year old, growing up near Salisbury, and my family watched and supported Hampshire – except that my mother decided that her first allegiance would be to Northamptonshire. She had lived there, in a little village called Farthinghoe, for the first two years of her life.

In winter, when the football results came on the television, she extended the fun by cheering whenever Northampton Town won.

And what fun it was when little Northampton Town started their improbable climb up the ladder. A fourth division side in 1961, they were winning promotion to the top flight in the spring of 1965.

Then in August of that year, while the footballers were training in readiness for Arsenal and Manchester United, the cricket team in the next door field spent all month at the head of the county championship table. On paper there was nothing special about their eleven players but somehow, under Keith Andrew's leadership, they had become winners.

Everything my mother touched seemed to have turned to gold.

*

Before I met Keith, I had listened to many of the players of the 1950s talking about the best wicket-keepers of their generation.

Godfrey Evans was the showman who thrived in the limelight. In Test matches his whole performance was inspirational. But in county cricket, they told me, he rarely bothered.

When they talked about the best county keepers, other names were proffered. There was Surrey's Arthur McIntyre, standing up all day to Laker, Lock and Bedser on the awkward Oval pitches. There was Somerset's Harold Stephenson, nimble and undemonstrative but never getting the whiff of an England cap. Yorkshire's Jimmy Binks, Nottinghamshire's Geoff Millman, even Gloucestershire's miscreant Peter Rochford.

But one name would always come up: Keith Andrew. It was as if it were a secret of their professional fraternity that he had gone about his business with such superb technique, with such style, for so long. His Northants team-mate Dennis Brookes summed it up: "Keith wasn't showy. Sometimes it can act against you if you are not flamboyant. On the big occasion Godfrey turned it on. Day to day Keith was far better."

One day, in his *Daily Telegraph* column, Michael Parkinson set about selecting an all-time team of cricket's greatest stylists, and his final twelve would be a joy for any spectator. For batting, there was Barry Richards, Jack Robertson, Tom Graveney, David Gower and Greg Chappell. For all-rounders, he had Keith Miller and Garfield Sobers. For bowlers, Dennis Lillee, Michael Holding, Fred Trueman and Bishen Bedi.

And the wicket-keeper? He lingered on the decision. 'If a definition of style is making a difficult job look easy, then Keith Andrew is my choice. If style is making a difficult job look impossible, then Godfrey Evans would have few rivals.' He plumped for Keith.

Yet such is the strange status of the wicket-keeper and his skills that there will be many who will read the names of this team with pleasure, only to falter at the end. 'Keith Andrew?' they will ask. 'Who did he play for?'

*

In that special summer of 1965 he set a world record. It is not listed in *Wisden* or the *Playfair Cricket Annual,* but among wicket-keepers it still occasions disbelieving admiration.

It started on Saturday the 12th of June 1965 at the United Services Ground, Portsmouth. Keith was 35 years old, nearing the end of his career, and this was his first match back after a fortnight's absence, recovering from a finger injury. He had played for England, and now his only remaining ambition in cricket was to lead the little county of Northamptonshire to an improbable first championship.

On paper they were not contenders. Yorkshire had nine Test players, including Trueman, Illingworth, Boycott and Close. Worcestershire, seven. By contrast, the little-rated Midland county had only two: David Larter, their injury-prone fast bowler, and Keith.

Yet they had finished third the previous year, and there was something about their gritty determination and their team work that made them hard to dismiss from consideration.

At Portsmouth they took their places in the field and, with the pitch quick and green, their captain stood back to the bowling of Larter and Brian Crump.

Larter was six foot seven, as tall and as fast as any bowler in England at that time, but he was not always the most accurate. "He bowled some phenomenal deliveries," Keith recalls. "He had such height, and he could swing the ball, too. But sometimes he was all over the place."

Crump was entirely different. At five foot five he was fourteen inches shorter, and his skidding deliveries had none of the pace of his partner. "He could really swing a new ball and quite late, too. So I tended to stand back at the beginning of the innings and look to cover the leg-slip area for possible catches. Later, I might go up to the wicket. It would depend on the batsman."

Keith kept wicket for 109 overs as Hampshire crawled to a total of 206. On Tuesday morning he kept for another 42 before rain arrived to bring the contest to an end. Then he boarded the team coach back to Northampton where the next day they were playing Somerset.

The Northampton pitch was slower, favouring the spinners at first, but further rain made it awkward. At that time, if play had not been abandoned for the day, the pitch remained open to the elements, and Keith found himself keeping on a surface that was described as 'tricky' in the Somerset first innings, 'spiteful' in the second. The visitors required 227 for victory but, after the effects of the roller had worn off, they managed only 95 against Larter's 'venomous pace bowling'. The tall man, finishing with eight wickets, could be almost unplayable in such conditions, but he needed a captain who knew how to let him loose in short spells. So the keeper who was concentrating keenly on taking the ball off the unpredictable pitch was also masterminding a series of bowling changes.

The next day they were at Headingley, playing on another testing pitch. It had been a wet week, and the batsmen all struggled on the soft turf. Yorkshire's first innings of 151 took 94 overs, then after more rain they found themselves chasing 178 for victory – and contending with Larter at his hostile best. Keith remained calm behind the stumps, the quick bowler struck seven times and the final Yorkshire wicket fell with ten minutes to spare.

After the light relief of a Gillette Cup match at The Oval, with its vast playing area, the Northants team re-assembled at the small Kettering ground. Here the spinners came into their own, with Peter Watts breaking the back of the Leicestershire middle order. "Leg-breaks, flippers, googlies, he bowled the lot. He'd even fire a fast one down the leg side. 'What the hell do you think I am?' I'd tell him. 'A coconut shy?'"

Another victory, their third in a row, was followed by an innings defeat on a surprisingly quick wicket at Northampton, where Surrey's John Edrich batted all day for 188. "He made us look ordinary. The ball would be swinging or turning, but he'd still be hitting it with the middle of the bat. I thought he was a great player." All the bowlers were tried – the erratic pace of Larter, the relentlessly accurate Crump, the mixed bag of Peter Watts, the steadier seam of his brother Jim and the drifting slow left-arm of Malcolm Scott – but there were few balls coming through to Keith. Keeping on such a day was not so much about taking the ball as about retaining concentration.

'Concentration is everything,' Keith recommends to young keepers in his book *The Skills of Cricket*. 'Even concentrate on concentration!'

Bob Taylor, who kept wicket 57 times for England in the 1970s and '80s, elaborates on this. "You've got to imagine that every ball is coming through to you. Even as the batsman is playing his shot, you have to imagine yourself taking the ball. You might have been in the field for five hours 55 minutes, and it's the last over. And you're in India, and there's 90 degrees of heat and 85% humidity, and the wicket's flat and Gavaskar's been in all day and hardly a ball's passed the bat. And maybe you've got Delhi Belly. That catch or stumping in the last over in those conditions, that's what wicket-keeping's all about."

There were no such catches or stumpings for Keith while Surrey were batting, nor while the New Zealanders made 370 for nine in the next match. But at Trent Bridge, on what was an even-paced batting wicket, he took four catches in a Notts first innings that lasted only 59 overs. Then, with spinners Malcolm Scott and Peter Watts in control, he led them to an innings victory that saw them rise to second place in the table, just four points behind the leaders Middlesex. His ambition to win the championship was starting to seem less far-fetched.

He had played in seven matches since his return from injury, on pitches as varied as Portsmouth and Kettering, Headingley and Trent Bridge, pitches that changed with every passing shower, and he had combined keeping wicket with captaining a young and successful side. At the age of 35 he had been in the field for nearly 45 hours, bending down ball after ball, more than five thousand times, as the various bowlers ran in.

He was the busiest man on the field, but he remained unostentatious as a keeper, just as he was calm as a captain.

"I can never remember Keith raising his voice," Brian Crump says. "He did everything quietly, and everybody respected him."

Then Jack Mercer, their elderly scorer, spotted something unusual in his large dark blue scorebook. "Dear old Jack," Keith says. "He used to whistle all the time he was scoring. I'd walk past the scorebox, and I'd hear him."

As he turned back the pages of the last seven matches, his eye was caught by the extras in each innings.

"It wasn't a big thing, but he said to somebody, 'You know Keith hasn't conceded a bye for several matches.' Well, I never thought about byes, but apparently, when they looked into it, I'd gone over 2,000 runs without conceding a bye."

It is a feat unequalled in the whole history of cricket. In seven matches Keith had stood behind the stumps while 2,094 runs had been scored and not one of them had been a bye. Add the 38 runs scored in the next match at Leicester before a Brian Crump delivery cut back and went down leg for four byes, and he had gone 2,132 runs.

He had kept for almost nine hundred overs, nearly half of which had him standing up to the wicket. Wearing compact gloves, free of the modern webbing and pouches, he received the ball from a variety of bowlers on a variety of playing surfaces, and all the time he was captaining a side that was winning matches and moving towards the top of the championship table.

"Byes didn't bother me much," Keith says, making light of his record. "In fact, sometimes, when I wanted to gee up the bowlers, I used to say to them, 'No wonder I don't give any byes away. You guys can't get past the bat.'"

Perhaps a brasher, more exuberant man would have championed his own reputation more effectively but, among wicket-keeping connoisseurs, his greatness has not been missed.

Bob Taylor has no doubt about his quality. "He's my number one," he says.

'Tiger' Smith played for England before the First World War, keeping to the great Sydney Barnes, and he maintained an eagle eye on the game, as umpire and coach, till his death in 1979 at the age of 93. "Both Bob Taylor and Keith Andrew suffered from one of the curses of modern cricket – the need to have a batsman/wicket-keeper," he said at the end of his life. "Alan Knott and Godfrey Evans gave England great service, yet neither had the class of Keith Andrew or Bob Taylor behind the stumps."

A different man, faced with a compliment like this, might feel a touch of bitterness at having had such little opportunity to demonstrate his skills at the highest level, but Keith's reaction is all pleasure.

"How wonderful to think of all these great names of cricket and to find myself associated with them."

As John Arlott wrote, 'Few cricketers of his considerable gifts can have been quite so modest. Had he been more self-assertive, he must have played far more often for England.'

*

Keith rang me towards the end of 2001. He was thinking that perhaps he might like to do a book after all. Would I be interested?

"Yes, I would," I told him.

But why?

First, I was drawn to the subject of wicket-keeping: how little noticed or understood are its skills, how little valued in the modern game is its art form. Keith could well be the best person to throw some light on that.

Secondly, I suspected that his years of county captaincy were rather special. Many a lesser captain has been garlanded for success leading teams stacked with much greater talent. I had followed the sporting rise of Northampton through my mother's enthusiasm, and I knew that it was a good story.

Thirdly, I liked it that he was an independently-minded man. He was a boy from the back streets of Oldham, a mechanical engineer by training, and, before the abolition of the amateur, he had risen to be one of the youngest professionals ever to captain a county side. Later he spent twenty years with the National Cricket Association, working to improve the often neglected world of the recreational game. He is not a natural conservative, with a small or a large 'c', but then neither is he a card-carrying radical. He is a free thinker.

But, more than any of these three reasons, I found myself remembering that afternoon in the hotel, how he recounted with such excitement the day he went to a Karachi bazaar to sign up Mushtaq Mohammad, how he reflected with anguish on the overbearing influence of one-day cricket and its diminution of the skills of attacking bowling, how he spoke with such passion about Colin Milburn and the slowness of the English game to awake to his genius.

He was an engineer, a man who could perform stress calculations, and he could look at a cricket ball as an object that could be redesigned to improve or diminish the game. But he was also a man of passion, a man who had experienced the joys of a lifetime in cricket, and he wanted to share that and to pass it on.

"I'd like to have something that I can give my grandchildren and say, 'That's what my life was all about.'"

I said yes, and I began the regular journeys: starting after breakfast among the rolling hills of the south Cotswolds, bypassing the rush hour traffic of Oxford, negotiating the countless roundabouts on the outskirts of Milton Keynes, and ending in mid-morning at his front door.

"Would you like a coffee?"

"Yes, please, Keith."

He stands in the kitchen and, after some minutes of pleasantries, with the kettle slowly boiling, he turns to me. "Now, you said you didn't want a coffee?"

This all started, I remind myself, because I asked Andrew Radd to recommend me a Northants player with a good memory, and he came up with Keith Andrew. "Definitely."

"No, I would like one, please, Keith."

To his team-mate Frank Tyson, he was 'the absent-minded professor of wicket-keepers'. To the younger David Steele, who played under his captaincy, 'there was a touch of Walter Mitty about him, always a bit of a dreamer.' And when I tell Brian Crump that I am writing a book with Keith, he bursts into laughter. "Keith? A book about his memories? That'll be interesting. He'd put me on to bowl, and ten minutes later he'd have forgotten I was on."

I repeat this to Keith, and he smiles mischievously. "I used to pretend to forget their names. David Steele could be very intense, and he was always wanting to bowl. I remember pointing at him one day, 'What's your name? Steele, Steele, isn't it? You bowl, don't you? Come and have a go.' And he'd be muttering, 'He doesn't even remember my name.' It was just my way of lightening the atmosphere. But of course he thought I was being serious."

Later, when Keith was with the National Cricket Association, he had further opportunity to engage in such strategies. "When he chaired meetings," Doug Ferguson, a regional coach, recalls, "he'd give the impression that he was a bumbling professor, and you'd think, 'This meeting's getting nowhere.' But he had such a keen brain, and he was full of ideas. And you gradually realised that the rambling was done with a purpose. It was his method, and the results always came out right."

Keith is a creative thinker, looking for new ideas, and as such he can seem quite abstracted at times. And without doubt he can be forgetful.

Many is the time he tells me about some episode in his career, only for me to find that twenty minutes later he is saying, "Here, you'll like this," and he is away with the same story. Nevertheless, when we have got into the mood and the conversation is flowing, fresh memories bubble up. He will retrieve a detail from fifty years ago, then stop in astonishment. "Fancy my remembering a thing like that. And everybody says I've got a bad memory."

Even then the flickering memory can play tricks.

Several times he has told me how his winning Northamptonshire side was built on a happy atmosphere beyond the boundary. They travelled everywhere by coach, they had a scorer who enchanted them with exotic tales and magic tricks, they had a Push Ha'penny League in the dressing room, and collectively they owned a greyhound.

"Lady Be Good, it was called. Crumpy got it for us."

"Lady Be Good," Brian repeats with bewilderment. "I don't know where Keith got that from. We called it The Cosmo Kid."

At such moments I have wondered if Keith was quite the right man to work on a book like this. But my doubts have never persisted for long.

I feel like Doug Ferguson. Initially I sat in Keith's front room, wondering how we were going to draw our rambling conversations into any coherence of form. Then, as the months passed, I started to realise what he was giving me.

I have had so much light thrown onto the art of wicket-keeping and how its evolution has reflected a changing game. I have come to understand better the sometimes lonely life of the keeper, how just a few moments of good or ill fortune can have such a major effect on the opinions that matter. I have relived with him the absorbing challenge of trying to win the county championship with an unglamorous county like Northamptonshire. I have reflected on the state of our national game, both at Test level and in the school playgrounds.

His is a fascinating story, one that his self-effacing quietness has allowed to go untold for too long.

CHAPTER 2

GUESS MY STORY

1954-1955

"We were on television, you know," Keith tells me. "A panel game. I think it was called *What's My News?* Is that right, Joyce?"

His wife pauses for a moment. "Or was it *What's My Story?*"

"*What's My Story?* Yes, that's right. *What's My Story?*"

I look it up later and find that it was called *Guess My Story*.

"That's it. *Guess My Story*. My word, you have been working hard."

"*Guess My Story*, what sort of programme was that, Keith?"

"It was a sort of *Have I Got News For You?*, only nicer."

I try to imagine that long-lost programme. The pictures are black-and-white, of course, and the television set is a large, clumsy thing with a dial that you turn to find the best reception. There is certainly no choice of channels.

It was a Sunday evening in August 1954. Fewer than one quarter of British households had television, and the BBC began broadcasting at four in the afternoon. The *Radio Times* lists *Out of Doors*, with Percy Thrower in the garden, followed by *Children's Hour*, featuring Muffin the Mule.

At six o'clock, with church bells ringing up and down the land, the station closed down, returning at 7.30 with the News.

The news of the summer of 1954. There was the final end of rationing, unrest in Cyprus, an outbreak of myxomatosis, the breaking of the four-minute mile, and American research suggesting a link between smoking and cancer.

Then at 7.55 came *Guess My Story*, in which people in the news appeared and the panel of Helen Cherry, Eunice Gayson, Michael Pertwee and Jack Train tried to work out their claims to fame. Peter West was in the chair, and artist David Langdon doodled an introductory sketch to give the panel a clue.

The first guest that evening was Jim Peters, the marathon runner who had collapsed from heat exhaustion half a lap from victory in the Empire and Commonwealth Games in Vancouver. Then came a trio, two young men sitting on either side of a young woman.

What was their story?

"It was Frank Tyson, Joyce and me," Keith explains. "Frank and I had been selected to go to Australia, to leave on the 15th of September, and Joyce and I had been planning to marry in October."

They had been taken through a rehearsal earlier in the evening, to make sure they were at ease in the studio. "Frank and Joyce were quite worried about it all, but I was full of confidence. 'Oh, you'll be all right,' I said to them."

The programme went out live. They stepped onto the set to applause from the studio audience, but it soon became apparent that they were not the same threesome they had been in rehearsal. "Frank and Joyce were as large as life, chatting away, and I was sitting on this box, of all things, and my leg was shaking. I couldn't speak."

Almost fifty years have passed, and there is no trace of any edition of the programme in the BBC archives. So all we have are their flickering memories.

"How long did they take to guess your story?"

"Oh, not very long," Joyce says. "They guessed it quite quickly."

"You and Frank were so articulate," Keith says. "I'd gone. They'd never have found out from me. We'd have been there all evening."

"We got paid," Joyce adds. "A cheque each for three guineas. Or was it five?"

"Joyce handled it all very well. In fact, Peter West wanted to know whether she might be interested in developing her talents."

"Ah well," she says with a laugh in her voice. "I'd had my five minutes of fame."

"So when did the two of you get married?"

"We brought it forward to the fourth of September. We'd been planning to go down to Cornwall for our honeymoon but, instead, we had a week in Eastbourne."

The traditional chimney sweep provides a lucky omen.
The picture appeared in the magazine The Sketch.
"Goodness me," Joyce's mother complained before the event.
"You can't go out of the house for reporters."

The 24-year-old wicket-keeper from Oldham had only been in the Northamptonshire side for four months, now he was embarking on the greatest adventure in English cricket.

Four days after their return from Eastbourne, they were at St Pancras Station. The rain had been falling for several hours, but the sky brightened as the *Northampton Chronicle* reporter observed the scene.

> Coming into the station half-an-hour before the train was due to leave, the players, many of whom had brought raincoats, soon lost their anxious looks as the clouds cleared and shafts of sunlight gleamed through the glass roof of the terminus. Tearful Mrs Joyce Andrew, 10-days bride of Keith Andrew, hurried from platform six just before the train left for Tilbury. Unable to bear the strain of parting, 22-years-old Mrs Andrew kissed her husband goodbye and left.

There would be three weeks on the *SS Orsova*, then six months of touring before the cricketers flew back at the beginning of April.

After ten days of marriage she had to return to her parents' home in Lancashire and her job as a proof-reader with the Stationery Office.

"Nothing prepares you for it," she says.

*

Keith was a quiet man and he, too, was unprepared. He had only been abroad once, a short cricket tour of Germany with his army side, and down the Mediterranean and through the Suez Canal both he and his cabin-mate Frank Tyson suffered sickness. "Frank was quite bad at one stage. He lost a lot of weight."

At 24 years old, the two of them were not the youngest in the party – that tag belonged to the fresh-faced Colin Cowdrey – but they were probably the least travelled, certainly the least experienced in the world of first-class cricket.

Keith Andrew had a career tally of 28 catches and 33 stumpings. His cabin-mate had taken just 105 wickets.

'I was beset with a wave of doubts and questionings,' the young bowler later wrote. 'Was I good enough? Was I experienced enough? I could bowl fast, but could I bowl fast enough?'

"I didn't even know half the people on the tour," Keith says. "I must have been a good taker of the ball for them to have picked me. But, looking back, I think it was a mistake to pick me at that stage. I wasn't ready."

They were two young men travelling out to a new world. In the months that followed, the course of their lives would start to take shape.

There was a fancy dress party and various deck games – "Tom Graveney and I won the table tennis doubles," Keith recalls – but the newcomers from Northampton did not yet feel relaxed in the company of their more established companions.

At Aden, with Frank laid up, Keith went ashore to buy cameras for both of them. "Two Zeiss Ikons. They were magnificent. I've still got mine."

Keith and Colin Cowdrey

But Keith's greatest ambition was to record the tour on the 16 millimetre movie camera he and Frank had brought with them.

"It was a crank Bell and Howell motion camera. I'm afraid we didn't know anything about it at first. In fact, I think Frank and I did well to start it off."

The old spools of film have been converted into a video tape, and he runs it through on his television set. There is no sound, but he has added explanatory captions each time the scene changes. In fact, the film starts grandly with a title frame.

THE MCC EXPEDITIONARY FORCE IN AUSTRALIA. 1954-5.
FILMED BY F.H. TYSON AND K.V. ANDREW.

The images flash past.

They are at St Pancras – "There's Joyce and me." – then they are at Tilbury Docks – "Denis Compton waving us off. He stayed behind for treatment on his knee." – then on the open sea – "Bill Bowes leaning over the rail. He was reporting the tour for one of the Yorkshire papers. Trevor Bailey smoking." – then at the ruins of Pompeii.

"It's a bit like the Keystone Cops at times," Keith apologises, "but it gets better later on – when we find out how the camera works."

Strolling among the ruins is the MCC manager Geoffrey Howard, impeccably dressed and looking like a 1940s film star.

"He always looked so debonair, didn't he?" Joyce adds.

Some distant figures walk along the banks of the Suez Canal. Then there is a game of deck quoits before another title appears.

COLOMBO AT 104° IN THE SHADE.

"We stopped there for a one-day match. The pitch was so hard that Frank bowled a ball that bounced once and hit the sightscreen on the full. And the ball itself was like a rock. I was keeping to Tyson, Statham, Loader, and, when I came off, I had a vein in my hand that had swollen up."

George Duckworth, the old England keeper who was scorer and baggage man for the tour, grins at the camera. "He took me aside before my next game. 'Get down to the kitchen and put a steak on it,' he said."

The film runs on. There are shots of the pressmen having a net and an Aboriginal bareback rider: "He was the top man. Look at him riding the horse backwards." There is Australian Rules football, then Pancho Gonzales playing tennis. "I was very taken by him. They don't hit the ball as hard as some of them do these days."

But mostly, as the camerawork improves, there is precious film of the cricket.

"I've got some good shots of Frank bowling."

The young fast bowler runs in repeatedly, a rushing, awkward action that generates its pace from the great slinging movement across his shoulders.

"He was extraordinarily clumsy," Keith laughs. "It was dangerous on the squash court when you played him. He used to swing the racquet round."

"Look at him," Joyce adds. "His arms and legs are all over the place. If he came to the house, you had to watch out."

"He'd break anything he sat on. I used to have a special chair for him."

On modern tours of Australia there are barely three weeks between departure and the start of the first Test match, but on the 1954/5 tour there were eleven weeks, giving time for the party to acclimatise, to find some form, to get to know each other.

The role of second wicket-keeper is never an easy one on tour, particularly if one has no pretensions to being a batsman and if the first-choice keeper is as well-established as Godfrey Evans was. Len Hutton the captain was not one to initiate conversation – "He hardly spoke to me all tour" – and the net practice rarely required Keith to do more than serve up gentle off-breaks.

His room-mate was a possibility to play in the Tests, his sheer speed creating much talk, but for the first weeks in Australia they were inclined to withdraw to their hotel room.

"Then one evening there was a knock on the door. It was Denis Compton and Bill Edrich. 'Come on out, you two,' they said. 'You're going to a party tonight.' And that in a way started the tour off for us. We suddenly realised that people wanted to be friends. It was our own fault that we were a bit raw."

The Saturday Night Club was set up by Geoffrey Howard. Every Saturday the whole tour party assembled for an evening together, with drinks and fines, with singing and laughter. "That was one of the highlights. I got to know the chaps better there than anywhere else."

The film shows many shots of the early matches, but there is little of Keith. In seven weeks in Australia he played just ten days, and he was not in the team that took the field for the final warm-up match at Brisbane.

Godfrey Evans was the first-choice keeper. Carmen Miranda at the Fancy Dress Party, leader of the singing at the Saturday Night Club, in the field he galvanised the whole England side, as he had done in every big match since his debut in 1946. 'The fulcrum of inspiration,' Len Hutton called him. 'He was more than the stumper,' Frank Tyson reckons. 'He was the chief whip.'

Keith was at close quarters with him for the first time, and it was a revelation. "His effervescent personality brought the whole day to life and very often part of the night."

The First Test was due to start on Friday the 26th of November and, on the Thursday evening, as Keith sat quietly in his room in the Lennon's Hotel, Brisbane, he was looking forward to five days with his movie camera. Then a voice on the radio startled him. "It announced that Godfrey had got a temperature."

He lay awake during the night, trying to absorb the shock.

Only in May had he stood behind the stumps for the first time in a county championship match. In late July he had stood in the huddle in the Northampton dressing room, around the Vidor portable radio that gave out the names of this touring party. In September he had stood in front of the altar at Christ Church, Chadderton, and kissed his bride.

Now he was to be a Test cricketer, taking the field with Hutton and Bedser, Compton and Edrich. "They were like cigarette card names to me still, I was so starry-eyed."

"You'll be all right, lad," George Duckworth told him in the morning, but he was nervous as Alec Bedser ran in to bowl. A caption on the video tape marks the moment – THE FIRST TEST AT BRISBANE – and one of his team-mates films two of the first deliveries. Alec Bedser is bowling to the left-handed Arthur Morris. The camera is somewhere behind long leg, so it is not easy to make out the path of the ball, but the second delivery seems to pitch on the stumps and to cut sharply to the left-hander's leg side, where Keith is in position to catch the ball cleanly.

"It's funny, isn't it," he reflects, "how that match at Brisbane so often comes up in cricketing talk."

At the Heart of English Cricket, my book written with Geoffrey Howard, starts on that very morning at Brisbane – with Len Hutton surprisingly asking the Australians to bat first and seeing his strategy turn to disaster.

By the time the manager arrived by tram from Lennon's Hotel, the innings had started, and he took his seat to see Alec Bedser running in to bowl to the left-handed Arthur Morris. The England wicket-keeper was Keith Andrew, making his Test debut in place of a feverish Godfrey Evans. He stood up to the stumps, as Alec Bedser always demanded, keeping to him for only the second time in his life, and in

Bedser's third over the ball caught the inside edge of Morris's bat and deflected sharply to Andrew's right. It was at best a quarter-chance, but it was not held. A day of misfortunes had begun.

George Duckworth, Keith and Godfrey Evans

After tea and with 55 to his name, Morris top-edged a hook that was spilled by Bailey at long leg. At close of play he had reached 82, with Australia two wickets down for 208. The captain's gamble had failed spectacularly but Norman Preston, editor of *Wisden*, filed a Reuter's report that found some consolation in the performance of the debutant keeper:

> The quiet efficient wicket-keeping of Andrew was one of the bright features of the English cricket. A vastly different personality from Evans, he did everything with the minimum of fuss, reminiscent of Leslie Ames. ... He could feel well satisfied with his first day as a Test player. Certainly he has not let down the side.

The next day there were more missed catches in the field. Morris scored 153, Harvey made 162, and the day grew long for the young keeper.

He was in Australia after just one summer of English county cricket, and he had never stood in an innings that had lasted more than six hours or seen more than 360 runs scored. His home pitch at Northampton was slow, and he had made his reputation standing up to the stumps to take the spin of George Tribe.

Yet here he was having to keep session after session to quick bowlers on a fast pitch. The early coolness had long given way to a baking sun, the Australians going past 500 and looking to bat on into the third day.

"The sweat was pouring from my brow, I could taste the salt in it. And I remember walking down the pitch from the Pavilion end and noticing a sign over the top of the sightscreen. 'Atlantic,' it said in huge red letters. It was a brand of petrol, I think. And I started to think of the Atlantic ocean and the beaches in Cornwall, where we'd been going to have our honeymoon. My concentration was in tatters. I think I'd got a touch of the sun."

By the time Australia declared at 601 for eight, the journalists had totted up twelve missed chances. In addition, 'England's throwing was so bad that Australia's running between the wickets became increasingly a point of impertinent and finally reckless attack.'

Hutton later wrote that it was 'the worst exhibition of out-cricket I was obliged to endure in my term of office.'

Everything went wrong. Compton broke a bone in his hand on the first morning, the excitingly quick Tyson took just one wicket for 160 runs, and on a still good wicket the first five batsmen – Hutton, Simpson, Edrich, May and Cowdrey – managed only three scores of over 15 in the match. The game was lost by an innings and 154 runs. It was a collective failure of great magnitude.

How hard Fate can be! At the end of the first day, Keith's keeping had been 'one of the bright features' and, if Morris had been bowled for ten or Australia all out for 250, that is how history would have left it. But at the end of the game the story came to be told otherwise. England had missed their talisman, Godfrey Evans, and it had all gone wrong from the moment Morris had been dropped on nought.

Eighteen months later, when *Wisden*'s definitive record appeared in print, Norman Preston was hinging his description on that moment:

> England allowed about twelve possible chances to go astray, including one from Morris to Andrew before he scored. If the England fielding had approached any decent standard, Hutton might well have achieved his objective.

Dennis Brookes, the Northants captain, recalls a conversation with Crawford White of the *News Chronicle*. "He was still talking about that catch two or three summers later. The reporters all damned Keith for it."

Hutton had been crouched at leg slip when Morris's edge had flown between him and his substitute keeper. Thirty years on, he too saw the failure of his decision in terms of the change of the man behind the stumps: 'I should have shied away from my intentions when Evans was pronounced unfit. It was almost like a warning from fate not to go ahead.'

Hutton was not a talkative man, but the young keeper knew what his captain was thinking. "I don't think I impressed Len very much."

The years have passed, and the dropped catch has become a cornerstone of almost every telling of the story. For Alec Bedser, manfully struggling to bowl while suffering from shingles, the match marked the effective end of a glorious Test career, and in 2001 his biographer Alan Hill sought to capture his subject's ill-fortune:

> 'I tried to bowl at 95 in the shade, with my back full of sores,' he says. He deserved a better reward for his fortitude. Morris was dropped off him before he had scored. That lapse by Keith Andrew occurred in the third over.

The Bell and Howell camera did not capture the moment so we are left to rely on memories.

"Lapse?" Geoffrey Howard repeats with indignation. "No, no, no. That's most unfair. It was off the inside edge. Keith was playing in his first Test, standing up to Alec Bedser, who was medium-pace. Alec always made the ball hit the ground hard, it bounced a lot, and he got late swing. An edge like that, any wicket-keeper would be lucky to take it."

And Keith's memory of the chance?

"It was a thick inside edge. When you're standing up to medium-pace, you can only take the line of the ball. You don't have time to adjust to edges like that. A lot of people don't understand wicket-keeping, they don't really know what is or isn't a chance. I didn't keep that well but, as God is my judge, I never got my hands anywhere near that ball. When I went into lunch, I never felt that I'd missed a catch. Within a day or two of the Test, though, I knew that that was what was being said."

'It was hardly a chance,' Frank Tyson wrote, 'but substitutes for Godfrey Evans must expect comparisons.'

*

The film moves on.

THE SECOND TEST AT SYDNEY
THE TIDE TURNS

This time, with Godfrey Evans recovered, Keith is back at the controls of the camera. "I was bobbing about in front of the Prime Minister, Robert Menzies, at one stage. I met him later in the lift of the hotel. 'How's the filming going?' he said to me."

England, 74 behind on the first innings, are 55 for three in the second when Peter May and Colin Cowdrey come together. The film moves occasionally onto half-speed – "Ah, we've found the slow motion." – and there is time to admire the correctness of May's movement as he covers his stumps and watches the ball onto his bat.

But the most important moment of that match is not recorded. "I was representing MCC at the Rotary Club of Sydney, and the news came through that Frank had been felled by a Lindwall bouncer."

Tyson was mostly an easy-going man, a university graduate of literature who enjoyed reciting Wordsworth and Gerard Manley Hopkins, but he could be roused. An ambulance took him away for an x-ray and, in his own words, 'When I returned from hospital, I was in an ugly mood.'

"I think that blow on the head changed his whole career. He was the only bowler I knew, of any quality, who was quicker and better when he was angry. I used to try to rile him sometimes."

Keith's memory wanders to a game in Cardiff in 1957.

"He'd gone out somewhere the night before. I know it sounds ridiculous, but somebody cut his tie off and he was really upset. Glamorgan had got to bat in the morning, and we were on our way home just after lunch."

Wisden confirms the detail. Tyson, 15 overs, seven wickets for 25.

The blow on the head at Sydney seemed to have much the same effect. The next morning began with Australia 72 for two, chasing 223, and Tyson ran in with purpose off his shorter run.

In the words of William Wordsworth,
Bliss was it in that dawn to be alive,
But to be young was very heaven!

He shattered the stumps four times before taking the final wicket with a catch by Evans. The series was level, and Tyson's six wickets captured all the headlines. "That was his first great bowling performance. From then on, he was the Typhoon."

THE THIRD TEST AT MELBOURNE

The position at the start of the final day was almost a carbon copy of the one at Sydney. Australia were 75 for two, chasing 240, and Keith recalls the moment that transformed the match, perhaps the whole series.

"It was the greatest wicket-keeping catch of all time. Neil Harvey glanced Frank for four – well, that's what everybody thought. And there was Godfrey – you've seen the photograph, haven't you? – with the ball in his hand, almost forty-five degrees to the wicket."

Here was wicket-keeping of a class that Keith could hardly comprehend. Harvey had given him a similar chance at Brisbane, and he had barely got his fingertips to it.

27

"Nobody else but Godfrey would have got near it."

'At the end of my follow-through,' Tyson wrote, 'I could scarcely believe my eyes. It did not seem possible that Godfrey could have caught it.' 77 for two became 111 all out, and cricket's newest sensation was leaving the field with figures of seven for 27.

As Gerard Manley Hopkins wrote of the windhover,
The achieve of, the mastery of the thing!

In Middleton, near Oldham, Frank's mother was opening her front door from 6.30 a.m. to a stream of celebrating neighbours. 'The house hasn't been empty all day,' she told reporters.

"Australia really suited Frank. The steaks. The warmth. And of course he met his wife out there."

Joyce smiles. "His mother told him not to come back with one of those Australian girls."

"He had such phenomenal success. I'd pick up the phone, and it would always be for him. 'Frank?' I'd say sometimes. 'Frank who?' He was the great attraction of the tour. And, being his room-mate, both being Lancastrians, both Northamptonshire players, I was always included in all the invitations he got. There were people coming up to him, saying amazing things. It gave me quite a close-up of how fame works."

But there was to be no such fame for the reserve keeper. He played a two-day match at Rockhampton, starting on December the 4th, then nothing till a three-day match at Hobart on January the 8th.

"One day I knocked on Len Hutton's door and asked him if he minded if I went and played golf. He was an unusual fellow. 'When I was your age,' he said, 'I was eating, sleeping and breathing cricket.' I said, 'Well, I've been doing a lot of watching, skipper.'" Keith smiles mischievously. "I should have asked him how he got his own handicap down to eleven."

THE FOURTH TEST AT ADELAIDE.
HUTTON LEADS ENGLAND OUT. 97°

The camera roams round the ground. "It was the loveliest ground in the world in those days, with the cathedral and the trees and all the hills in the distance. Now, of course, they've built it all up. You can't see the hills."

The film breaks for a visit to the Australian Open tennis, for a match between Lew Hoad and Ken Rosewall. "When they were warming up for the championships, I played a game of doubles with Lew Hoad – against George Worthington and Tom Graveney."

Then the scoreboard shows Australia 90 for eight in their second innings. Then Compton and Evans are completing the winning run.

AND SO AFTER MORE THAN 20 YEARS
THE ASHES WERE WON IN AUSTRALIA
WITHOUT THE USE OF BODYLINE

The reserve keeper has played no part in the three Test triumphs, but he has found himself another occupation with his movie camera.

The final Test at Sydney is an anti-climax. More than two days are lost to rain. Then, after some stylish batting by May and Graveney, a strip of film has been threaded wrongly onto the video tape and the cricketers are briefly upside down and going backwards. It rights itself, and the series ends with Hutton bowling a light-hearted over to Benaud.

"There, look, he's bowled him."

It is Hutton's first test wicket since 1939, and the players leave the field. OVER AND OUT, declares the final caption.

In New Zealand there might have been a consolation Test for Keith but, opening the batting against Canterbury, he sustained a broken rib.

"It was amazing that I got selected for that tour," he says now. "I was still learning the skills. I wasn't anywhere near ready."

So would it have been better for his career if he had never gone, if the stigma of that chance at Brisbane had not stuck to him?

"Oh no. I wouldn't have missed it. It was a great tour, a wonderful experience. It gave me a start in a world in which I had no idea. It was a huge benefit. When I came back, I was a different man. I had a much wider view of the world, and I was determined to improve my wicket-keeping. And by jingo I did get better. In my heart I know I didn't drop any easy catches, but I wasn't at all the wicket-keeper I became later."

*

The years passed, and the apprentice keeper became the master craftsman. At the Scarborough festival in September 1963, he represented England against Young England, the next generation of hopeful apprentices.

The previous September at Scarborough he had stumped Ken Taylor down the leg side off Trevor Bailey's fast-medium bowling, a special moment he treasures in his memory. Now he turned in a polished display that caught the eye of at least one of his young opponents.

It was Richard Hutton's 21st birthday, and in the evening they all gathered in the marquee to celebrate.

"You've improved a bit," Len's son said to him.

"What do you mean?"

"Since you were in Australia."

"Well, I hope I have."

AUSTRALIA v ENGLAND – FIRST TEST

Brisbane. 26, 27, 29 & 30 November, 1 December 1954

AUSTRALIA WON BY AN INNINGS AND 154 RUNS

AUSTRALIA

L.E. Favell	c Cowdrey b Statham	23
A.R. Morris	c Cowdrey b Bailey	153
K.R. Miller	b Bailey	49
R.N. Harvey	c Bailey b Bedser	162
G.B. Hole	run out	57
R. Benaud	c May b Tyson	34
R.G. Archer	c Bedser b Statham	0
R.R. Lindwall	*not out*	64
G.R.A. Langley +	b Bailey	16
I.W. Johnson *	*not out*	24
W.A. Johnston		
Extras	*b 11, lb 7, nb 1*	19
	(8 wkts, dec)	**601**

1-51, 2-123, 3-325, 4-456, 5-463, 6-464, 7-545, 8-572

Bedser	37	4	131	1
Statham	34	2	123	2
Tyson	29	1	160	1
Bailey	26	1	140	3
Edrich	3	0	28	0

ENGLAND

L. Hutton *	c Langley b Lindwall	4	lbw b Miller	13
R.T. Simpson	b Miller	2	run out	9
W.J. Edrich	c Langley b Archer	15	b Johnston	88
P.B.H. May	b Lindwall	1	lbw b Lindwall	44
M.C. Cowdrey	c Hole b Johnston	40	b Benaud	10
T.E. Bailey	b Johnston	88	c Langley b Lindwall	23
F.H. Tyson	b Johnson	7	*not out*	37
A.V. Bedser	b Johnson	5	c Archer b Johnson	5
K.V. Andrew +	b Lindwall	6	b Johnson	5
J.B. Statham	b Johnson	11	(11) c Harvey b Benaud	14
D.C.S. Compton	*not out*	2	(10) c Langley b Benaud	0
Extras	*b 3, lb 6*	9	*b 7, lb 2*	9
		190		**257**

1-4, 2-10, 3-11, 4-25, 5-107, 6-132, 7-141, 8-156, 9-181, 10-190
1-22, 2-23, 3-147, 4-163, 5-181, 6-220, 7-231, 8-242, 9-243, 10-257

Lindwall	14	4	27	3	17	3	50	2
Miller	11	5	19	1	12	2	30	1
Archer	4	1	14	1	15	4	28	0
Johnson	19	5	46	3	17	5	38	2
Benaud	12	5	28	0	8.1	1	43	3
Johnston	16.1	5	47	2	21	8	59	1

Umpires: C. Hoy and M.J. McInnes

CHAPTER 3

EARLY DAYS AT NORTHAMPTON

1953-1954

It is hard to imagine the emotions that Keith went through when he heard that voice on the radio telling of Godfrey Evans' temperature. He was a young man who had never witnessed a Test match, and suddenly he was England's keeper at the start of an Ashes series. His night's sleep, as he anticipated the coming morning, was fitful and full of anxiety. And, when the match began, nothing went right for England. Morris and Harvey, the two Australian left-handers, accumulated big centuries, and the game was lost by an innings.

Strangely he had been through a similar experience little more than a year previously. Only on that occasion his reputation, and that of his team-mate Frank Tyson, had been greatly enhanced.

At the start of 1953 Northamptonshire signed him to become their wicket-keeper, in place of the retiring Ken Fiddling, and he had to spend the next twelve months completing a residential qualification. He took a job in the design office at British Timken, a company that manufactured roller bearings for the fast-expanding motor industry and whose chairman John Pascoe was the county club's chief benefactor. He was directed to lodgings at 18 Roseholme Road, a three-storey Victorian house just one hundred yards from the main gates of the county ground.

His predecessor in the attic bedroom was Frank Tyson, who had also been completing a residential qualification and who was now away, finishing his degree at Durham University.

Northampton was a market town in those days, with a population of fewer than 100,000 and a reputation as the centre of England's boot and shoe manufacturing. Keith's landlord, Mr Berrill, was a retired shoe-maker. With his wife and unmarried middle-aged daughter Emily, they had been letting out rooms to cricketers since the 1920s when Vallance Jupp and Nobby Clark had stayed there. They also put up visiting umpires.

Joyce was given the spare room on her regular trips down from Oldham to see Keith, and she remembers the atmosphere. "It was like stepping back into the 1870s."

"Mr Berrill had white hair and a white moustache," Keith says. "Every day he went off to his allotment, and every evening he came back with his fruit and vegetables. Mrs Berrill used to sit in her armchair, never letting go of this huge handbag."

"It never left her side," Joyce says. "I think she had the Bank of England in it – all her money, all her bank books, the lot. And Emily, their daughter, worked like a skivvy for the whole house."

"Emily was a great cook, but we always had the same meals on the same nights of the week. On Sunday it would be roast beef and Yorkshire pudding.

On Monday it was served up cold and the Yorkshire pudding had got a bit soggy and had sunk."

There was no television set in the household, and Keith was expected to join in the card games that were part of the weekly ritual.

"I had to play crib every Tuesday night in winter. Mr Berrill was quite an expert but, when he'd got more than one five, he'd get excited and start whistling."

"They played Newmarket every Wednesday," Joyce adds. "The football trainer came round. Mrs Berrill gave out these toffee tins with the money in from the previous week. That was Harry's. That was Dad's. That was Keith's. That was Emily's. But she never played herself. She'd sit in her armchair with her handbag – she was like a duchess – but she never participated in the game. Apparently back in about 1915 Mr Berrill had cheated, and she vowed she'd never play with him again."

Keith did what was expected of him. He was a better lodger than his predecessor.

"I conformed. Frank didn't. One thing he did was to rig himself up a switch from a string so that he didn't have to get out of bed to turn the light off, and apparently it knocked over his hair oil on Emily's best carpet. He went away, and he didn't get back again."

So there in that attic room Keith lay on the evening of Friday the third of July 1953. He had played two non-championship matches for the county – one at Fenner's against Cambridge University, the other at Peterborough against Scotland – and tomorrow he was to play his third, against the touring Australians. That was an altogether different prospect.

Frank Tyson's qualification period was over. He had played just once for the county in 1952, against the Indians, and he was now returning from Durham to play his first game of the summer.

People were still talking about his opening over against the Indians, how Pankaj Roy had edged him to slip and the ball had hit Freddie Jakeman on the knee before he had started to move for it. After that, they all stood much further back. His return to play the Australians was eagerly anticipated in the town.

"I didn't sleep well that night," Keith recalls. "I had a dream – a nightmare, I suppose. I was standing behind the stumps, and from the football end this man called Tyson was firing a cannon at hundreds of miles an hour. The balls were flying past me and, when I looked up at the scoreboard, it was 500 for no wicket and they were all byes."

In the morning Emily climbed the stairs to the attic room with a jug of hot water for shaving and, as Keith prepared himself for his big day, he became aware of the noise outside the house. He looked down from his high window, and he saw the crowds streaming towards the ground. "I thought, 'What's going on? They didn't tell me it was going to be like this.'"

How could they? Never before in the history of the little Midland county – nor, for that matter, since – had a crowd of anything like that size gathered at the ground. According to the local paper, 'Huge queues began to form long before the scheduled time for the opening of the gates.'

The Australians had not lost a Test series against any opponents for twenty years. Their 1948 side, under Donald Bradman, had remained undefeated throughout their tour of England, winning 17 of their 34 matches by an innings. Now Lindsay Hassett's side had reached the halfway stage of its tour, and they too were unbeaten. With Lindwall and Miller, Morris and Harvey, they were a team guaranteed to produce early morning queues.

On that Saturday, the *Northampton Chronicle* reported, 73-year-old Jack Harris was the first to arrive. He had got up at 5.15 that morning, and, he told the reporter, it was his first visit for fifty years.

The gates opened early at nine o'clock. Within ten minutes, 'a thick, unbroken ring of spectators' was settled on the grass round the boundary. Ten minutes after that, every cushion in the ground had been sold. By the time play started, the boundary rope had been brought in several yards to accommodate the vast numbers.

Taking the field against the Australians: (left to right) Des Barrick, Jock Livingston, Keith Andrew, Bob Clarke, Norman Oldfield, George Tribe

The ground record of 13,000 against the 1950 West Indians was quickly surpassed. By early afternoon there were about 18,000 there and, with little in the way of tiered seating, as Dennis Brookes says, "I don't suppose fifteen thousand of them could see."

But they did provide atmosphere and, with the Northants captain Freddie Brown asking the Australians to bat first, Frank Tyson did not disappoint them.

'In a sensational opening over,' the *Chronicle* told, 'Northamptonshire's T-bomb exploded with a bang. Tyson opened with the new ball from the football end and began his 25-yard run-up with a field of three slips, two gullies, a leg-slip, a backward short-leg, silly mid-on and a cover point.'

McDonald sliced the first ball over the head of Oldfield at gully, and it sped away for four. The second delivery 'kept lower to rap the pads of the 24-year-old Victorian schoolmaster', and such was the pace of the hard, new ball that, when the umpire's finger went up, it was as much as McDonald could do to hobble back to the pavilion.

'A lone figure against the background roar of the crowd,' Frank Tyson later called him.

The third delivery 'rose sharply to strike Hole a powerful blow on the thigh'. The fourth 'speeded through his guard to send back the middle stump.'

Australia were four for two after four balls and, Frank remembers, 'Keith wandered over, bemused, and shook me by the hand. I don't think he could believe it any more than I could.'

When de Courcy was bowled by Bob Clarke at the other end, it was ten for three, a very different score from the one that Keith has seen in his nightmare. "Once I'd taken one or two balls I was OK. In fact, I felt really good. I had a strange calmness about me all day."

'It could not last,' Tyson says, 'and it did not.'

Arthur Morris was still there, and he was joined by Neil Harvey who, Keith says, "played phenomenally". Hitting his seventh century of the tour, Harvey took the score to 185 for three by early afternoon.

George Tribe was bowling, the left-arm chinaman bowler who had migrated from Melbourne to Northampton via the Central Lancashire League. He was one of several Australians who, unable to make their national side, had made their way into the county championship. One was his team-mate Jock Livingston, second only to Hutton in the national batting averages. Another was Nottinghamshire's Bruce Dooland, the country's leading wicket-taker, while Tribe himself was the only man that summer to complete the all-rounder's double.

"George was probably the best cricketer I ever played with," Keith reckons. "He was the supreme wrist-spin bowler. He had the chinaman, the googly, two or three kinds of flipper, the whole shooting match. And he studied the batsmen. His attitude was so good, too. With the bat he was a real fighter."

Tribe's Test career had ended six years earlier, and now he had the opportunity to demonstrate what his compatriots had been missing. Not long after lunch he flighted the ball and, according to the Chronicle, 'Harvey, becoming even more adventurous, went down the wicket but was deceived by the spin and stumped by Andrew.'

Harvey, stumped Andrew, bowled Tribe, 118. It was Keith's first great moment.

Better still was to follow.

Freddie Brown, the captain, tried his seamers. A whole-hearted cricketer, even at the age of 42, he drifted one down leg that the young Ian Craig shaped to play and missed. "Nobody knew where it had gone," Keith remembers. Then, when they saw the bails off, they thought he must have been bowled. It was a moment before anybody realised that I had stumped him."

Craig, stumped Andrew, bowled Brown, 18.

It was Keith's second great moment, a much more special stumping than the first, and his captain knew it. "I saw him dancing this little jig," Keith recalls.

He looks back across fifty years. "So much followed from that moment." he says now. "The bad luck in my cricket career all seemed to stem from that chance at Brisbane. But so much of the good luck came from that stumping of Ian Craig."

Freddie Brown had played just once previously with Keith – against Cambridge University – and he would not play with him again. Yet that winter, when he sat down to write his memoirs and he picked his own tour party for the following winter in Australia, he had no hesitation in naming Godfrey Evans' deputy: 'A lot of cricketers may never have heard of Keith Andrew. They will. When he kept wicket for the county against the Australians, he impressed several of them with his efficiency. He is unobtrusive and good. Moreover he is a promising right-hand batsman who would get in at number eight in most county teams.'

"I think in a way, because of that stumping, Freddie thought that I was better than I was. But it was such a special one, one you remember all your life."

Even with the Australians as visitors, Northampton was not a popular ground for the leading cricket writers. The *Times* correspondent was at Lord's, watching Colin Cowdrey score a century in the Varsity match. But Keith's stumping had caught the most important eye of all, that of Freddie Brown, also chairman of the England selectors.

Brown had retired from that role by the next summer, but there was undoubtedly opportunity for him to pass on his views. His memoirs got another tour selection right, too: Frank Tyson. He described him as the fastest English bowler he had seen since Harold Larwood in Australia in 1932/3.

Australia were all out for 323, with George Tribe taking five wickets, and on the Saturday evening there was a dinner for the two teams at British Timken. Radio's Kenneth Horne was the guest speaker.

On Monday evening, after Northamptonshire had lost by an innings and 62 runs, the two teams were entertained by the County's Supporters' Association at the Salon-de-Danse. Some of the Northamptonshire cricketers liked to drink on such occasions, but the *Chronicle* reporter spotted that the Australian tourists had a different approach.

'They were rarely seen in the bar and seemed more intent on keeping their muscles in trim by dancing with pretty girls to the music of the Northamptonshire Regimental Dance Band. They needed plenty of stamina to get through the energetic motions of the Gay Gordons on such a hot – oh, so hot – night.'

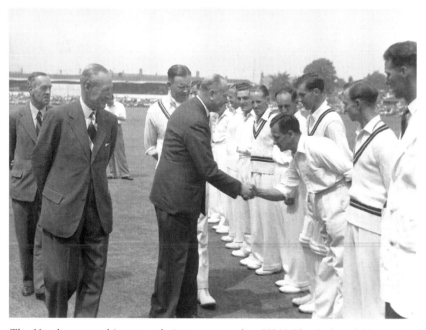

The Northamptonshire team being presented to HRH The Duke of Gloucester
(left to right) Colonel Coldwell (secretary), T.E. Manning (chairman),
Freddie Brown, the Duke, Bob Clarke, Brian Reynolds, George Tribe,
Jock Livingston, Keith Andrew, Norman Oldfield,
Doug Greasley (12th man), Laurie Gray (umpire)
"Norman Oldfield was brought up at Old Trafford in the thirties.
I don't think the rest of us would have bowed that low."

The Australians lost only one match that summer, but alas for them it was the final Test at The Oval. It was Coronation year, Everest had been climbed, and the Ashes were regained by England.

Tyson played the rest of the season in the county side, earning the brief comment in *Wisden* that he 'did enough to suggest that he might become a very fine fast bowler.'

Keith, meanwhile, returned to the design office at British Timken, to the occasional Club and Ground games and to the weekly routine of life at the Berrills.

At the end of the summer he and Joyce went on holiday to Bournemouth, and he remembers the moment when he realised what he had left behind at

Roseholme Road. "We were sitting on the beach one day, and I said, 'Oh God, I've left the cold Yorkshire pudding in the drawer in my room.'"

Keith and Joyce on Bournemouth pier

Nothing was said when he returned, and the card games and the meals continued. He grew ever closer to Joyce, and she still recalls one particular day when they were on the brink of engagement.

"I went down one weekend, and we went out on the Saturday morning looking at rings. Well, we came home for lunch and he said, 'I've just got to pop out for something.' I said, 'OK', and off he went. 'That's it,' I thought. 'He's gone to get the ring.' And, when he came back, I was all flushed and excited. And he put his head round the door and said, 'Come into the hall. I want to show you something.' So I went into the hall, and sheepishly from behind his back, he produced .... a set of golf clubs."

"It wasn't clubs," Keith chips in. "It was a leather golf bag."

"I said, 'Oh how lovely.'" There is laughter in her voice as she recalls the moment. "I should have taken heed."

*

Such was the impact Keith had made in that one match against the Australians that, at the start of the following summer, when he was still to make his county championship debut, he was selected to play for the MCC at Lord's in a prestigious season's opener against Yorkshire.

Rain limited him to just one hour's keeping, and it was not the only game so ruined. It was the coldest, gloomiest summer of the twentieth century and Keith's batting entirely failed to fulfil the promise that Freddie Brown had found in it. By early July he had scored 97 runs at an average of 6.93, and he was batting at number eleven.

"If I've one regret in cricket," he says now, "it's that I didn't push my batting more. I feel I didn't do my best somehow, and I'm annoyed with myself."

In his memory he was only an apprentice behind the stumps that summer, though his new captain Dennis Brookes remembers otherwise. "I never thought of Keith as learning his trade. He was a top-class keeper from the outset."

So it was a great shock to the young man when in mid-July he heard from Colonel Coldwell, the Northants secretary, that MCC had written to the county, enquiring about his availability for the winter tour of Australia.

Less than a fortnight before the picking of the party, the fixture list sent Northamptonshire players to Lord's to play Middlesex and, with influential eyes on them, events in that match advanced two more reputations.

Saturday brought more rain, time only for Northants to make 63 for two, but on the Monday there was a full day's play. Jock Livingston scored 133, Tyson weighed in with a powerful 60, and there was even an innings of 14 by Keith that occasioned the *Times* correspondent to remark that 'Andrew is certainly not the worst of number elevens.'

In the evening Northants bowled just seven overs. Jack Robertson was caught by Keith off Bob Clarke and, with the pitch much livelier than the slow Northampton square, Tyson set about the incoming Bill Edrich with a sequence of short balls. Edrich, never short of courage, took him on.

"He hooked Frank early on, and Frank bowled him another short one, only this time a bit quicker. Bill went to hook him again, that's the kind of guy he was, and the ball hit him on the jaw."

'He fell like a log with a sickening cry,' *The Times* reported. 'He was last seen being helped in on Tyson's shoulders before leaving for the hospital.'

The next morning Frank dismissed both Sharp and Compton, and 'to a reception of great warmth' Bill Edrich reappeared, having spent the night in hospital. 'His face was swollen and plastered, and his first ball, a short one from Tyson, hit him over the heart.'

Edrich, though 38 years old, had been a bomber pilot in the war and was undeterred. 'He hooked, if unsuccessfully, at each of the four bouncers he received.'

"The whole episode put the pair of them on the tour, I think."

Edrich was not the only casualty that match. "In the second innings Frank was bowling so fast that Bob Clarke at the other end felt like medium-pace. So I thought, 'I'll stand up to him', and he sent one down the leg side that hit me on the chin. I had to have several stitches. In fact, I'm still careful every time I shave."

They went down to Maidstone for the next match, and the press was buzzing with word of the lightning-fast Tyson. "They took a side-on picture of Frank at the start of his run-up and me in the keeper's position, speculating whether there had ever been a greater distance. But really, when they took the photograph, I was chatting to George Tribe. I still had to go back a couple of paces."

At Maidstone, with the stitches

Within the week Colonel Coldwell was opening another letter from Lord's, this one enquiring about the availability of Tyson.

The tour party was to be announced on Tuesday the 27th of July, on the sports bulletin at 6.15 on the Home Service, a five-minute slot wedged between the News and the piano duets of Rawicz and Landauer.

Northamptonshire were completing their return game against Middlesex, and Keith was padded up, hoping not to have to bat. Rain had ruined the match, but there did remain the excitement of playing for the four points for first innings lead. Middlesex had scored 309 and, when the ninth Northants wicket fell, the home team were on 308. The nervous number eleven had to put out of his mind the approaching bulletin.

'He walked away from the portable radio,' the *Chronicle* reported, 'and made his way slowly to the wicket.' He shouldered arms to the last ball of the over, and his partner John Wild struck the first of the next for four. With the clock approaching 6.15, he thoughtfully chipped up a catch, allowing Keith to return to the pavilion, to 'listen and fidget, nervously sipping a drink as the BBC announcer rattled off the seventeen names.'

According to *The Times*, it was a party with several places hard to forecast. 'It is possible to think of 35 players whose hearts will understandably be beating more quickly than usual today.'

All round England they were listening, and there were gasps as the names rushed past. Hutton, Compton, Bedser, Evans, Bailey, these were all expected. But no Laker, no Lock, no Trueman, and amid them all there were two men who seemed to have come from nowhere. They were the only two who had neither played in Tests so far that summer nor been on show at the Gentlemen-Players match at Lord's. 'The two surprises,' *The Times* called them.

Dick Wells (2nd XI captain), Keith Andrew, Vince Broderick, George Tribe

Tyson had taken just 52 wickets at an average of more than 22 – where Trueman had 87, the perennially ignored Les Jackson 93, both of them averaging under 15.

And Keith? *The Times* suggested that 'there will probably be those who feel that Evans's understudy should have had ability with the bat and accordingly would rather have seen Stephenson, Spooner, Harrison or McIntyre included.'

Tyson and Andrew. They were the first Northamptonshire professionals ever to be selected to tour Australia, and their team-mates, bursting into a chorus of 'For they are jolly good fellows', carried them back out to receive the general applause.

Jock Livingston, Freddie Jakeman, Doug Greasley, Keith, Des Barrick,
Vince Broderick, Frank Tyson, Johnny Wild, Ray Hogan, Dennis Brookes

The drinks flowed. Then the pair set off with George Tribe to honour an engagement, visiting patients at Manfield Orthopaedic Hospital.

Their new-found fame had to be kept in perspective.

"To see all those men in hospital, severely disabled, it was awful. So many of them had had motorbike accidents, and their lives were ruined. I've always had an abhorrence of motor bikes. I still feel, why don't they play soccer or cricket? It had a very great impact on me."

On Midsummer Meadow in Northampton, Chipperfield's Circus had set up the largest marquee in Europe. Five thousand spectators crowded into the tent to see a man and woman fired out of a cannon, then a tiger riding on the back of an elephant.

At the Repertory Theatre, T.S. Eliot's 'Cocktail Party' was on. A bemused *Chronicle* theatre critic concluded, 'Nothing is what it seems to be.'

"It took a while for the news to sink in," Keith recalls. "Then I realised that I was getting married in October – and not only that. I was still a reservist in my regiment, and I had a fortnight's training starting in September."

The last month of the season passed in a blur of excitement. His summer's tally of 25 stumpings, the majority of them off George Tribe, broke the county record – while, off the field, he was measured and fitted for a tour blazer and cap, vaccinated against smallpox and inoculated against typhoid. There was a wedding and honeymoon to rearrange, a trip to be made to London for *Guess My Story* and final goodbyes to be said at Roseholme Road.

"By then," Joyce recalls, "Mrs Berrill had become ill and taken to her bed. I was allowed to go in and see her but only after Emily had made the room immaculate. She sat up in this snowy white, starched bed, with her long ear-rings on and of course her handbag beside her."

It was as if a part of an older Northampton was passing away. Keith was their last lodger.

At the Repertory Theatre the county members laid on a farewell evening for Keith and Frank, and the two of them had to stand up and sing a duet.

Now is the hour
When we must say goodbye.
Soon we'll be sailing
Far across the sea.

The young wicket-keeper was an England Test cricketer when he returned the following April. He had been round the world, and he had shared the excitement of his team-mate's triumph. He was a married man, too, setting up home with Joyce in Weston Favell, on a newly-built estate on the outskirts of Northampton.

What a change twelve months had brought – but he was not looking to rest on his laurels.

"I'd watched Godfrey in Australia and, although I didn't have a bad tour, I knew in my heart that I had a lot to learn."

NORTHAMPTONSHIRE v AUSTRALIANS

Northampton. 4 & 6 July 1953

AUSTRALIA WON BY AN INNINGS AND 62 RUNS

AUSTRALIA

C.C. McDonald	lbw b Tyson	4
A.R. Morris *	c Brown b Tribe	80
G.B. Hole	b Tyson	0
J.H. de Courcy	b Clarke	4
R.N. Harvey	st Andrew b Tribe	118
I.D. Craig	st Andrew b Brown	18
A.K. Davidson	b Tribe	12
R.G. Archer	b Tribe	58
D. Ring	b Tribe	0
G.R. Langley +	c Livingston b Brown	12
J.C. Hill	*not out*	8
Extras	*b 3, lb 4, nb 2*	9
		323

1-4, 2-4, 3-10, 4-185, 5-218, 6-245, 7-246, 8-246, 9-284, 10-323

Tyson	15	2	62	2
Clarke	14	1	62	1
Brown	24	3	66	2
Broderick	10	0	27	0
Tribe	24.3	1	97	5

NORTHAMPTONSHIRE

D. Brookes	c Langley b Archer	9	c Langley b Davidson	8
N. Oldfield	c & b Archer	25	b Davidson	3
L. Livingston	c Hole b Archer	5	b Ring	30
D. Barrick	b Davidson	27	run out	19
B.C. Reynolds	c McDonald b Archer	21	lbw b Ring	8
V. Broderick	lbw b Archer	6	c Ring b Archer	10
G.E. Tribe	*not out*	25	c Hill b Ring	16
F.R. Brown *	c Hole b Archer	0	c Hill b Ring	8
K.V. Andrew +	c Langley b Davidson	5	b Hill	3
F.H. Tyson	c Hole b Ring	11	c Harvey b Ring	7
R.W. Clarke	c Davidson b Archer	0	*not out*	0
Extras	*b 4, lb 3*	7	*b 3, lb 4, nb 1*	8
		141		**120**

1-34, 2-35, 3-50, 4-78, 5-92, 6-103, 7-103, 8-119, 9-140, 10-141
1-8, 2-19, 3-67, 4-71, 5-78, 6-100, 7-102, 8-110, 9-120, 10-120

Davidson	20	4	62	2	9	2	21	2
Archer	15.4	1	56	7	10	3	18	1
Hill	9	6	9	0	11	6	11	1
Ring	3	1	7	1	22.3	7	46	5
Hole					4	1	12	0
Harvey					1	0	4	0

Umpires: A. Skelding and L.H. Gray

CHAPTER 4

A LAD IN LANCASHIRE

1929-1952

The class of boys and girls lined up in the form room in Waterloo Council School, Oldham. There were about forty of them, eight- and nine-year-olds, and, as the teacher read out their exam results, they took their places in the line. Education meant competition, and the last place of all in that line was occupied by a quiet, slightly solitary boy – a boy from the rougher streets on the other side of the park, a boy who was still quite new at the school.

"I had never felt so embarrassed," Keith says. "I looked up the line at all the boys and girls. Then, when I turned and looked the other way, there was nobody there."

His childhood memories are fragmentary, but this moment of humiliation has stayed with him.

He had started his education at Wellington Street School, near where he lived. It was not one of the better parts of Oldham, and his class-mates showed little inclination to study. "We had a lady teacher. I felt very sorry for her; she wasn't in control of the class. There was pandemonium in the room, fighting and shouting. I was getting nowhere. All I remember is sitting there and learning nothing, not to mention getting involved in a few fights."

He was a quiet child, living with his hard-pressed, mill-working mother, but even at the age of eight he had a determination to improve himself. On the way to his grandmother's house he would pass Waterloo School, and he knew one or two boys who went there. "And it dawned on me that they were going places more than I was. I don't know why, but I had this urge to do better so I got myself transferred. I don't remember the details, but I do know that I arranged it all by myself."

He started again at the new school, and after those first exams he was standing at the end of the line. He had a long way to go, but he did not lose heart.

"I told myself that next year I was going to be at the other end."

He held tenaciously to his ambition throughout the following months and, when the names were read out again, his was indeed the first to be called.

"I didn't get to grammar school. I went for the interview but, when they asked the questions, I didn't really know what they were talking about. But I won a place at the Junior Technical School, and that was another world. I was going to be an architect, I was going to build the Empire State Building, but I finished up in engineering."

His father, Sam Andrew, was the youngest of five, from a wealthy business family who lived in Frederick Street. His father's older sisters were women of importance in the town – one was a headmistress, another the wife of a mill-owner – but he had failed to maintain the family's status. He had married

Gladys Kershaw, a girl who worked in a mill and whose father was unemployed. The Andrew family never accepted the marriage.

By the time Keith was eight, his father had 'gone to Barrow', to work in the shipyards, and was never seen at home again.

It was barely a mile from their two-up, two-down home in Eldon Street to the grand houses in Frederick Street, but in Oldham in the late 1930s it was a journey into another world.

"My mother went to see them once, when she was in a desperate state, and they kept her standing at the door. That was enough. She never went again."

"This was when I was about seven years old. I was sent down to London in the school holidays to stay with my Uncle Sydney. I can still remember my mother taking me to Manchester and putting me on John Bright's express. They put me in the luggage van. I had a raincoat on and a label."

In the streets around his house the boys played football and cricket, sometimes heading off to the park, and Keith joined in. "People would have called it a tough district, and I do remember once or twice, when the grammar school boys from up in the hills went past, we threw snowballs at them. But there was no real nastiness. Mostly we were playing games. I had a very happy time."

Keith was an only child, however, and he had to learn to enjoy his own company. "I had an old billiards table in my bedroom, a small-scale one. How I got it, I'll never know. I used to play cricket on it, with a marble and cigarette cards. I made a bat out of wood and, if I hit the marble into a pocket, I scored runs."

His morning walk to Waterloo School took him along Queen's Road, beside the park, where the large, double-fronted houses each stood grandly behind a generous front garden and a low stone wall. "I always seemed to have a tennis ball with me, and I used to walk along, throwing it at the base of the wall – so that it bounced back at different angles. I never thought anything of it at the time; I certainly never thought I was having catching practice or anything like that. I just did it – with no idea of what it would one day lead to."

In the school playground, where they played impromptu cricket and football matches, he developed a reputation as a ball player. One lunch-time, when he was eleven, a master pulled him aside.

"'There's a trial for Oldham Boys cricket team,' he said. 'It's down at Abbey Hills. I'll put your name down.' I'd never played a proper game."

It was the summer of 1941; the war was nearing the end of its second year. Many of the young men were away in the forces, and the facilities for sport were rudimentary.

"The ground for the trial was all shale, no grass at all, and this tall, grey-haired man came up to me. I found out later that his name was Mr Bailey. I've always remembered him with affection. 'What's your name?' he said. 'Andrew, sir.' 'You can sit on the side, Andrew. We'll get you on later.' And I sat there, feeling miserable, watching the match.

"Then, by the grace of God, the ball hit the wicket-keeper on the head and cut him. So Mr Bailey came across to me, 'Do you want to have a go, Andrew, keep wicket?' And I did. Anything to get in the game. And I enjoyed it so much, I was involved the whole time, and I got picked for the Oldham Boys' team."

The next summer he was on the train that rolled across the moor to Huddersfield. He was keeping wicket for Oldham Schoolboys against Huddersfield Schoolboys on the Fartown ground where Yorkshire had played every summer before the war. "Malcolm Hilton was in our team – and Alf Alker, who became a lifelong friend. I remember them in the carriage. They were already playing at Werneth Cricket Club. That's how I came to play there. They got me to go along with them."

And his memories of the game at Fartown?

"We had greengage jam for tea."

The Werneth ground was situated in the Coppice, a respectable part of Oldham just before Frederick Street where his father's family lived. The club president was Granville Mills, the town's leading stock-broker, while Clifford Stott, captain for many years, was a bank manager. It was another world for Keith – "In the pavilion they had the best billiards table I'd ever seen." – but his mother, ever anxious to give him a chance in life, made sure that he was not out of place. "I don't know where she got them from, but I had the cleanest flannels in Oldham."

The club was a leading member of the Central Lancashire League, hiring a professional each summer and attracting sufficient spectators to have seven turnstiles around the ground.

Keith had been there once with his father. "I have a memory of sitting on the far side of the ground, and out of the pavilion came 'Ted' Badcock, who was the Werneth pro. They say he used to drink a couple of whiskies before he went in to bat."

Badcock was a colourful character – 'tall, dark and handsome,' according to his *Wisden* obituary. Born in India, educated at Wellington College in England, he had played in New Zealand's first ever Test team before arriving in Oldham. He hit the ball hard, he bowled fast, and his fielding electrified the large crowds. 'Men would work a four hour shift on a Saturday morning,' the club website tells, 'then hurry to the ground to stand for five hours, three or four deep, to see him.'

When Nelson came to Werneth for their traditional two-evening friendly match, he did battle with Learie Constantine, and the club had to erect a large stand to provide extra seating.

It was not difficult for the young boy to feel the magic of it all, but his father left and Keith did not return to Werneth till Malcolm Hilton and Alf Alker took him along with them.

His mother worked long hours. "In most of the mill families, it was the women who kept things going. They started work as girls when they were twelve or thirteen. They got up at five o'clock, then many of them would come home from the mill to make breakfast. My mother worked near Hathershaw Road. She had to walk down the valley and up the other side. A mile and a half, maybe. And, when I had a dog, she used to come home at lunch-time to feed it."

There was no sign of his father, only word that he was working on the submarine Thetis. It had sunk on its first trial, but they had raised it and he was on board when they tried again with greater success. "I held onto that in my mind. It gave me a little bit of credibility – my father going down in the Thetis – but really I hardly knew him."

One night in Oldham the air raid siren went and, as he and his mother knelt under the table, they heard the sound of a flying bomb. "That's at my mother's," she said and, after the all-clear, they walked together in the dark up Queen's Road. "It was after two o'clock. I can see it now. Windows were in everywhere, one or two walls were down, and, when we got to my grandmother's little two-up, two-down house – number 12, Kenton Street – it was quite a relief to find it still standing. She came to the door. She'd been in the cellar, but my grandfather was still in bed. He didn't work very much, but he always wore a thick leather belt that used to terrify me. We went upstairs, and there he was, fast asleep, with plaster all over him."

In his younger days Keith's grandfather had been a hard-drinking rugby player, and on the sideboard was a heavy lump of green glass. "He'd been playing rugby in St Helens, he went drinking, and he picked it up. It needed a lot of lifting, but apparently he brought it back overnight, walking most of the way. It must have been twenty miles or more."

For Keith's mother they were years of poverty and hard work. She was an intelligent and a determined woman, and the great priority of her life was to give her son – 'our Keith', as she called him – a good start. "I was her pride and joy. I tried for her. And I was a very happy boy. So it wasn't hard. I was as free as the wind, that's how I felt, but I wanted to work."

Mother and son

Keith prospered at the Junior Technical College, he played football for the Hope Sunday School side, and with each passing summer the cricket grew in importance.

In the ginnels, the alleys that ran between the houses, he played with a younger boy, Jack Dyson, whose mother worked on the market. They were rough and ready games, with little equipment. but they would both graduate to county cricket and Jack would score a goal for the winning Manchester City side in the 1956 F.A. Cup Final.

In 1943, at the age of thirteen, Keith was captain of the Oldham Schoolboys. In 1944 he played for the Werneth Under-15 eleven. "Alf Alker, Malcolm and Jimmy Hilton and I were all in the side. Turner Warrener used to take us. A tiny, old man, five foot nothing. He was such an enthusiast. I kept wicket in his cap, with its black, yellow and green circular stripes. One day we played at a place called Droylsden, and he was umpiring. I can see him now. I stumped this lad out, and he gave him out from the bowler's end."

Keith progressed from the third to the second eleven, then in 1945, with the war over, he made his first appearance for the first team.

"It was Oldham Wakes week, and Harry Wright, the first-team keeper, went on holiday. We played at Heywood. Bill Farrimond, the old Lancashire and England keeper, was playing for them. He came in to bat at number six and, when a wicket fell at the other end, he put his bat down and came over. 'Now, lad, who taught you to go down the leg side like that?' 'Nobody,' I said. I think I'd quite impressed him. But he showed me how to stand more to the off side and to put more weight on my left foot."

It was the first real coaching Keith had received.

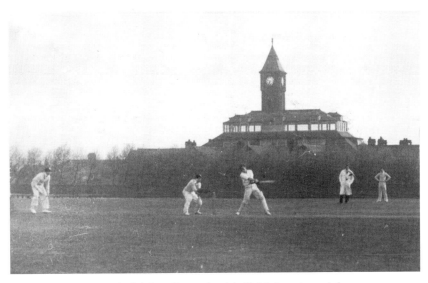

Werneth Cricket Ground, with Keith keeping wicket
"I carried this picture for years – as a memory of a very happy time."

That summer, the chief draughtsman at Dronsfield Brothers visited Keith's school and selected his friend Fred Brock and him for the two vacancies in the Drawing Office. They continued their studies at Oldham Municipal College: four evenings a week and Saturday mornings, for a National Certificate in Mechanical Engineering. "Brocky was cleverer than me. I was just a trier, but I was very competitive. I used to use reams of paper, writing down all the formulae so that I could fix them in my memory. I really worked hard."

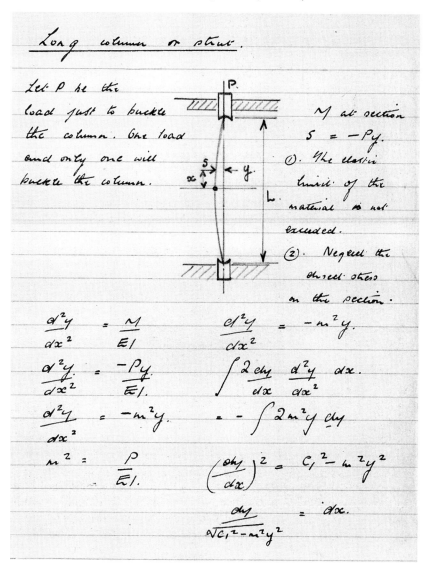

Werneth's professional in 1946 was Eric Denison, a Yorkshireman from the same village as Hedley Verity. In the late '30s there had been talk that one day he would succeed Verity, but he had had a hard war. Escaping from a prisoner-of-war camp in Italy, he had been on the run for three years and, with nobody in England knowing his whereabouts, he arrived home to find that his league club Middleton had offered terms to another professional. Meanwhile Yorkshire had had to find a replacement for Verity, who had died in a prisoner-of-war hospital in Italy, and they had settled on the 43-year-old Arthur Booth who had been taking wickets all war in the Bradford League.

Denison worked in Schofield's, Oldham's sports shop, and he persuaded the local education authority to pioneer some indoor winter coaching for youngsters.

"He used to coach us at Werneth, too. On Wednesday evenings. The first time I saw him in the net, I wondered what he was doing, I'd never heard of coaching. But he'd got such a lot of lads that sometimes, by the time I got my turn, it was going dark."

When the sun went down, they retired to the Werneth pavilion, and Eric Denison sat and told stories, many about the now legendary Verity. "I was spell-bound," Keith recalls.

It was Verity who had the best bowling figures in all cricket's history, with ten wickets for ten runs in a county match at Trent Bridge. It was Verity, also, who had taken fourteen Australian wickets at Lord's one Monday in June 1934. In the rationed world of 1946, there was something golden about such past glories.

One day in August Keith decided to find out about cricket beyond the Central Lancashire League. He travelled by bus to Old Trafford to watch Lancashire play Somerset, but the cricket did not catch his imagination as Badcock at Werneth had done. "It was a warm day, and I remember M.M. Walford batting. But I got a bit bored, to be honest. It took me a hell of a long time to get there, and it cost so much. I didn't go again."

At the end of that summer of 1946, with English cricket still recovering from its six-year hiatus, Wally Hammond led a team to Australia – and it seems probable that Hedley Verity, had he survived the war, would have been at St Pancras station, catching the same boat train that eight years later in 1954 was boarded by the young wicket-keeper who, as a sixteen-year-old lad, had listened spell-bound to Eric Denison's stories.

The *Northampton Chronicle* had their reporter at St Pancras that day in September 1954, and he had a moving detail for the readers: 'Keith Andrew had a famous bag stored away in the team's luggage. It belonged to Hedley Verity, the great Yorkshire and England bowler who was killed during the war. Mrs Verity gave the bag to Andrew as a souvenir.'

"Eric Denison gave it to me before the tour," Keith explains. "It was an old leather bag in good condition, but the name of Hedley Verity was very faint. I had it for some years, but in the end it fell apart, and I bought a big case."

Through 1947 his studies progressed – second each year to Fred Brock – and by July 1948 he was playing regularly for the Werneth first eleven, not only keeping wicket but batting at the top of the order.

Malcolm Hilton, the Oldham schoolboy who had introduced him to Werneth, had already graduated to Old Trafford where in May that year, in only his third appearance for Lancashire, he hit the headlines by dismissing Bradman twice in one match.

Malcolm's younger brother Jim was in the Werneth first eleven while Jack Dyson and Geoff Pullar were learning the game in the third team. Werneth was just one club out of fourteen in the Central Lancashire League, yet in the late 1940s they produced five county cricketers, three of them going on to play for England.

The summer of 1949 was a golden one. It was dry, sunny and warm – with more dry days than any other summer in the twentieth century – and the league professionals broke all the records. Frank Worrell came from Barbados to hit over 1,500 runs at Radcliffe, George Tribe from Melbourne topped 150 wickets for Milnrow, and Vinoo Mankad arrived at Castleton Moor from Bengal for a summer's work of 1,466 runs and 124 wickets, the first league cricketer to do the double in his debut season.

The previous summer Charles Barnett had batted for England against Australia, now he was scoring stylish centuries for Rochdale. George Pope had bowled for England at Lord's in 1947, now at Heywood he – like Tribe – was beating the league's wicket record. Werneth had the Jamaican JK Holt, who in five years' time would hit Len Hutton's England for 166 in the Test at Bridgetown. Walsden had Ellis Achong, the West Indian chinaman bowler. Royton had Jock Livingston, who might have toured with Bradman's Australians, had it not been for the emergence of the young Neil Harvey.

Then there was Oldham's Stan Crump, the gritty Staffordshire all-rounder, a professional who had never been able to play first-class cricket but who was certainly not out of place in this company.

It was a happy summer for Keith. He passed his National Certificate exams, for the first time outscoring his great rival Fred Brock. "I was top of the whole shooting match, and I won a scholarship to Manchester University worth two pounds a week. But I had to wait a year before I could go. I'd got to take an English exam."

There was the thrill of the cricketers he was meeting. "One of the greatest pleasures of my years in cricket is that I became such good friends with Frankie Worrell. He had a magical personality. I played against him in the very first match he played for Radcliffe, in 1948. The first ball he drove so hard that he knocked the stumps over at the other end. The second ball he was bowled – by Raymond Lees. I couldn't believe it. I can see his face now. The sadness of his eyes. Normally he was so happy, but sometimes you could see a sadness. The week after, he got 151."

There was also the thrill of his own achievements at this level. "I used to get half a crown a victim from the Werneth Cricket Club. I once caught a catch at

Walsden. JK Holt was bowling, the batsman had a swing, and the ball went high into the air – with the wind blowing. Cover-point could have caught it easily, but 'Mine,' I shouted. I finished up catching it on the boundary and sitting down on a form. 'You'll do anything for half a crown,' they said, but it went in the kitty for a big party at the end of the season. We all went to Blackpool.

"I got fifty in a night match against Burnley, with Cec Pepper bowling. How I got it, I don't know, but I did, and there was a collection made among the crowd. I'd never seen so many coins. It was a huge bag."

Keith kept enough for a slap-up fish-and-chip meal at the Riverside Café with Alf Alker, but for the professionals it was an important part of their earnings. "Dorothy Tribe always said that George lived on his collections. He used to get at least five wickets every game."

Frank Worrell

Frank Worrell started on five hundred pounds a summer, better than most county cricketers at the time, but this was only the half of his real earnings, as he revealed in his autobiography: "It was nothing to see forty or fifty pounds jingle out of the boxes in pennies, sixpences and shillings."

It was a golden summer. The post-war austerity was slowly receding, and nowhere was busier than the North-West. "England's bread hangs by Lancashire's thread," the Mayor of Oldham declared, and there were eight million spindles at work in the cotton mills of the town.

In August, the town of Oldham celebrated its centenary, and two cricket matches were staged. The first, at the Oldham club, was between a Central Lancashire League eleven and a team of Australians. The second, on the afternoon of Thursday the eighteenth of August, at Werneth, saw the League eleven take on the full Lancashire side, with only Cyril Washbrook absent.

Keith was still working in the drawing office at Dronsfield Brothers. "I'd just done my first design for one of the textile machines. The Roller End Grinding Machine." But he slipped away without permission when he was selected to play for the League eleven at Werneth.

"It was the day that changed my whole life. I'd played once or twice with the pros on Sundays, in charity matches, but only as a batsman. Jock Livingston was the captain, and he used to keep wicket himself. But that day at Werneth he turned to me. 'You're a wicket-keeper, aren't you? ... Well, you can keep today.' And I thought, 'Oh crumbs, we've got George Tribe and Wally Walmsley, spinners who bamboozled everybody, and I'm going to be keeping in front of all these people.' But somebody was smiling on me."

It was a Thursday afternoon, a working day in Oldham, but more than two thousand people crowded into the little Werneth ground. The bar below the scoreboard did good business with its beer, and the League eleven declared on 157 for nine. Frank Worrell scored 49, Jock Livingston 46, while Keith at number eleven was left with 0 not out.

Five of the Lancashire side had already completed 1,000 runs that summer, but in truth there were several county attacks less testing than that of the League eleven. Worrell and the Australian Des Fitzmaurice opened the bowling, with Tribe and Walmsley, two more Australians, both spinning it from the back of the hand.

Keith caught Ikin off Worrell. He watched as Geoff Edrich fell to a brilliant, one-handed catch on the boundary. Then he settled to the challenge of keeping for the first time to the left-arm mysteries of the Australian George Tribe.

"George was very good to me. I couldn't tell which way he was turning it, but he kept nearly everything on the off side."

Winston Place progressed serenely to 44, and Tribe pitched a ball on leg stump. It was his chinaman, the ball turned further to leg and the batsman went forward and missed.

"I don't know why I went down the leg side. I suppose I must have read it off the pitch and gone after it. I certainly didn't read it out of his hand. And I stumped Winston Place. It was one of the most special moments in my whole life in cricket."

Place, stumped Andrew, bowled Tribe, 44.

The *Oldham Chronicle* was full of praise:

> A feature of the Lancashire innings was an outstanding display by amateur Keith Andrew, the Werneth wicket-keeper who took two fine catches and brought off a one-handed piece of stumping on the leg side. His entire work behind the stumps was clean, unostentatious, most workmanlike and quite up to county standard.

"If ever there was a moment in my life that was responsible for my playing first-class cricket, that was it."

Lancashire ended the day on 157 for seven, with the scores level. 'TIGHT GRIPPING GAME WAS A HUGE SUCCESS,' read the *Chronicle* headline. But at Dronsfield Brothers the next day the triumphant young keeper was brought back down to earth. "The chief draughtsman, Fred Bates, sent for me. 'I believe you were playing cricket yesterday, lad,' he said. I think it was only my success with the Roller End Grinding Machine that saved me from getting the sack."

He moved soon afterwards to the National Gas and Oil Engine Company at Ashton, looking for more experience of the workshops. "I played for their football team, at inside left, and in one match I was alongside Hughie Gallagher."

Gallagher had been a legendary goal-scorer in the 1920s, the darling of Newcastle when they won the championship in 1927, one of the Wee Blue Devils, the great Scottish forward line that had beaten England at Wembley. But he was a plain-talking Glaswegian, he fell out with authority and, by the time he was appearing with Keith in this works match, he had come a long way down from his glory years, heading for a lonely suicide in front of an express train.

"They brought him on for ten minutes. He was working there as a labourer, he was 51, and he wasn't in good shape. It was very sad."

Needing a wage to bring home to his mother, Keith turned down his university scholarship, preferring to continue his education on day release at Manchester Municipal College of Technology. "They made me work hard there, but I was fuelled by so much desire. I never felt that studying was hard work."

Meanwhile he continued to play occasionally for Jock Livingston's Sunday side, mixing not just with Tribe and Worrell but with the pros of the Lancashire League: Everton Weekes, Cec Pepper, Bill Alley. "It was like a travelling band of players, with Jock Livingston – the Doctor – its mastermind."

Worrell was the gentlemanly stylist, who returned the following summer as part of the victorious West Indian Test team. One of the great three Ws: Weekes, Worrell, Walcott. "Everton wasn't an artist, like Frankie was. He was a ruthless square cutter, and he hit the ball very hard off his legs. He was more of a Bradman type. But Frankie, in terms of the aesthetics of the game, he was the best batsman I ever saw."

Tribe was the thoughtful craftsman, accepting philosophically that his three-match Test career was over and studying every batsman for a chink of fault in their technique. But the character who provided the real combustion was Cec Pepper. He had been one of the Australian stars of the 1945 Victory Tests, but somehow he had had too many scrapes with authority to feature in the real Test sides that followed. 'I cannot imagine any match involving Pepper following a peaceful course,' one Manchester journalist wrote.

"I remember batting with him one day. He had 99, and he came down the wicket to me. 'I'm not f---ing getting out now,' he said. 'I'm here to impress these f---ing people.' And he hit the next ball straight over the pavilion. 'Wow,' I thought. I was still a bit starry-eyed.

"He was given out lbw one day at Oldham and, as he went off, this little man with a broad Oldham accent said to him, 'You're a bloody Australian twister, you are.' And Cec got hold of him. 'I'll twist your f---ing nose,' he said, and he grabbed this chap's nose. He used to wind them up a bit. They had to smuggle him out of the back of the pavilion about two hours later.

"But I liked him. He was good with our youngsters, and of course later he was a good umpire."

For these professionals the golden summer of 1949 ran into an equally glorious winter. The MCC had pulled out of their commitment to send a team to India, and in their place George Duckworth, the old Lancashire and England keeper, assembled a Commonwealth side, captained by 'Doctor' Livingston and based largely on his travelling band.

From early October till March they journeyed about the sub-continent, scoring runs at a sparkling pace and providing so much entertainment that they were invited back the following winter. Worrell scored 684 runs in the five unofficial Tests, George Tribe took 99 wickets on the tour, and only Cec Pepper missed out. Furious with the local umpires, he returned home after the first Test.

The young Indian all-rounder Polly Umrigar impressed the tourists, and the following summer he was Werneth's professional, bowling brisk swing that Keith stood up to the stumps to take. Jock Livingston had left, signed by Northamptonshire after being spotted by their coach Jack Mercer, so he was not present at Blackpool when Keith stumped Jim Parks senior off an Umrigar in-swinger that drifted down leg. "But I'm told that Jock got hold of the report of the match."

Keith was invited to play for Lancashire second eleven – but only as a batsman – and, when the game was ruined by rain, he decided that he would not pursue the possibility of county cricket.

"I played cards with Ken Grieves and one or two of them. Stan Worthington the coach approached me, he thought I might make it as a batsman, but I knew in my heart that I wasn't good enough. I was just a plodder. And I'd played with Jock Livingston, Everton Weekes, Polly Umrigar, Frank Worrell – so I didn't rate myself at all. Batting didn't interest me that much, anyway, and I wanted to finish my engineering training. I had a living to earn and, if they'd known what I was really like as a batsman, they wouldn't have paid me in washers."

Keith was an Oldham lad, and the pull of Lancashire County Cricket Club was not strong.

"Every Yorkshireman aspires to play for Yorkshire, but every Lancastrian doesn't aspire to play for Lancashire. I don't know what the reason is. Perhaps it's because Old Trafford is the centre of Lancashire cricket and it's in Manchester, whereas Yorkshire cricket is everywhere. Later, when I did play county cricket, there was a part of me that wished I'd played for Lancashire.

Old Trafford was a great place to keep wicket, and I always felt very at home whenever I played there."

Cricket remained a pastime as he became a graduate of the Institute of Mechanical Engineers and passed a course in Business Administration. From the day he stood at the bottom of his class at Waterloo School he had set his heart on educational success – as his young cousin Les was also doing. Keith's mother had a younger brother Sam who drove a laundry van, and his boy Les also followed the twin paths of education and sport.

"He became Doctor Kershaw, a Senior Lecturer in Chemistry at the University of Salford, but he was football mad. He used to go to all the matches and analyse the way the teams played. And Terry Venables, when he was manager of Spurs, took him on. Les would watch their opponents two weeks beforehand and send in all his findings. So there'd be fifteen or twenty sheets of graph paper on Terry Venables' desk each week. Now he's the director of the academy at Old Trafford, and his son is a consultant orthopaedic surgeon."

Keith and Les had found their way out of the back streets of Oldham, but do the same opportunities exist for the youngsters today?

"Not in the same way," Keith thinks. "I was a free spirit, because my mother trusted me. But you can tell from my story that I had a lot of luck. I was in the right place at the right time."

He was never more in the right place than on that day in August 1949 when he stumped Winston Place off George Tribe. It would be three years before the significance of that moment finally registered.

*

In the spring of 1951, with his qualifications completed, it was time for Keith to become Craftsman K.V. Andrew in the Royal Electrical and Mechanical Engineers, stationed at Arborfield, near Reading.

"After I'd been through the basic training, I had the opportunity to go to Sandhurst or to become a mathematics instructor at Arborfield. And I opted for that. The equipment was brilliant. I was involved with the Centurion tank and with all its electronic circuitry."

National Service brought new cricketing adventures.

"I put my name down for a battalion cricket match. We all went to the ground for the trial, and this boy from Middlesex, quite a cocky chap, had the gloves on before I knew what had happened. I didn't keep. But in the first match he had his nose broken, and I finished up later that summer playing for the Army at Lord's."

He did not bat against either the Royal Navy or the Royal Air Force, Signalman D.B. Close scoring the runs, but for the Combined Services against the Public Schools he walked to the wicket to bat at Lord's for the first time.

"I was bowled for nought, by Colin Smith – Sir Colin, as he is now. My stump cartwheeled out of the ground and stuck in the turf. And, as I went back through the Long Room, this chap – I'll never forget him as long as I live –

was looking at me through an enormous eye-glass. And he said to his friend, 'Who was that one?'

"I asked the attendant which bath Bradman had used. 'That'll do for me,' I said. 'I won't be here again.'"

The corps magazine carried a report on his century against the Royal Army Service Corps – "I still dream of that innings." – and the next May he was in the Combined Services side for the three-day match against Glamorgan at Cardiff. "I knew it was a first-class fixture, but I didn't think of myself as a first-class cricketer."

In late June he was at Gillingham, playing the touring Indians in a two-day match. Every one of that Combined Services eleven went on to play county cricket, five of them – Jim Parks, Ray Illingworth, Micky Stewart, Fred Trueman and Keith himself – receiving Test honours. Trueman had already become a Test cricketer, his debut at Headingley sensational as India were reduced to nought for four, but at Gillingham the bowling honours were taken by Gloucestershire's rough-hewn off-spinner 'Bomber' Wells.

"Bomber was a great bowler," Keith says. "He should have played for England."

Fifty years on, Bomber is quick to return the compliment. "There was no better keeper than Keith. You never noticed he was there, and that's how keepers should be."

He was back at Lord's in August, but the real developments in his life were not in these Services matches.

A weekend trip home during the winter had taken him to Boundary Park, the Oldham Athletic football ground, and there he set eyes for the first time on Joyce Lancaster.

Meanwhile in Northampton the county club was busy trying to assemble a successful side. Jock Livingston had joined them in 1950, and he recommended his friend George Tribe in Lancashire. Tribe was qualified to play by May 1952, when he began his championship career with 40 wickets in his first four games.

Ken Fiddling was the Northants keeper, but he had brittle fingers, struggled to read Tribe's chinamen and googlies and by mid-summer was out of the team with appendicitis. There was an urgent need to find a young replacement.

Jock Livingston had been the mastermind of the Lancashire League's travelling band of players. He had captained that day at Werneth when Winston Place had been stumped, and he volunteered the answer.

"There's a lad up in Lancashire who can read George."

"They contacted me at the barracks. At first I said 'No, I'm going to make a career in engineering.' But then they mentioned the possibility of a job at British Timken."

He was summoned from Arborfield to play for the Northampton Club and Ground side against Peterborough Town.

Arborfield to Northampton was not an easy journey. By train it would have been expensive, involving a trip into Paddington, so Keith resolved to hitch-hike across country with his hold-all.

"I finished up in an open-sided Walls ice-cream van. I had two shillings and sixpence in my pocket, and the driver suddenly decided he had some deliveries to make and dropped me on the bend by Wolverton Station. And I only had just enough time and money to catch the train to Northampton for the start of the match."

Ken Turner, the assistant secretary, was confused about the regulations concerning registration of players born in other counties, and he entered Keith on the scorecard as K.V. Smith. Hugh Wright the captain asked him to open the batting.

His partner that day was Peter Arnold, a New Zealander who had turned up for trial in Spring 1950, having spent £65 on a boat ticket.

"It was a wonderful voyage," he recalls. "The Empire Games had just finished, and we had all the teams in the boat. The majority of the passengers were in their teens or early twenties so it was a fair old time."

Arnold arrived at the County Ground in April and stayed for a two-day trial.

"I went back to London on the train with Jack Mercer. He said, 'They haven't told you, but they're taking you on. I'll sort you out with digs.' I finished up out in Colwyn Road, by the racecourse. I was in the attic, sharing a double bed with a Scotsman called John Dennis. I couldn't understand what he was saying, and probably he couldn't understand me, either. Having come from a reasonable family in New Zealand, I thought to myself, 'Life's changed a bit now.'"

And his opening partnership with Keith against Peterborough?

"We put on some runs. Keith was a very good straight player. But I'm pretty certain he ran me out."

"I did," Keith confesses, "and not for the last time."

By the summer of 1953 Keith was working in the design office at British Timken, living in the Berrills' attic and playing against the Australians, keeping to Tyson and Tribe in front of 18,000 spectators.

"And of course I couldn't read George consistently at all. Well, not then. I did later."

In April 1954 he reported to the Northampton County Ground, ready to take his place in the championship eleven.

CHAPTER 5

LOOKING FOR REPLACEMENTS

Northamptonshire County Cricket Club

Northamptonshire had a population of less than 400,000 in 1954, substantially fewer than any of their competitors in the county championship. Lancashire, with five million, and Yorkshire, with four-and-a-half, each drew their support from populations more than ten times as great, with even the city of Leeds more populous than the Midland county.

The market town of Northampton was the main conurbation, but the surrounding club cricket lacked the passion of the northern leagues and produced few first-class players. For a few years at the start of the century, the county side had boasted enough fine cricketers to gain elevation on merit to the championship. After a shaky start, including a record low total of 12 all out at Gloucester in 1907, they became a formidable side, finishing as runners-up in 1912. Alas, the war changed all that, and the '20s and '30s were an unremitting struggle.

Eleventh place in 1925 was the pinnacle of their inter-war success, with the '30s yielding one year at 13th, two at 16th and seven at 17th and last. There were regular proposals to return to minor county status or to amalgamate with Leicestershire.

Dennis Brookes, a promising sixteen-year-old batsman from near Leeds, arrived in 1932 for a trial, making his debut for the county in 1934. He remembers how threadbare the playing staff was in those years.

"The first team was made up of eight professionals and three amateurs, and the only other players on the staff were myself, a young man called Cullen from South Africa and Norman Grimshaw, who came highly recommended from Yorkshire. There was no second eleven. I used to try to get a game on the Racecourse. Mostly we were bowling to members in the nets."

Vince Broderick of Bacup in the Lancashire League arrived as a teenager later in the decade, and he also remembers bowling to members. "We used to call it mincing. There was one chap: Mr Barrett, of Barrett's Boots and Shoes, 'Walk the Barrett Way' was their slogan. If you bowled him out, he gave you sixpence. He had a bad leg so we used to get him playing forward, then slip in a short one."

The summer of 1933 saw a slight revival, five victories in 24 matches taking them to 13th place in the table. "I believe that there was even talk of Northants being a dark horse for the championship," Dennis says. "We had some fine players: Nobby Clark, Fred Bakewell, Vallance Jupp, Austin Matthews."

Clark and Bakewell both appeared in the Tests that summer – but Clark, a left-arm fast bowler, was already 31, and three summers later Bakewell's career ended with injury in a motor accident that also killed R.P. Northway, the amateur. Jupp was past his best at 42, and in any case he spent the summer of 1935 in gaol as a result of another motoring accident. All the promise of this team was gone by 1937 when Matthews, frustrated at the committee's decision to delay his benefit, left for Glamorgan.

"They all grew old and left," Dennis says, "and there was nobody behind to replace them."

Dennis himself made his first appearance in May 1934 when one of the amateurs pulled out of the trip to Bradford to play Yorkshire. They lost by an innings in two days and so short-staffed were they that, when Bakewell damaged his knee, Len Hutton had to field for them. At the end of the summer they were back at the foot of the table, with just two victories to their name.

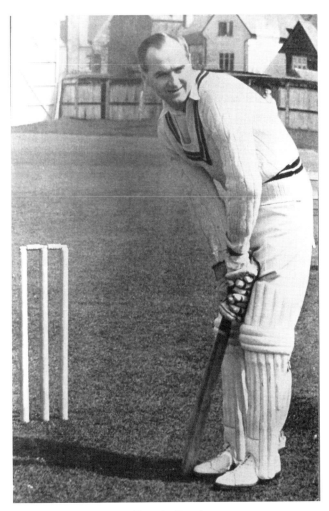

Dennis Brookes

In May 1935 the nineteen-year-old Brookes was in the side for the opening fixture at Taunton, making 20 in a first innings total of 171. When he was lbw for a duck in the second innings, Northants were just 31 runs ahead with six wickets down. But Timms completed a century and Somerset, chasing 124 for victory, were dismissed for 75 by Clark and Matthews.

In the scorebook, in the distinctive copperplate with which Leo Bullimer had adorned the pages since 1900, were written the words: 'Northamptonshire opened their Season with a great victory, mainly through fine bowling and fielding in the Second Innings.'

For the young Dennis Brookes, starting a fresh season, the victory seemed unremarkable – but another did not follow till May 1939. And by then only Jack Timms and Reg Partridge survived of his Taunton team-mates.

From the conclusion of that first game in 1935 to the end of the summer of 1938, the county's record in all matches was: Played 101, Won 0, Drawn 40, Lost 61. Only twice in the 58 cricketing summers that have followed has a county failed to win a single first-class match: Notts in 1967, Durham in 1996. Yet Northamptonshire managed it three seasons in a row in the '30s. In 1937 they even contrived to lose by nine wickets to Cambridge University.

But there was not the demand for success that exists in the modern world. "We didn't get depressed," Dennis reflects. "We loved the game, and we enjoyed playing." And their scorer remained eternally optimistic: "Bully was a great enthusiast. He used to come in the dressing room every morning. 'This is the one,' he'd say. 'We're going to win this.'"

Dennis Brookes scored a century against Cambridge University in the first match of 1939, and that brought to an end their long sequence of matches without victory. But the celebrations at Fenner's were as nothing compared with those at the County Ground three weeks later.

In their championship season they started with a draw after following on against Hampshire, then three defeats, the last two of them suffered within two days. Only their neighbours and great rivals Leicestershire stood below them in the table when the two teams met at the County Ground on the Saturday of the Whit Bank Holiday weekend.

The omens were not good. Leo Bullimer had broken his kneecap while alighting from a train and was not there to encourage them. Dennis was feeling ill: "I woke up in the morning with a sore throat and a boil on my neck. I felt dreadful. But I had to play because, in those days, if you didn't play, you didn't get paid." And the Leicestershire players were unusually high-spirited when they arrived.

In the Whit match the previous year Northants had collapsed to a heavy innings defeat, unable to fathom the mysteries of the Australian Jack Walsh's chinamen and googlies. Walsh, however, had been brought to England by Sir Julien Cahn, a wealthy businessman with his own ground and team, and his appearances in county cricket were rare.

Dennis went through the gates at the same time as his fellow Yorkshireman, Leicestershire's batsman Frank Prentice. "'It'll be all over in two days,' Frank said. 'We've got Walshy playing.'"

At five past twelve the scoreboard showed five wickets down for eight runs – only it was Leicestershire who were batting. "I think they'd come off a slow wicket somewhere, and they were all playing back when they should have been playing forward."

The *Northampton Chronicle* confirms this: 'The only explanation that could be offered for this sorry state was that the Leicestershire men were beaten by the pace of the pitch.'

So great was the excitement that the *Chronicle* even suggested that the county might remove the ignominy of more than its long barren run in the county championship: 'Spectators were beginning to ask their neighbours whether Northamptonshire was going to get rid of that lowest total record which has been held since 1907.'

The later Leicestershire batsmen lifted the score to 134, but even these runs were a blessing to the home side, in particular Dennis Brookes. "It was a warm day. I put a scarf round my neck and, during their innings, the boil burst – so it eased the pain." By close of play Northamptonshire were 280 for two, with Dennis unbeaten on 120.

On Monday he went on to 187, playing 'copy-book cricket', according to the *Chronicle*. 'He moved to the ball as all good batsmen move. His defence was watchful, and there was hardly a scoring shot to which exception could be taken.' The declaration came at 510 for eight, and more than seven thousand excited Bank Holiday spectators saw Bill Merritt, Northants' New Zealand leg-spinner, working his way through the Leicestershire batsmen.

The eighteen-year-old Vince Broderick was twelfth man, and he was on duty in the pavilion. "I had to man the pay-phone next to the secretary's office," he recalls. "People were ringing all afternoon for the score."

Dennis Brookes, a veteran of telephone duty earlier in the decade, explains. "The secretary in those days hadn't got a telephone."

Sometimes twelfth man Broderick had to step aside to let committee members make calls out. "One was the coroner. He wore a top hat and a frock coat. He was getting on a bit, and he would leave his money in the machine if he didn't get through. We used to press Button B and get his two pence back."

When the telephone rang during the tea interval that Whit Monday, "Fifty-three for no wicket," he told each caller. Then it was 60 for one, 100 for two, 136 for seven, and at half past six the last wicket fell at 183. "I always remember a lady running from the West Stand to grab a stump, and the groundsman chasing after her from the other side."

'Most of the people,' the *Chronicle* reported, 'cheered wildly, forming an avenue through which the players walked to the pavilion. The last man had not reached the entrance when the gap was closed, and everybody seemed to be shouting at once for a speech from the captain.'

Robert Nelson was in his second year as captain and, in the words of the Honorary Secretary, W.C. 'Beau' Brown, 'He had quietly and imperceptibly moulded a disorganised rabble into a team which it was impossible to recognise as the same lot who had done duty before he took over the captaincy.'

"Disorganised rabble?" Dennis Brookes repeats quizzically. "It could well be. Mind you, W.C. Brown was captain himself for some years."

The *Chronicle* added its own praise: 'Mr Nelson is one of those leaders whose charming personality extracts the best from every man serving under him, so that the exercise of authority is not needed.'

"He was one of Nature's gentlemen," Dennis adds. "A good cricketer and a nice man. He wasn't a fancy cap."

It was Robert Nelson's finest hour. 'At the top of the pavilion steps Mr F. Ince-Jones called for three cheers for the team, and these were heartily given. Then Mr Nelson thanked the spectators for the manner in which they had received the victory.'

The *Chronicle* was full of fresh hope – 'Now that the bogey has been disposed of and the stigma of a long succession of defeats removed, further successes are confidently expected.' – but it was not to be. There were no further victories, the only comfort being that this one triumph was sufficient to lift them above their neighbours in the final championship table.

Whatever improvements the county made under Robert Nelson's charming leadership were overshadowed by the political developments that summer. By the Saturday following that victory, men were registering under the Military Training Act.

In the final home fixture at the County Ground, Lancashire's captain Lionel Lister received a summons from his Territorial regiment while waiting to bat. Quietly he unbuckled his pads and departed. "We didn't know a great deal about what was happening," Dennis Brookes remembers. "We read what Chamberlain was saying, but even then we didn't think there was going to be a war. It was only when Lionel Lister left that we realised that something was afoot. But we still went down to Clacton and Taunton to play."

At Taunton, in the season's final match, they lost by an innings. 'Nelson tried hard to make a fight of it,' *Wisden* records, 'but the collapse could not be checked.' The match ended, and their captain departed hurriedly.

In October 1940 the newspapers reported the death of Lieutenant Robert Nelson in a bomb raid on his Royal Marine barracks. 'His promise to carry on for at least one season after the war,' Secretary Brown lamented, 'has been the mainspring of the Committee's exertions to keep the club together since county cricket lapsed. His loss has left a great gap.'

*

Dennis Brookes was a P.T. Instructor in the Royal Air Force and, in a match against the Army, he encountered Maurice Leyland, the great Yorkshire and England batsman. "He asked me if I'd play for Yorkshire after the War, and I said I'd think about it. But the Northants chairman said, 'If we take away Brookes, we might as well fold up.' And I didn't want to spend a year qualifying in the leagues. I'd had six years away as it was. So I stayed."

He scored nearly 15,000 runs in the first seven summers after the War, but he played only one Test match – in the West Indies, when neither Hutton nor Washbrook had made themselves available. "I've no doubt that, if I'd signed for Yorkshire, I'd have played more times for England."

Northamptonshire, however, showed no improvement: 16th in 1946, then back to 17th in the following two summers. "We were a poor side in 1946," he thinks. "If I didn't get runs, we were struggling. But, if we'd had a reasonable captain in '47 and '48, we'd have started to climb. By then we'd got some better players."

The captains in those years, Peter Murray-Willis and Arthur Childs-Clarke, have become part of Northamptonshire folklore. The latter "changed the bowling by the clock," according to Dennis Brookes, while Keith Andrew had not been long at Northampton when he heard the professionals telling the story of Murray-Willis fielding one day at square leg. "Somebody hit the ball to him, he only half-stopped it, and it trickled on towards the boundary. Apparently his cap blew off, and he turned and went after his cap – while the batsmen ran five. He was a lovely character by all accounts but, with due respect, the bowler's playing for his living as a professional cricketer. I can't think that he would have been very amused."

Despite these difficulties, a new seam of players was found. Albert Nutter and Buddy Oldfield had both been capped by Lancashire before the War, Oldfield playing once for England, but neither signed contracts for 1946, preferring to play in the thriving Lancashire League. Yet in 1948 they were tempted by the prospect of winter work at British Timken to join the staff at Northamptonshire, bringing with them their fellow Lancastrian Gordon Garlick.

In 1949 Freddie Jakeman was recruited from the Bradford League, together with fellow Yorkshireman Des Barrick. "Des got 147 against the New Zealanders in his first game, wearing his little white Pontefract cap," Keith tells. "He came back into the dressing room and said to Percy Davis, 'Run me the bath, will you, Percy?' Percy had been on the staff since the mid-30s. The story lasted for years."

Then in 1950 there came Jock Livingston, the mastermind of the Central Lancashire League Sunday eleven – and, within three years, he had been joined by three of his colleagues: George Tribe, Frank Tyson and Keith Andrew.

All this coincided with the appointment of a new captain in 1949. Freddie Brown, the old Surrey and England amateur, had not played regular county cricket since 1936, but he too was persuaded onto the payroll of British Timken and he returned to cricket in style, the third all-rounder that summer to complete the double of 1,000 runs and 100 wickets. 'He took charge of the team,' *Wisden* recorded, 'and the dark clouds of despondency immediately rolled away. The players seemed to reflect Brown's own character in keenness, enterprise and determination.'

Northamptonshire 1950
back row (left to right): Eddie Davis, Jock Livingston, Bob Clarke,
Gordon Garlick, Ken Fiddling, Bill Barron, Percy Davis
seated: Buddy Oldfield, Dennis Brookes, Freddie Brown, Albert Nutter,
Vince Broderick   in front: Freddie Jakeman, Des Barrick

Dennis Brookes concurs: "By the force of his personality, he dragged the county with him. And, of course, he brought a first-class all-rounder in himself."

Unlike his predecessors as captain, he was not tolerant of indifferent fielding, though sometimes his own whole-heartedness could backfire – as it did at Lord's in only his second match in charge.

"We were playing on the Tavern side," Vince Broderick recalls, "and the boundary on the other side was almost the full ground. Bill Edrich hit my first ball away to mid-wicket, and Percy Davis – 'Sparrow' – ran after it. His legs went fast, but he never seemed to cover the ground. Freddie Brown backed up his throw and, instead of throwing it to me, he threw it straight over the wicket-keeper's head for four overthrows. That was nine off my first ball, and I was bowling at Compton and Edrich."

It still stands as the most runs scored off a single delivery since 1900, and Freddie Brown rubbed salt in the wound: "'You'll have to bowl nine maidens now to catch up,' he said."

"He wouldn't have Percy's brother Eddie in the team," Dennis tells, "because of his fielding. Freddie was the sort of man who, if you were afraid of him, he'd chase you."

"He was a strong autocratic personality," Keith says, "but there was a great soft side to him. He had a heart of gold. He never asked anybody to do anything he wouldn't do himself. I got to know him very well in later years, and he told me about his war. He was a prisoner in Italy for three years, you know. He lost several stone."

The wooden spoon of 1948 was forgotten as the county prospered. In August three successive matches were won by an innings, they reached sixth place in the table, and Brown was rewarded with the England captaincy for the last two Tests against New Zealand.

The progress was not maintained in the last four years of Brown's captaincy, but by then he had acquired other commitments: captain of England till the end of 1951, then chairman of selectors in 1953.

The team continued to evolve, however, and, when Keith made his championship debut in May 1954, Northamptonshire were represented by six who had come down from Lancashire (Livingston, Tribe, Broderick, Starkie, Tyson and Keith himself), three from Yorkshire (Brookes, Barrick and Jakeman) and only Bob Clarke and Brian Reynolds who were home-grown.

They might be playing under the flag of a small, semi-rural Midland county, some might nickname them Timkenshire, but their cricket had a grit and, under the quietly perceptive captaincy of the professional Dennis Brookes, they rose year by year – seventh in '54 and '55, fourth in '56 – till they finished as runners-up in 1957. They had reached such heights in 1912, but that was in the years when they played only an 18-match fixture list, avoiding most of the stronger counties.

Wisden was clear. It was 'the most successful season in their history', and the key factor was their 'astute team building'.

Behind the scenes another ingredient was the county's early embrace of the idea of raising extra revenue through a county-wide football pool. Worcestershire and Leicestershire began such a scheme in 1952, and by the autumn Northamptonshire were following suit.

At first it seemed a peripheral activity. The Supporters' Association employed a Secretary and an Organising Secretary to handle the venture: the former quit before starting work, the latter after a week with the extraordinary statement that he did not believe in gambling. Their next candidate found the downstairs bar too attractive, and by November they were running out of hope, turning as a last resort to the county's Assistant Secretary Ken Turner to lend a hand.

The MCC did not approve, Ronnie Aird the secretary calling it 'easy money, which I believe to be a dangerous thing'. There were attempts to have it declared illegal, resulting in some amendments to the competition procedures. But armies of volunteers collected weekly shillings down streets and in factories, and by the late '50s there were 79,000 subscribing members.

As Ken Turner himself put it, 'it was equivalent to Wembley Stadium being three-quarters full every Saturday.'

The sparsely-populated county had not only assembled a competitive team to shake off the long years of failure, it had found relative financial prosperity. At a time when greater clubs were struggling to make ends meet, it was able to increase the playing staff to 29 and still to bank a surplus.

Ken Turner succeeded Colonel Coldwell as Northamptonshire's Secretary in April 1958, and his first full year in charge produced the following accounts:

Income	£41,854
Expenditure	£39,536
Surplus	£ 2,318

Within this figure of £41,854 for income, the total for all gate receipts, stand tickets and members' subscriptions was £10,554. MCC provided £1,825 from tour and Test receipts and £2,527 from television fees. There was £2,305 from various smaller items: scorecards, yearbooks, the indoor school and interest from investments. The remaining £24,643 came from the Supporters' Association.

The football pool was contributing 59% of all the club's income.

"Ken Turner was the greatest man in the history of Northamptonshire cricket," Keith Andrew reckons. "Almost single-handed, he raised the money to keep the club in the first-class game."

Ken Turner

K.C. Turner, Assistant Secretary, 1949-58. Secretary, 1958-85. He could be a hard man in dealing with players' contracts, he did not court popularity, but he sustained the county at a level of achievement unimaginable in the '20s and '30s. "He upset a lot of people, but as Secretary he did everything. When I retired in 1966, I wrote to him 'There's only one Mr Cricket in this county,' I said, 'and that's KCT.'

"And do you know? After he died, his wife found my letter in his wallet. For nineteen years he'd carried it with him everywhere."

CHAPTER 6
TECHNICAL DEVELOPMENT
1953-1961

By 1953 Keith was pursuing two careers.

The boy at the end of the schoolroom line, the boy whose mother worked long hours in the mill, had studied hard to become a qualified mechanical engineer, and he had landed a good job with prospects in the design office at British Timken, undertaking stress calculations on motor vehicles and aeroplanes.

All the while, the boy who had tripped to school 'free as the wind', bouncing his tennis ball against the low walls in Queens Road, had turned into a professional wicket-keeper, merely by pursuing the recreation he loved. He had a natural talent and, by a series of happy chances, he found himself qualifying by residence to become Northamptonshire's next wicket-keeper.

At Werneth he had not been tempted by Lancashire's interest in him, not wanting to jeopardise his engineering career, but, uprooted from his home town by National Service, he was now eager to settle in Northampton and to see what life had to offer.

"I was an Oldham boy, out in the wider world. I loved Lancashire people, I still do, but I had a chance to spread my wings, and I was meeting such a range of people. And, because I had another job, I never felt under any pressure with my cricket. In fact, I earned more money in winter than I did in summer."

The same could not be said of his captain Freddie Brown. "He was a PR officer at British Timken. I don't think he did very much. He was only on the payroll so that he could play cricket. I respected him immensely, but really I think I was as much an amateur as he was."

The winter after he toured Australia, Keith was working on a stress analysis of the Timken wheel bearings specially designed for the new Bristol Britannia Aircraft. "I was working under the leadership of Alec Edwards, a very clever engineer. I was responsible for checking his stress calculations relating to the forces generated on landing. And one day we received the news from Bristol that the undercarriage had partially collapsed when landing during testing at Filton. It was a serious business. Alec and I were sent for immediately.

"Eventually they tested it on a stress pad at Farnborough, and they found out – by the grace of God – that we weren't to blame. The problem had been caused by a small strut on the under-carriage itself. I shall never forget the worry. It was hanging over our heads when I went back to cricket the following summer. If it had been our fault, I don't like to think what the consequences would have been. They would have been a lot worse than dropping Arthur Morris at Brisbane."

As in his rivalry with his fellow student Fred Brock in Oldham, Keith was more of 'a trier' than a natural, but in his cricketing summers, although he enjoyed thinking about the game, nothing generated the same anxiety or pressure. It was never hard work.

"The cricket was such an adventure, out in the fresh air with this wonderful atmosphere: the different personalities, the different styles of playing, the spin bowling, the competition, the camaraderie between the teams, the travelling, the whole feeling of being part of a way of life. Somehow there was a magic about it all."

Nobody captured cricket's magic better than the Northamptonshire coach, Jack Mercer. With Colonel Coldwell, the secretary, no great judge of a cricketer, it was left to Mercer, the former Sussex and Glamorgan bowler, to travel the north of England in search of possible signings – among them Jock Livingston and Frank Tyson.

But he was not a coach, as we now know the word, and Keith soon discovered this when he reported for pre-season practice in 1953.

"I'd been there a few days when I said to one of the chaps, 'Who's the old bloke behind the net with the trilby on?' A smart man, with a raincoat and a brown trilby. I knew he was a bit deaf because, when you spoke, he never answered. 'That's the coach, Jack Mercer,' they said. 'He doesn't do much coaching, but he gives the Colonel some great tips."

He was an enigmatic figure with lodgings in town and a fashionable apartment in London's West End. He was already 58 years old, but he would still be on the staff in thirty years' time, retiring to the scorebox when his coaching was no longer required.

"He gave me the scorecard of the day he took ten wickets in an innings at Worcester. He was a member of the Magic Circle, and he could manipulate a cricket ball just like he did a pack of cards. He'd be running up, showing the batsman an off-spinner's grip, and he'd switch it and bowl a leg-cutter."

"He was wonderful with the children," Joyce adds. "He would mesmerise them with his tricks. And he had this fanciful way of speaking. He was a mystery man. He'd talk about the past, and it was always very glorious."

He had served with the White Russians before the Great War. He had hit Wilfred Rhodes for four sixes in an over. He had become a hero in the Caribbean.

"'I shall go to the West Indies this winter,' he'd say. 'They'll all be out in Jamaica to see me.' And you knew full well he wasn't going to be going."

MCC were due to tour the West Indies in the winter of 1953/4 and, though Keith was still completing his residential qualification, Jack Mercer took him aside.

"'I know the West Indies,' he said. 'I'll have a word. I'm sure we can get you on the boat.'"

The Oldham boy, 'out in the wider world', did not know quite what to make of him. If this was coaching, it was nothing like any instruction he had ever received in a technical college.

It was certainly nothing like the new initiatives that MCC were developing at this time.

Back in 1948 Gubby Allen, the former England captain, had asked his colleagues on the MCC committee what could be done to develop cricketing experience among boys in the state schools. As a result, an enquiry was established with three main areas of concern: facilities, coaching and finance.

Within four years MCC were running coaching courses at Lilleshall. A Youth Coaching Certificate was established, and the MCC produced the first edition of its Coaching Book.

The emphasis was not on small group work focused on talented youngsters in nets with good playing surfaces. Rather, schoolmasters were to be shown ways of initiating large classes, in halls and rough playgrounds, into an appreciation of cricket and its skills.

'The main object,' the final report declared, 'was to train coaches who in turn would instruct schoolmasters and youth leaders on the best methods of teaching boys to play the game and to foster their love and understanding of it. A target of 5,000 trained masters for one million boys was visualised.'

Gubby Allen was an Old Etonian, now a leading figure at Lord's, and his main ally in the venture was the Winchester schoolmaster Harry Altham. They appointed Harry Crabtree, PE co-ordinator and former opening batsman in Essex, as the first Director, and groups of professional cricketers started to attend Lilleshall.

Early ventures were primitive. Harry Crabtree recommended marshalling boys into lines to play the forward defensive. "He had this way of getting them to pick the bat up," Keith says. "One, two, three, four." Meanwhile Gubby Allen talked enthusiastically to the professionals about leg-break bowling. "They say that he spoke for an hour and a half, and he'd got his arm hanging in the air the whole time."

Though Keith was a young man, setting out in the game, he was quick to sign up, attending with Maurice Tremlett of Somerset, Vic Cannings of Hampshire, Arthur McIntyre of Surrey and Bill Voce, the former Notts and England fast bowler. There were coaching careers ahead for Cannings at Eton, McIntyre at The Oval and Keith, but most of the professionals were suspicious of the scheme.

"They thought that the schoolmasters were going to be taking their jobs. But that wasn't the idea at all. You can't expect a mathematics teacher to be an expert cricket coach, but he could learn how to organise group coaching and that wasn't what the professionals were good at doing.

"The old pros didn't like the technical side of it, either – things like the five positions in the bowling action – but, of course, I had a technical background so that fascinated me."

Keith had been an instructor in the army, and in Northampton he continued his teaching at evening classes at the Technical College: "mathematics, engineering drawing, applied heat". Now he was getting drawn into the analysis of cricket's skills.

But, if Keith had only been interested in cricket for its technical challenges, he would have spent his summers in the design office, working on helicopter gear boxes and earning more money.

Like Allen and Altham, he never lost sight of the coach's most vital quality, the ability to transmit a love of the game.

"The techniques are important," he says, "but you've got to create enthusiasm. And cricket is such an adventure. I think back to Jack Mercer, sitting in the dressing room and telling his stories. 'When I was coming in to bowl,' he'd say, and he'd jiggle with the ball. It made you envisage a situation that you wanted to be in."

Four sixes off a Wilfred Rhodes over. All ten wickets at Worcester. A VIP's welcome in Jamaica. "He was a magical man. Nobody ever got miserable in the dressing room when he was there."

*

Keith returned from Australia in early April 1955. He had been with Joyce for only ten days of their seven-month marriage, and she had spent the winter back in Lancashire with her mother.

"She saw quite a bit of my mother, too," Keith says. "I remember my mother saying to me, 'You've got a good girl there.' Well, I knew that, but it was nice that she said so."

Keith's mother was in her early fifties, still working hard but now battling with a cancer that would kill her by the end of the following year. His father, meanwhile, remained out of contact. Once or twice he had appeared as a face in the crowd at Werneth but nothing more.

There were four weeks between Keith's return and his first match of the summer, but this was no time for a rest. He went back to Oldham and, within a week, he and Joyce were travelling down the old A5 in a removal van, ready to move into their Wilson home on the large new estate in Weston Favell.

While he had been away, Joyce had been choosing carpets and curtains – and cleaning up after the painters. "It was before the days of emulsion paint, and they'd splashed all this white distemper over the floorboards. I had Dorothy and George Tribe with me, and I had them each with a bucket and brush, scrubbing the floor."

No sooner had the newly-weds arranged their furniture than it was time for Keith to report back to the County Ground.

"The committee offered Frank and me contracts for £200 each for the summer. I remember saying to them, 'We can get more than that emptying the dustbins for Northampton Corporation.' So eventually they agreed to our having £250 – plus, of course, our win bonuses."

There was even a one pound bonus for first innings lead. "In my first summer little Freddie Jakeman was playing. A tubby Yorkshireman and a very fine striker of the ball. People still talk about his batting. He got 500 runs in a week once, without being out, and he hit a six that cleared the pavilion at Northampton. He'd sit in the dressing room after he'd batted and, as soon as we'd got first innings lead, he'd be up to the office to collect his pound note. Then straightaway he'd be putting it in an envelope to send to his wife back in Holmfirth.

"The county used to bank at the Westminster Bank on the corner of the main square. It had a lovely mahogany counter and they say that, when Colonel Coldwell arrived to pay in the money for the salaries, Jakey would already be there, waiting down the other end of the counter to draw his out. Most of that went back to his wife, too."

The contracts were signed, and the pre-season training began. The cricket season was only three weeks away, and his wicket-keeping had to be taken back to the drawing board.

"Australia was a wonderful experience. I wouldn't have missed it for anything. And I must have been a good taker of the ball for them to have picked me. But as a keeper I still had a lot to learn."

His rise had been rapid. In the Central Lancashire League he had rarely kept to anything above medium-pace, almost always standing up to the stumps. In the Army he had been here and there with a variety of teams. Then after less than three months of county cricket at Northampton, his name was announced in the winter's tour party. The selectors had seen little of him, and six months in Australia left him with few illusions.

"I didn't keep that badly, but I looked at Godfrey and I realised that I could never be like him. When he stood back to quick bowling, he could get to positions to take catches that I couldn't reach. So I knew I had to reappraise my technique."

He had not impressed Len Hutton, the journalists had blamed him for missing Morris at Brisbane and, though nothing was said, he soon realised that he was no longer in the selectors' minds.

Godfrey Evans broke a finger in the third Test that summer, and the selectors turned to Hampshire's Leo Harrison to replace him in the Players–Gentlemen match. Then, for the remaining two Tests, they picked Surrey's Arthur McIntyre and Dick Spooner of Warwickshire. The following summer, looking for a second keeper for the winter tour to South Africa, they opted for Brian Taylor of Essex.

It was starting to look as if his Test career would be limited to that one last-minute call-up at Brisbane.

"Other than Turner Warrener at Werneth, nobody had helped me with my keeping, but I brought in my training as an engineer. When we were batting, I'd sit and put a rolled-up newspaper to my eye, and I'd focus entirely on the wicket-keeper."

The greatest of all the keepers framed by his *Daily Telegraph* was Godfrey Evans. What was it that Keith worked out about him?

"He was the strongest man I've ever seen. He'd been a professional boxer, and he had these terrific legs like steel springs. He could get down to the squatting position and take off to first slip without getting up, almost like a rocket being launched. I don't think I've seen any other wicket-keeper do that. That catch off Neil Harvey, it must be the greatest catch in the history of cricket."

Was that what Keith had to learn to do?

"He really set me back. In fact, he ruined a whole generation of wicket-keepers. Everybody copied him. Alan Wilson at Old Trafford even developed his perky walk between the wickets. They all started to crouch down like him, but they didn't have his legs. You never see a goalkeeper getting ready for a penalty on his haunches, do you?

"They squatted down when they were standing back but, other than Godfrey, I noticed that their first movement was to get up again as the ball was delivered. From that realisation I never again squatted down. I just stood with my hands near my knees, like a goalkeeper. I found I could get quite wide by picking up the line of the ball and moving across. If you squat down and you haven't got legs like Godfrey's, then you've got to come up before you can go across.

"When I was standing up to the stumps, I would crouch down, but I would concentrate on coming up with the bounce of the ball. The ball down the leg side is the most difficult because there's a spot where you can't see it. A lot of the keepers were taking the ball by moving backwards with their left foot, but what you should do is to cut it off by narrowing the angle. That way you can get your gloves back to the wicket more quickly. The key to standing up is not catching the ball but the speed at which you move your hands after you've got the ball.

"Sometimes, when we played exhibition matches on Sundays, I'd stand back and throw myself about. 'Well caught, Godfrey,' they'd shout. But, if you think about it, the tell-tale sign of a poor keeper is that he is late on the ball. He is making excessive late movements instead of anticipating – and that's almost the opposite of what the crowd sees. I was a much better keeper once I realised that I should move to the ball rather than dive."

It was a different style of wicket-keeping from that of Godfrey, less theatrical, and, once he had perfected it, there were many who thought him the better keeper.

"As far as we were concerned," his team-mate Peter Arnold says, "he was the best in the world for many years. He wasn't a Godfrey Evans. He didn't fall all over the place or dive but, if he had one miss during the season, everybody stopped with their mouth open."

But this was not a unanimous view at Northampton.

"I remember talking to Frank Tyson about it once," Peter Arnold says. "I said, 'Who would you rather have?' He said, 'I'd rather have Godfrey. He does drop more, but the way he makes catches puts me right on top of the world as a bowler. Keith is so methodical and easy, you hardly realise you've taken a wicket."

Keith is more modest. "As a wicket-keeper to a fast bowler, I wasn't in Godfrey's street. I wouldn't even want to be compared with him."

On Sundays Keith practised taking fielders' returns without looking. "I used to duck my head and catch the ball behind my back. It became a bit of a circus performance, but it did help, especially with those leg side deliveries when you can't see them. You learn how to become a friend of the ball."

At heart Keith was always an engineer, quietly working to re-design and improve his technique.

"I trained myself to maximise the speed at which I could take the bails off after receiving the ball. The key to that was to get my weight moving towards the wicket, mainly on the inside foot. Then, as I was taking the ball, my weight was already on the foot nearer the wicket. The difference was amazing, especially with run outs. When you watch the replays on television, you can see how quickly the batsman is covering the ground, and how close the outcome often is – so, if the wicket-keeper can save himself a split second, it can be all-important."

Unfortunately, playing for Northamptonshire, it took him some time to gain the opportunities to put his new ideas about standing back into practice. The Northampton wicket was naturally slow and, even with the world's fastest bowler in its ranks, the county was happy to accept that and to work on increasing the turn on a spinner's length. 'Go back to Lancashire,' Len Hutton told Frank Tyson bluntly. 'If you carry on playing for Northants, you'll be out of Test cricket in two years.'

The summers of the mid-1950s were wet and, with no covering either of the pitch or of the bowlers' run-ups, conditions often made it neither rewarding nor easy to run in and bowl fast. Added to this, Northamptonshire often found when they were travelling away that their hosts, fearful of Tyson's pace, had prepared a docile pitch.

The statistics of the summer of 1955 underline the story. Keith kept wicket for the county for 3,800 overs, more than two-thirds of which were bowled by spinners. With Tribe and Broderick often in tandem, 51% of all the overs were by slow left-armers, a figure that rose to an extraordinary 65% in 1957 when Mick Allen and the Australian Jack Manning joined the side. Keith was rarely standing back for long – and certainly not on pitches like the one at Brisbane.

"On a slow wicket it's more difficult to stand back. You have to stand closer, and you don't get the time. On a pacy wicket, it comes through at a nice height. You can almost take a walk and catch it. But on a slow wicket the ball comes through much lower, and you have to take the ball much nearer the ground, much nearer the wicket also. It can be very hard on the hands."

Frank Tyson returned from Australia as English cricket's brightest star. He had taken 25 wickets in the three victories over Australia, and he had been part of the side that had demolished New Zealand, reducing them to a new Test low of 26 all out at Auckland.

"The day after that 26, he had his bowling speed measured by some people at the University at Auckland. They'd rigged up a machine, with a beam, and they clocked him at over 90 miles an hour. But what they didn't realise was that he didn't want to do it.

The speed test in Auckland

"The phone went in the hotel room. 'The taxi's here,' I said, and he started moaning. 'Come on,' I said. 'We're going to be late. It might rain.' And, when he got there, he wasn't really interested. In fact, he bowled in two jerseys. If that was 90 or so, then I'm sure he must have bowled at over 100 miles an hour at times.

"The other factor to take into account, of course, is that in those days they called no-balls off the back foot and he had quite a drag. So, when he released the ball, he was a lot nearer the batsman than they are today."

It was the end of six glorious months under Southern hemisphere skies, a world away from the Park Avenue ground at Bradford where in early May Tyson played his next first-class match.

On paper the game promised one of cricket's great showdowns: 'Typhoon' Tyson, England's new fast bowling sensation, against 'Fiery' Fred Trueman, still smouldering from his omission from the Australian tour. Yet, on a rain-affected wicket, they sent down just twelve overs between them. Yorkshire were dismissed for 94 and 104, with George Tribe taking fifteen wickets for 75 runs, while Northants managed just 61 and 59 against the bowling of Appleyard and Wardle.

Keith draws breath at the mention of the two Yorkshire spinners. "What a pair they were! I can't think of a better two bowlers in tandem. Maybe Laker and Lock."

Jock Livingston, a fine player of spin, was the highest scorer for Northants with 19 and 1, which was eighteen runs more than the cheerful Bob Clarke managed, batting at number eleven. He was not known as one of the game's great analysts, and it might even have been in this match that he set off to bat and turned back to his team-mates.

"What's this chap bowling?"

"Off-breaks."

"Off-breaks? Which way do they go?"

After retirement he became the cricket coach at Christ's Hospital.

A barrel-chested left-arm bowler, he was not likely to be taking notice if Jack Mercer did ever start showing the various grips. "Bob could swing it," Dennis Brookes says, "but he didn't know how he did it. He just came up and bowled as fast as he could. He never shone the ball. Albert Nutter used to complain, 'Here I am, rubbing the ball up, and, when it comes back from Bob, it's all gone.'"

At Bradford he bowled three overs in the first innings and scored 0 and 2, but at least he contributed three catches in the second innings. "Dear old Bob," Keith says. "He was our specialist mid-wicket. He used to catch them one-handed."

"He was magnificent," Dennis says. "He could catch birds."

'The safest catch of anyone away from the close positions,' Freddie Brown wrote, 'but there are times when he doesn't seem to be playing in the same match as his colleagues. He wanders haphazardly about, and often I have felt impelled to scratch a mark to indicate where I want him to stand.'

"Vic Wilson hit this ball towards him once," Dennis Brookes tells, recalling a match two years earlier at Headingley, "and he realised that Bob wasn't with us. He went for a run, and suddenly Bob sprang to life and threw his wicket down."

But, in George Tribe's repertoire of bowling tricks, there was a key role for a dependable catcher at mid-wicket.

"George was a great thinker about the game," Keith says. "He'd take me out to the wicket in the morning, get a feeling for the background, analyse the conditions. We'd throw a ball about and talk cricket all the time. It was fascinating. I was learning so much.

"We'd go into the nets together, and he'd bowl all his different deliveries. It did take me a bit of time to pick him. Even after a season or two he'd do me now and then. He even bowled three types of flipper. He squeezed it out of his fingers so that it appeared to gather pace. And sometimes he would bowl a deliberately bad ball, a short googly but a little quicker. The batsman's eyes would light up like organ stops, and they'd try to whack it. And, because it tended to bounce more, it would hit high up on the bat. And there would be Bob at mid-wicket. 'Woodbines,' he'd shout, I don't know why, and he'd catch it one-handed."

Lancashire's captain Cyril Washbrook was a fearless batsman against quick bowling, but he had no answer against Tribe, his humiliation at Blackpool in 1957 still recalled with amusement.

"I'd scored a century," Denis Brookes recalls, "and Washy said to me that it was the worst hundred he'd ever seen. He couldn't remember a shot in it. Then he went out and faced George Tribe. In five overs he hardly got the bat on one ball."

Washbrook, bowled Tribe, 0.

"I can see him there," Geoffrey Howard the Lancashire secretary told me. "He struggled for about three quarters of an hour to get off the mark, with no idea which way George Tribe was turning the ball."

"If you play that type of bowling from the crease," Dennis says, "you're in trouble. And that's what he did. He never got his front foot up the wicket. So he was giving the bowler everything he wanted to do."

The second innings at Blackpool brought no relief. "On the third morning of the match George Tribe got a fifty, and I declared, leaving Lancashire about half an hour before lunch. It was a soft wicket with rain on it, and Frank Tyson knocked the first two down very quickly. Washbrook came in at number four so I said to George, 'You'd better have a bowl.' He said, 'I'm a bit tired. I've been batting all morning. I'll have a shower at lunch, then I'll get him out.' And he got him first ball of the afternoon."

Washbrook, caught Livingston, bowled Tribe, 1.

At Old Trafford the following summer the Lancashire captain was not on the team sheet and, according to Geoff Edrich who led the side in his absence, the whole Lancashire team knew the reason why.

While all eyes at Blackpool were on the floundering Washbrook as he played in vain at the spinning ball, did anybody notice the unobtrusive ease with which another figure was gathering it each time into his gloves?

"Keith had very soft hands and good balance," Dennis says. "He had so many difficult bowlers to take. George Tribe and Jack Manning, when the wickets were turning. Frank Tyson was rapid, and even Bob Clarke wasn't easy, because he swung the ball both in and away. I used to get a shock if Keith ever missed a chance. That's how good he was."

That first summer back from Australia, standing up to the slow bowlers, Keith made 29 stumpings, more than any other keeper in the country, indeed more than any keeper has made in any of the 47 summers since.

George Tribe prospered, his 176 wickets owing much to the keeper who was now taking his bowling as nobody before had done – neither Keith's predecessor, the brittle-boned Ken Fiddling, nor the great Australian keeper Don Tallon, whose uncertain handling had been a significant factor in the shortness of Tribe's Test career.

But, if Keith wanted to work on standing back to Frank Tyson, he had fewer than 300 overs of practice – and the fast bowler, frustrated by the unresponsive pitches, only once took five wickets in an innings.

They were a long way from Australia.

*

Frank and Keith had got to know their fellow tourists in Australia at the usually high-spirited gatherings of the Saturday Club. So, recognising the international flavour of the Northamptonshire team, they initiated the Cosmopolitan Club, known as the Cosmo, meeting for an hour each Saturday night. 'An adolescent concept,' Frank Tyson calls it now, but together they sang bawdy songs, fined each other for ridiculous offences and pooled the money for a slap-up end-of-season celebration.

While other counties started to let players travel to away matches by private cars, Northamptonshire – haunted by the two accidents in the 1930s that saw Jupp gaoled, Northway killed and Bakewell invalided out of the game – stuck firmly to their coach, and that was also good for team spirit.

"We had two card tables," Keith says. "Freddie Brown was on the coach one time, and we were playing a game called Twist. It was lethal, a pure gambling game, and little Fred Jakeman off-suited him. He threw the cards out of the window."

However hard they all tried, though, there was never any doubt who was in control at the table. "We'd be halfway to Cardiff, and Jack Mercer would always be the one with all the money. He'd be sitting there, telling his stories, but somehow in the end he'd manipulate it so that nobody won or lost anything. His hands with the cards were a bit special."

Frank Tyson remembers sitting next to Keith, trying to engage him in conversation.

"I wonder what time we'll get back," he said.

"I'll tell you," Keith replied and lapsed into a long silence.

Such unfinished snatches of conversation were not unusual with Keith so Frank said no more. Then suddenly, after several minutes, Keith broke out of his reverie to announce their expected time of arrival.

"I estimated the distances between the telegraph poles," Keith explains. "Then I looked at my watch and worked out our speed and, if we kept going at that speed, what time we'd be back in Northampton."

Frank looked at him in amazement. Side by side on the coach seat, they were the very embodiment of C.P. Snow's two cultures but, in the happy mix of Northamptonshire's cosmopolitan side, they were the closest of friends.

*

Frank and Keith were still Lancastrians at heart, and for them the visits to Old Trafford were a highlight of the season's fixture card. Frank went off to stay with his mother while Keith returned to Oldham. In 1958, by a happy chance, he was there for the start of Wakes Week. His own mother had died by this time, but his Uncle Sam and Auntie Hilda put him up. Sam was no longer driving a laundry van but delivering Brooke Bond tea all around the county.

"In the evening," Keith recalls, "I went up with Jackie Dyson and Alf Alker to Tommy Field, the market area that they used for the fair. And I won a goldfish on the coconut shy."

It is a long story, one that has been told many times over the years.

Determined to get the goldfish, now named Archie, home for his daughter Clare, he left it overnight in the back sink. Then, waiting for the bus next morning, he let the bag slip out of his grasp and, with the fish flapping on the pavement, rushed into a nearby shop, pleading urgently for more water.

Malcolm Hilton boarded the bus further down the road – "I tried to hide the fish, but halfway to Manchester he suddenly saw it. 'Oh my God, KV, what the hell's that?'"

But the real fun started at Old Trafford. The county had just installed plush new showers and baths, and the Lancashire secretary Geoffrey Howard, a sheaf of papers as ever under his arm, looked in to what he thought would be an empty visitors' dressing room, to discover not only Archie swimming in a half-filled bath but a barking corgi which Frank Tyson had bought for his wife.

"But by jingo I got Archie home for Clare, even with George Tribe on the coach trying to stick a safety pin into the bag."

Forty-five years on he smiles once more. "There was so much laughter in my time in cricket. And that's my memory. The laughter."

*

Freddie Brown's captaincy had lifted Northamptonshire from the foot of the table, but it was only under their first professional captain Dennis Brookes that they started to occupy the upper reaches with consistency. Seventh in 1954 and

1955, they rose to fourth in 1956, their highest placing since the first world war. Then in 1957 the little Midland county – with 15 victories and only two defeats – finished in a heady second place, sandwiched between the giants of Surrey and Yorkshire.

"Perhaps the earlier years had conditioned Dennis's approach," Keith thinks. "He may have been more cautious. But it didn't affect me. I knew we were a little county, but you can't look like that at a team with players like George Tribe, Jock Livingston, Frank Tyson and Dennis."

Jock Livingston

"He'd have been thrilled if he'd known this picture was here.
He was a great player of spin bowling. He used to hit Jim Laker
into the bowling green at Northampton. Then Jim would start
looking at his finger, as if to say, 'I don't think I can carry on.'"

The statistics bear out the achievement of those years.

Most championship points, 1954-57

1. Surrey   1004
2. Yorkshire   780
3. Northamptonshire   650

Surrey were champions in each of the four years, yet between August 1955 and May 1957 they were beaten four times in a row by Northamptonshire.

In those four summers George Tribe took 548 championship wickets, second only to his fellow Australian Bruce Dooland at Nottingham. In the first three summers, before a knee injury handicapped him, Jock Livingston was the leading batsman with 5,715 runs. Jack Manning's spin was as sharp as any in England, Dennis Brookes was still stroking the ball with copybook precision and, when the pitches were lively, they had in Frank Tyson the fastest bowler of them all.

Keith had become a Northamptonshire cricketer just as the county was entering the most successful period in its history. "As far as I was concerned," he says, "we were a top six side from day one."

Dennis Brookes was one of only four professional county captains in 1957 and, for all his success, he had his detractors.

"Jock Livingston was always trying to depose me," he says with a smile. "Because he'd been captain of the Commonwealth side in India, he thought he should have become the Northamptonshire captain when I was appointed."

"Jock was a breath of fresh air on the cricket field," Keith says. "He was a magnificent attacking batsman and a brilliant catcher. And his interest in cricket knew no bounds. He was a good friend of Don Bradman, and he had a great knowledge of the game. His house in Fife Street was like a home from home for every Australian who visited England, with Marjorie feeding them all.

"Dennis was a different type of man altogether. Quiet, intelligent, amiable. Very modest in every way. He was an English batsman of the old school, a forward player, very difficult to get out. On a good wicket you could put him down for a hundred. He was a great example to professional cricket."

And as a captain?

"He was very good. I admired Freddie Brown so much, but Dennis was a gentler man, as honest as the day is long, and he had a better understanding of the professionals. He was probably the most respected cricketer I've ever met."

Unfortunately this view of Dennis's captaincy was not shared by everybody involved in the management of the club.

"There were those on the committee who wanted an amateur and did right through his captaincy."

Dennis had been inculcated into the ethos of county cricket in the 1930s, when a professional captain was unthinkable, so he was able to accept the rumblings with stoical good humour. "'Where did you go to school?' they used to ask me, and I'd say, 'I went to an elementary school, but it *was* on top of a hill.'"

In 1955, the second year of his captaincy, the county recruited from Surrey the talented young batsman, Raman Subba Row, a Cambridge blue who had been educated at Whitgift School. He hit the Lancashire bowlers for 260, the highest score in England that summer, finished near the top of the national batting averages and departed for two years of national service in the R.A.F. But, unknown to his team-mates, the committee promised him the captaincy when he returned in 1958.

In 1957 Dennis Brookes led the county through the most successful season in its history, but at the end of it he stepped down with a good grace, recognising the social forces that were at work. It was not a change that the younger players accepted as readily.

"Raman was a fine batsman," Keith says. "He wasn't the greatest stylist, but he knew how to get runs. And he was a very pleasant bloke. But he didn't have the knowledge and the experience that Dennis did, and he wasn't a natural leader like Freddie Brown. I'm afraid that some of the players didn't support him to the degree that they supported Dennis."

Nevertheless, the summer of 1958 saw them once more challenging for the championship. At Northampton they dismissed Yorkshire for 67 and 65, with George Tribe taking fifteen wickets for 31 runs. Then, after six successive victories in July, they were only eight points behind Hampshire at the head of the table. But August proved a barren month, and they slipped to fourth place.

The team that had been assembled so astutely in the early 1950s started to break up. Livingston retired after 1957, Manning, Tribe and Brookes after 1959 and, when Tyson went into full-time teaching at the end of 1960, only Brian Reynolds, Mick Allen and Keith remained of the first-choice team that Dennis Brookes had led to second place three years earlier. It was not an easy assignment for Raman Subba Row who, by then, was often away at Test matches, and the county slipped rapidly down the table.

Subba Row scored eleven centuries in his first two summers as captain, including a triple one on his first return visit to The Oval. "He was very keen to make his mark," Keith says, "but I always had this feeling that he was really a Surrey player. He wanted to play brighter cricket, and he tried to keep the traditions of cricket at the forefront. But sometimes we'd be 150 for six at lunch, and you don't win matches that way. And it is important to play to win, especially if you're playing for a living."

When Subba Row told the committee in 1961 that he planned to retire to develop his public relations business, they turned their attention to Roger Prideaux, the young Kent batsman who had been educated at Tonbridge School. A recent graduate of Cambridge University, he was to be offered the nominal post of Assistant Secretary so that he could retain his amateur status.

The development did not impress Keith, now 31 years old and established both as a county cricketer and as a mechanical engineer.

"Roger Prideaux's coming down," they said.

"Where from?" he asked. "Heaven?"

"Don't get me wrong," he says. "But here we were, over halfway through the twentieth century, and we were still living in the Middle Ages, still treating professional cricketers as if they weren't intelligent. Men like George Tribe, Dennis Brookes, Frank Tyson. It was a legacy from the past, and it had outlived its day – if it had ever had one."

They were sentiments that had brought him a brief and memorable encounter with one of the great amateur figures in English cricket history, Douglas Jardine.

"I'd been four or five years at Northampton when I was invited onto a Cricket Society panel in Oxford, with an audience of about five hundred. Leslie Gutteridge was the chairman, and the panel was Douglas Jardine, the President of the Lawn Tennis Association and me. I can't think what I was there for.

"In the afternoon I'd been walking around Oxford, and I'd looked in the window of the Elmer Cotton sports shop. There were all these cricket bats, autographed by Peter May, Colin Cowdrey, Peter Richardson. Gray-Nicolls made my wicket-keeping gloves so I knew they were paying so much a bat to the players.

"One of the first questions was, 'Why is it that the first six batsmen in the England team are almost all amateurs?' And Leslie said to me, 'Keith, would you like to address this question?' Well, I just believe in what I believe in. Up in Lancashire that's how we were. So all of a sudden I was saying, 'Amateurs? I didn't realise there were any amateurs in the first six of the England batting order.' You could have heard a pin drop.

"I felt Douglas Jardine's head swivel and stare at me. 'What do you mean?' he said, and I said about the bats at Elmer Cotton's. 'If that's what an amateur is, I'm an amateur.' Then later there was a question about tennis. I said, 'Billy Knight's a friend of mine. Eleven months of the year he's playing tennis. His father owns a bed shop in Northampton. He can't live and drive the car he does without getting something from tennis.'"

The meeting ended, and Douglas Jardine stopped the outspoken youngster.

"Would you like to have a coffee with me before you go back?"

The villain of the Bodyline tour, the old Wykehamist whose autocratic bearing had incensed the Australians, sat across the table in the hotel lounge.

"We talked for ages, with this silver coffee pot between us. 'Young man,' he said. 'Always speak and believe as you do now.' His finger wagged at me. I can see him now. 'Speak with conviction and honesty.' And we shook hands. 'I'm very pleased to have met you,' he said. I was astonished."

Within weeks the newspapers were printing his obituary.

"I was very impressed with him. He had such great presence when he answered the questions. He reminded me of Freddie Brown. I could have played under him any time."

But not under Roger Prideaux?

"Roger was a hell of a good batsman. I saw him get a hundred in just over fifty minutes in a festival match at Blackpool, with Close and Illingworth bowling on a turning wicket. He was a great striker of the ball. But there's no way I could have played under his captaincy. I knew the players. I had a professional attitude to winning matches."

In late August 1961, with Raman Subba Row injured and unavailable, the county were back in last place in the championship table. Keith was the senior professional, and he took charge as they climbed into the coach to drive to Swansea, then on to Dover. They were two matches that would change his life.

"I think I'd completed my course on wicket-keeping by then. I'd found out all I was going to. I'd given up all thoughts of playing for England again, and I had an engineering career to progress. If the captaincy hadn't come up, I would have called it a day."

Always he was looking to move on. The boy at the end of the line at school. The hard-working student striving to beat his friend Fred Brock. The young wicket-keeper analysing the movement of his counterparts through a rolled-up *Daily Telegraph*. Now it was time to make progress in his engineering career.

He had qualified at the Manchester Municipal College of Technology, and there was always a part of him that regretted that he had never taken up his scholarship to the University of Manchester.

"I was a bit of a fool not to go, but two pounds a week wouldn't have done much for my mother. But, when I took on the captaincy of Northamptonshire, that gave me experience that I couldn't have got anywhere else. If you think about it, there's no difference between leading a team of engineers and leading a cricket team. You've got to know what you're doing, and that's how you get your respect."

Northampton had changed in the eight years Keith had been living there. The market town with its boot-and-shoe factories was gradually developing into a centre for light industry. The M1 motorway was opening up access from London, and there was talk of the town becoming a major area of population expansion.

Soon the Manchester Municipal College of Technology would be renamed UMIST and awarded university status.

"The captaincy of Northamptonshire was the happiest time in my whole working life. It was such a fascinating challenge. In a way, it was my university. I learned so much."

It would never have happened without those two matches at the end of August 1961, games that could both have been lost so easily.

"You've got to be lucky in life, haven't you?"

CHAPTER 7

WHERE IS WICKET-KEEPING GOING?

1955-1961

Cricket evolves – its skills, its manners, its artistry – and no role reflects that evolution more sharply than that of the wicket-keeper, the man who stands all day at the centre of proceedings.

It is his task to watch and understand the bowler and the batsman, yet who watches and understands him?

"I've heard so much garbage talked about wicket-keeping," Keith says, "especially from batsmen. It's amazing how little non-wicket-keepers know."

Perhaps it is not surprising, for there was a time when to go unobserved was the ambition of every keeper. "You never knew he was there till he had you out," they said of Bert Oldfield, the great Australian keeper between the wars, and thirty years earlier, before the end of the Victorian age, Ranjitsinhji was writing in similar terms of the England keeper of the time: 'Mr MacGregor holds the record for tranquillity at the wicket. He is sphinx-like in his fixity.'

That was the great tradition of wicket-keeping. It was a tradition which the quiet lad from Oldham, the boy who studiously worked his way from bottom of the class to a Higher National Certificate, had no difficulty in following – as his first county captain Dennis Brookes recognises: "Keith was a class keeper. You didn't notice him, and that's the hallmark of a good wicket-keeper."

But is it still the hallmark?

'One of the most marked characteristics of the great wicket-keepers,' Ranjitsinhji wrote in 1897, 'is their quietness. Every ball is taken easily without any fuss.' But for Simon Hughes, author of the recent Channel 4 book 'Jargon-busting', 'The keeper is the focal point of a team's fielding, and the vocal point – relied on throughout the day to urge on bowlers and fielders.'

"The vocal point?" Keith replies. "The wicket-keeper has to give one hundred per cent concentration to what he's doing. If a fielding team needs the wicket-keeper to be concentrating on them, then I think there must be something wrong with the captaincy."

The master craftsman has had to take on the role of cheerleader, nor is it the only change in the responsibilities of the keeper.

For Ranjitsinhji, 'One thing is quite certain – it pays to select the best wicket-keeper quite irrespective of his batting ability. A really good wicket-keeper saves more runs than any single batsman gets, besides helping the bowlers.'

The same view was expressed in the first edition of the MCC Coaching Book, published in 1952, the year of Keith's first-class debut: 'Of all positions in the field that of the wicket-keeper is at once the most important and the most exacting. It can therefore be laid down as an absolute principle in team selection that the best wicket-keeper, irrespective of all other considerations, should always be chosen.'

But, fifty years on, Hughes is writing: 'Wicket-keepers are the new all-rounders. They are no longer selected simply for their keeping ability – their batting talent is of enormous importance.'

The man with the gloves must not only be the cheerleader, he must also be a front-line batsman. And perhaps, in the modern game, it is no longer critical that he is an expert behind the wicket. He is likely to be standing back to fast-medium and medium-paced bowling, on predictable pitches that are covered during rain, often in one-day contests in which run restriction outweighs wicket-taking – and wearing gigantic gloves.

"Nobody is protecting the ethos of wicket-keeping," Keith says. "We're trying to get people watching cricket, and we're taking one of the skills out of the game. We're reducing the wicket-keeper to a nonentity, a man who stands next to the slips with gloves on. Is that what we really want?"

He pauses, searching his brain for a comparison that will drive home his point more clearly.

"It's like assembling an orchestra and getting some bloke to fill in on the first violin."

He sits quietly, reflecting on what he has said. The game has come a long way from the one he played in the 1950s, when he stood up to George Tribe and Jack Manning.

"In today's world, with my background and training, I can't see a place for myself playing county cricket. Keeping wicket without a spin bowler, on a bland pitch, I would find it very boring."

*

Back in the 1930s the England wicket-keeper was Leslie Ames of Kent. In the county game he kept all day to the leg-breaks of 'Tich' Freeman, with ͵posing batsmen more ready than their modern counterparts to leave their ͵rease in search of the ball's pitch. Consequently 'stumped Ames, bowled Freeman' was a regular entry in the Kent scorebook, and in all matches in 1932 Ames claimed 104 victims, of which 64 were stumpings. The majority were off Freeman, but there were also some off the opening bowlers.

"He stood up to everything," his deputy Hopper Levett recalled. "If you didn't stand up to medium-pacers, you weren't considered a keeper."

Geoffrey Howard was living in Kent in those days, and he recalled the same being true of Levett himself: "He stood up to all the Kent bowlers, even the ones who were too fast for him. He considered that he was part of the entertainment and that people went to see him standing up."

In combination with Freeman, Les Ames set stumping records beyond the modern imagination. But by the accident of his own great batting ability it was he who did most to advance the idea of the wicket-keeper as a front-line batsman.

He was good enough to hit 102 centuries, eight of them in Tests, and to score 3,000 runs in a season. Indeed, by temperament, he was more in his element as an attacking batsman than as a patient keeper – "Taking on the bowlers was my idea of cricket, not worrying about dropping a catch." – and after the war, when Godfrey Evans inherited the gloves for both Kent and England, he was happy to play five summers as a specialist batsman.

Evans was not a batsman in his class, but he was good enough to score two Test centuries and to go in at number seven for England. In any case, from 1949 Trevor Bailey fulfilled the role of all-rounder so it was never difficult to field a balanced side.

Post-war cricket had its moments of gaiety, never more than when Denis Compton scored eighteen centuries in the golden summer of 1947, but with austerity came a new professionalism.

"Before the war at The Oval," Dennis Brookes recalls, "you could have as many drinks at lunch as you wanted, and they used to have Pimms Number One. I can remember some of the senior players, they used to be a bit high by the time they went out. After the war they stopped that. It was just a pint of beer or its equivalent. In the pre-war days, it was very carefree."

The same change started to appear in the batting, as Gloucestershire's George Emmett identified in 1961: "People today don't take the risks. Shots that were termed good before the war are now termed risky."

A new method of playing leg-spin was devised, as Doug Insole recalls. "Batsmen used to dance down the wicket and smack 'em. But they'd get stumped, and gradually they started to think, 'What's the point? We can play the line of the ball. If it's pitched outside the off, assume it's the google. If it's not, it'll go past. And if it's pitched on the stumps, assume it's a leggie. Then just wait for the short or the over-pitched one.' It became a piece of methodology. Only Denis Compton kept going down the wicket, but he was in a class of his own."

The MCC Coaching Book of 1952 was an attempt to reverse these trends, as the foreword entitled 'The Spirit of the Game' makes clear:

> It would seem that of recent years the instinct for attack has tended to give place to a premature concern with defence in which the batsman's chief aim is to stay at the wicket rather than to make runs and the bowler's is to keep down the rate of run-getting rather than to get wickets. With the resulting development of defensive technique in batting, bowling and field-placing the game is in danger of becoming less vital and less enjoyable for players and spectators alike.

'The greatest wicket-keepers have always contrived to make their art look simple,' the section on keeping stated. 'With most of them it has been so unobtrusive that spectators take it for granted.' The advice was clear: 'The best wicket-keeper should always be chosen.'

"Harry Altham would have written that," Keith says. "Even at that time I don't think the county game accepted his view fully."

"People started to stand back to the medium-pacers," Geoffrey Howard noticed. "Haydn Davies of Glamorgan was the first."

But for England Godfrey Evans was a great keeper, and he stood up to the stumps whenever possible. He was the first-choice keeper by the Sydney Test of December 1946, and he was rarely missing in the following twelve years.

He was not quiet and efficient, in the tradition of Oldfield or even Ames, nor did he concentrate all day every day, but, when it mattered to him, he was supreme. At Kent he kept to the brisk leg-spin of Doug Wright who, according to Dennis Brookes, was not always happy to have England's best keeper taking his bowling.

"I remember Doug telling me, 'I'm pleased when Godfrey's playing in the Test matches. I prefer Derek Ufton.' Godfrey was always chattering. I've played when he's missed many, many chances, because he wasn't concentrating, but on the big occasions he turned it on. Day in, day out, I would have Keith in my side, his performance was always top class, but put Godfrey in a Test match and he was the best of the lot."

'Put an England cap on Godfrey's head, fill the ground, and he became supercharged with energy, a dynamic force,' Len Hutton wrote. 'His infectious enthusiasm was worth runs and wickets to England.'

"He was a born entertainer," Trevor Bailey says, "with a flair for the spectacular and audacious. It not only made him a favourite with the spectators, it acted also as a spur to the fielders."

Godfrey was not 'the vocal point' of the team, as Simon Hughes would have it, but he was certainly 'the focal point'. He missed his share of chances, even in Tests, but, Bailey says, "he could dismiss instantly from his mind any mistake he might make." His successor, however accomplished he might be, would have a struggle to fulfil the expectations he had created.

But who would be that successor?

Keith had the chance to advance his prospects in Australia in 1954/5, but the verdict on him was not a favourable one. So two years later, for the South African tour, the selectors turned to the Essex keeper, Brian Taylor. "He was a good batsman," Keith says, "and he was a good catcher, standing back. A strong man, with strong legs." But he was not the best standing up, as was made clear at Wisbech one Sunday when he asked to take Keith's place in a charity match. In South Africa he would be keeping to Johnny Wardle, and he wanted some practice with George Tribe.

"George turned him inside out. It was awful. George was naughty, really."

Neither Keith nor Brian Taylor was under serious consideration by the time the selectors sat down to choose a party to tour Australia in 1958/9. Evans was 38 years old, and for his deputy they looked to youth and to the promise of Roy Swetman, who was learning his craft in the Surrey second eleven. At 24 he was the youngest on the boat, a short man with quick hands and a chirpy ebullience that reminded many of Evans' infectious enthusiasm. 'There is only one Evans in the world,' *The Times* suggested, 'and Swetman, his substitute, has the same buoyant ability.'

On paper the sixteen cricketers on the *SS Iberia* were as strong a party as had ever set out for Australia, but they had an average age of 30 and, in the words of *Wisden*, 'long before the tour was over, it became apparent that several had turned the corner', among them Bailey ('not a match-winning quantity either as batsman or bowler') and Evans ('another stalwart who gave evidence of a decline in power'). The series was lost by four matches to nil, and the following summer, with weak Indian opposition, the selectors took the opportunity to look at a new generation – with Evans keeping in the first two Tests, Swetman in the final three.

By the time the selectors were considering the party for the following winter's tour of the Caribbean, Swetman seemed to have become their first choice, and *The Times* limited its speculation to the identity of his companion: 'The other wicket-keeper will come from Evans, Murray, Parks or Andrew, and it is an invidious choice. Sentiment points to Evans, who is still able to raise his game higher than all his rivals. Yet looking ahead it might be more provident to take Murray; and from the batting angle, it would be exciting to have Parks.'

John Murray had learned to keep as a teenager at Lord's, attracting much attention two summers previously. At the age of 22 he had emulated Les Ames, becoming only the second keeper in the history of the game to do the season's double of 1,000 runs and 100 victims.

Jim Parks, by contrast, was a specialist batsman, good enough to play for England in 1954. He was a fine cover point fielder, and only by the unconventional thinking of the Sussex captain Robin Marlar did he ever come to wear the gloves.

Sussex's regular wicket-keeper since 1950 had been Rupert Webb. The history books all record that he lost his place because of injury, but he tells the story differently.

"We went to play Essex at Brentwood. I'd changed, and I had my pads and my inner gloves on, in case we were fielding. I always got ready half an hour beforehand. I used to sit quietly in the corner, composing myself. And somebody came in. 'Here, you're not playing, Rupert.' 'I'm not playing? Who's keeping wicket then?' As far as I was concerned, there was no other wicket-keeper there. He said, 'Jim Parks.' 'What?' 'Jim Parks is keeping wicket. Young Richard Langridge has been brought in as a seventh batsman.'"

The first half of the strategy was a great success, with Langridge scoring 60 and lifting Sussex back from the depths of 102 for six, but in the field Jim Parks did not find life easy. "It did not take me long to realise that I did not possess the necessary concentration, while the physical demands were far greater than I ever imagined. My colleagues had to carry me back to the pavilion. I've never felt so stiff."

On the Friday evening they returned to Sussex, only to assemble the following morning for the highlight of the county season, the visit of the touring New Zealanders. "The most peculiar day I ever had in cricket," Rupert Webb calls it, and he tells the story with relish.

"I walked in the ground, and somebody said, 'Oh I see you're not playing again, Rupert.' I wasn't surprised this time, but my contract said to be at the ground for first team matches, unless given permission not to, so I wandered around while we were batting. I went into lunch, and about three o'clock, when we were five or six wickets down, somebody said, 'Hadn't you better get changed, Rupert?' 'I'm not playing,' I said. 'Yes, you are,' he said, and he showed me his scorecard. It was the second edition. I'd been put in instead of Richard Langridge.

"Wickets were falling. I got my bat and pads and got myself ready. Marlar went out. One more to go, I thought. Then there was another shout, another wicket, and I got to the gate before I realised he'd declared."

Sussex, 274 for nine wickets, declared.

"The New Zealanders had a chap called D'Arcy and, early in their innings, Ted James threw this half-volley down the leg side. D'Arcy went forward, I whipped the bails off, and off he went."

J.W. D'Arcy, stumped Webb, bowled James, 0.

"Alan Oakman was great to have in the side. He turned to Jim at cover-point. 'Would you have stumped him, Jim?' he asked. 'I don't think so,' Jim replied, and everybody laughed."

At Worthing a month later Jim Parks took over again, and this time the switch was permanent. "There was tremendous pressure put on Jim to do it. Marlar reckoned it would get him into the England team, but of course he stood back to bowlers I would have stood up to. And, as a result, the game changed."

A year later, Parks was one of four names being mentioned as a possible second keeper in the West Indies, along with Godfrey Evans, John Murray and Keith. The selectors plumped for the least fancied of the four – Keith Andrew – and *The Times* was not impressed. 'If it was thought that only the craftsman was competent to keep wicket to this attack, a preference for Andrew would be understandable. But to take him as reserve to Swetman seems to be wasting a place.'

"I'd have picked John Murray," Keith says. "He never dropped the ball, and that's the best way of judging a good keeper. And he was a good batsman."

Keith was 'the most accomplished technician', according to *The Times*, but already – in the aftermath of Godfrey Evans' long tenure – this was not sufficient, especially not for the second keeper who would have limited opportunities on a tour with five Tests in less than four months. With the previous generation all dropped after the fateful tour of Australia, Keith was at 29 the oldest cricketer on the *Camito*, and there were those who had been hoping for a younger man as Swetman's deputy.

The criticism, however, had misunderstood the intentions of the selectors, in particular their chairman Walter Robins, who was also manager of the tour.

"On the boat he told me that I was going out as the number one keeper and that I'd be playing in the Tests."

It was a judgement that had the full support of Gordon Ross, the editor of the *Cricketer* magazine. 'The choice of Andrew gives me immense pleasure,' he wrote. 'I have always imagined that Andrew was given pretty short shrift after his tour of Australia, and I have put him at the top of the tree in his profession for a long time.'

But Fate again intervened. If she had played a kind part in catapulting Keith from obscurity in Oldham to a county career at Northampton, then she allowed no such favours when it came to his Test career.

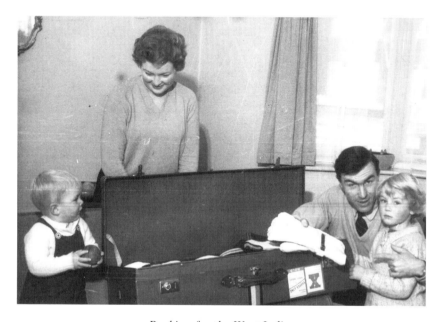

Packing for the West Indies

"I'd been on holiday with Joyce and the children, and I caught a touch of 'flu. I thought I was over it but, about halfway through the voyage, I went down. I was sick, night after night, and I lost weight. I can see myself now, lying in my cabin, staring at the dressing gown on the back of the door. It was swinging back and forth, about 45 degrees. When we landed at Barbados, they put me straight into hospital. I had a temperature of 103."

He missed the whole Barbados leg of the tour, including the first Test, and, when he returned to the team for the match against Trinidad in mid-January, he was still shaky. "I took my own temperature at lunch-time on the first day, and it was getting on for 102 then. In retrospect I feel pretty annoyed. I was trying to do the right thing, but I was ill. I should have gone home but, if you say you're not fit, people think you're making excuses. And it was a great opportunity for me. I was very disappointed."

By February, when they arrived in Jamaica, he was fully fit, taking four catches and two stumpings in the match against Jamaica, and the talk was that he would replace Roy Swetman, whose keeping in the first two Tests had drawn criticism – though not from Keith.

"He dropped two or three thick edges, standing up. There's no way they were chances, but I knew he was going to get the blame. He was a good keeper, quick on his feet, but his personality didn't always help him. He said what he thought, when he might have been better to get on with it."

Whatever Roy Swetman said on that tour, it was enough for Walter Robins to tell him at the end that he would never play for England again.

Robins was an amateur of the old school, and he was happy to turn back to his own first-choice keeper, the quietly efficient Northampton man. But the tour captain Peter May, who was Swetman's captain at Surrey, saw things differently. "Walter and I were not on the same wavelength on that tour," he wrote, and it was the voice of the captain that prevailed in selection. "I was going to play," Keith recalls, "but Peter May didn't want me."

Dennis Brookes remembers the story as it was told to him back in Northampton in April. "Peter May told Keith, 'I want Roy to play. He's had a bad time. I want him to get his confidence back.' So he played Swetman again."

With England one-up after the first Test, the selectors were keen to give the batting depth. Keith batted only once all tour – "I never even had a bat in a proper net." – but Swetman's thirteen runs in six innings in the second, third and fourth Tests and Peter May's return to England seemed to open the door once more for the original first-choice keeper.

But Fate was determined to play her unkind hand to the end.

There had been a vacancy for a coach in Trinidad that winter. "I was offered it," Dennis Brookes says. "I turned it down."

In his place Jim Parks took the posting and, when Ken Barrington looked a doubtful starter for the fourth Test, he was summoned as a replacement batsman to Georgetown. In the event he did not play, but he fielded as twelfth man and the idea became lodged that he might play as a batsman-keeper in the fifth Test at Port-of-Spain.

While Dexter and Subba Row saved the fourth Test with second innings centuries, Jim Parks practised his keeping with the England reserve bowlers and under the tutelage of Keith. "I shall always appreciate Keith's friendship and his valuable guidance," he wrote. "I quickly learned that I had to keep lower than in England, because the ball is liable to slip through, especially with the spinners. I also had to stand up closer to the stumps for the quick bowlers."

Keith's own memory is less clear. "I think I told him some of my thinking about weight distribution. He needed to bring his hands back to the wickets much quicker than he was doing."

For the intervening match at Berbice Jim Parks borrowed Keith's equipment, even his bat. Going in at number three, he hit 183, the highest individual score of the tour. Then in the Port-of-Spain Test he rescued the

England second innings with 101 not out and, according to *Wisden*, 'did all that was necessary behind the stumps.'

"During the Test," Keith recalls, "Tommy Greenhough and I were practising in the nets, and we had a mass of young West Indian lads watching us. When we went back to the pavilion, they were following us, thirty or more of them, and I remember saying to Tommy, 'Look, they're all walking like Gary Sobers.' They were all swinging their left arms and leaning forward at the same angle, as if they were walking into a gale. They were like little figures in a Lowry picture."

For Keith, *Wisden*'s only accolade was that 'he set a wonderful example by his cheerfulness and willingness to accept the situation.' Within a week of his arrival back in England, he received a letter from Colin Cowdrey, who had assumed the tour captaincy after Peter May had returned home ill.

> Dear Keith
> Just a short note to offer you most sincere congratulations on the way you accepted your misfortune on this tour and being such a wonderful tourist. You made a great contribution to our success behind the scenes, although you will never get the credit for it. Well done!
> I hope you found Joyce and family in good heart.
> With every good wish
> Yours sincerely
> Colin Cowdrey

In less than two years, Robin Marlar's far-sighted plan had come to fruition. Jim Parks was the England wicket-keeper, condemning to history the aspirations of the MCC Coaching Book.

Dennis Brookes at Northampton was not inclined to look charitably on this development: "Jim was a nice man and a fine player, but he was one of the worst wicket-keepers in the country at that time."

Keith, however, is more philosophical. "I'd like to have done the job but, when I look back, I think Jim was a good selection. He was a better keeper than everybody thought. He wasn't a wicket-keeper as such, he wasn't good standing up, but he had a good pair of hands. And, with the team they had, only off-spinners and no turning wickets, they were right to play him. He was a beautiful batsman. He had a touch of Denis Compton. If he'd had more encouragement early in his career, he could have played as a batsman."

So no regrets?

"Oh yes. I should have got stuck into my batting earlier in my career. I got in a terrible frame of mind, very defensive, and I lost confidence. I used to be good at cutting, and in first-class cricket I don't think I ever tried a cut. I could kick myself. It was my fault – and my fault only."

The American and British Chewing Gum Company issued a set of 48 cards of cricketers in the summer of 1959, and Keith Andrew was number 25. A brief summary of the statistics of his career ended with the sentence, 'His ambition is to play in a Test match in England.'

Jim Parks retained his place through the summer of 1960. John Murray took over against the Australians in 1961. There were Tests for Nottinghamshire's Geoff Millman in a winter tour of India and Pakistan and at the start of the following summer. Then once more it was Murray.

Keith still had just one cap, from Brisbane in 1954, when he deputised at the last minute for Godfrey Evans. But by 1962 his ambition to play for England had given way to the challenge of leading Northamptonshire in the county championship.

*

Jim Parks played 46 Tests for England. He averaged 32 with the bat, and he stood back to most of the bowlers. When he did stand up, there was nobody as challenging as Alec Bedser or George Tribe. The slow bowlers of those years were mostly not great spinners of the ball.

He won his place as a wicket-keeper with a century in the Port-of-Spain Test in March 1960, and it was there eight years later that he lost it finally to a young Alan Knott and a new era began. Knott played 87 of England's next 88 Tests, missing just one Test in New Zealand when he reluctantly stood down to allow his understudy Bob Taylor to win a cap.

Evans had put paid to the notion of the quiet, sphinx-like keeper. Parks had triumphed over the dictum that the best keeper should always be selected. Now Knott would change traditional thinking on standing up to the wicket.

In Knott's calculation, the stumpings he took off medium-pacers were fewer by far than the extra edges he caught when standing back. "The tradition of standing up to anyone who was a fraction short of genuinely fast was a stupid example of pride," he said. Ever health-conscious, he added that, by standing back and wearing larger, thicker gloves, he could keep free of injury. "Ideally I like to take away all sensation of the ball entering my hands."

He was a great wicket-keeper and, like Evans, his admirers started to copy him. With one-day cricket and covered pitches leading to a decline in spin bowling, the keeper came to be seen less and less at the stumps – and, from that development and the arrival of Alan Knott's larger gloves, it was not long before the England selectors returned to the example of Parks. The benefit of playing the top keeper was not equal to the extra runs that could be scored by an adequate substitute who could bat.

"I'd like to see a proper analysis of that," Keith says, reverting to the mindset of his engineering training. "I don't think that people are taking all the factors into account."

Inevitably the comparison comes round to the relative merits in the England side of Jack Russell and Alec Stewart in the past ten years.

"I'm an immense fan of Alec Stewart. Standing back, he's a very good catcher of the ball. As a batsman-keeper, rather than a keeper-batsman, he's head and shoulders above anybody else. But, standing up, he's too far back, and he's catching the ball, not taking it. He's got to reach forward to bring the ball back to the wicket.

"He had the potential to be a great batsman – after all, he scored a century in each innings in the West Indies, didn't he? – and they sacrificed that so that they could economise on a wicket-keeper. They've done that to bring in some all-rounder who doesn't score runs and sometimes doesn't even bowl. And Jack wasn't a bad batsman. I don't know the figures, but I doubt if there was that much difference between his average and Alec's when he's been keeping. Seven or eight runs, maybe."

The statistics in Spring 2003 confirm Keith's hunch. Jack Russell's batting average in Tests is 27.1. Alec Stewart is averaging 35.5 when playing as a wicket-keeper and 46.7 as a specialist batsman.

"Neither should we forget Alec's fielding. With the possible exception of Graham Thorpe, he was our most outstanding fielder in any position."

So, if Keith is right, this is the comparison. Add up Russell's runs, the advantages of his keeping, the extra runs that Stewart would have scored as a specialist batsman, even the quality of Stewart's fielding, and see if your additional player can contribute more than all that.

"But to do that, you have to be able to measure over a series of matches how many more chances Jack would take – and not just the catches and stumpings; his speed of hands may create an extra fraction of a second in a run-out. Then, if you could work all that out, you would still need to know the effect of each missed chance, how many runs it had cost. And, as far as I'm aware, nobody's ever done that analysis."

Keith is back in his element, his brain whirring away as it did when he estimated the speed of the Northants motor-coach between telegraph poles.

"But that isn't the whole picture. You have to look at the difference between a top-class keeper standing up to the stumps and a good keeper standing back. It's not just a matter of the chances. It's the effect on the batsmen, the inhibition of their foot work. When a keeper's stood up, the batsman has an entirely different feeling at the wicket against a medium-pace bowler who can swing the ball. Any good batsman will tell you that. Sobers said that to me, so did Frankie Worrell. They were free players, they liked the freedom of the crease. Look at Tendulkar."

He is animated now, finding an eloquence born of passion and of scientific comprehension.

"Is it all right my talking like this? I'm not going on too much, am I?"

"Carry on, Keith. You're talking a lot of sense."

"Then there's the effect on the bowler. Once you've restricted the batsman, you've enabled the bowler to pitch the ball further up, to a more attacking length, so it will do more in the air. And that will affect the field placings. If the batsman can't move about so much, you can set a more attacking field. Keep a man in his crease, and you can attack him better. After all, what does a batsman do if he wants to put off the bowler? He goes down the wicket.

"When the keeper is standing up to the wicket, he's working more closely with the bowler. The understanding between keeper and bowler is so important. That's why I loved keeping to George Tribe. We were always working to a plan."

"So what do you think of Simon Hughes, what he says about the wicket-keeper needing to be an all-rounder?"

"Simon is a good talker, and 'Jargon-busting' is a good book. But he's talking one of the skills out of the game. As a player he was a useful medium-pace bowler. In fact, if he'd had a wicket-keeper standing up to him, I've no doubt he'd have been a better bowler."

Slowly the scientific analysis which began our conversation has turned into a cry of passion – for the game he loves, for the game he sees being gradually transformed into a version that is less subtle, less artistic.

"The skills of the game, particularly the slow bowling and the wicket-keeping, have gone to the dogs in this country. If that's the way it's got to be, that's fine. But somewhere along the line, shouldn't there have been some sort of debate about it? Is everybody happy with it? Could it not be a better game with slow bowling? It's happened too easily, without a lot of thought. The wicket-keeping is just one aspect of it.

"Look at Test cricket. What would it be like without Warne, Muralitharan, Saqlain, Harbhajan, Kumble? It would be boring."

The man, whose reputation was for quiet unobtrusiveness, wants to be heard, and he is not the only one. He put a pair of his old gloves into auction, and they were bought by Jack Russell, who wrote him a letter that he treasures.

Where is wicket-keeping going? It does worry me. Heavens forbid. I have visions of a fielder with a baseball mitt. I hope I'm wrong, but it wouldn't surprise me.

"Look at the effect Jack Russell has had on Gloucestershire. They wouldn't have won all those one-day competitions if he'd been standing back."

CHAPTER 8

WHO, ME?

1962-1963

By July 1962 another tour party for Australia was under consideration, and the selectors gathered at Lord's for the annual contest between Gentlemen and Players. The MCC tour captain was announced during the match – with Ted Dexter the surprise choice ahead of Colin Cowdrey and the Reverend David Sheppard – and among the places still to be decided was the identity of John Murray's deputy. The two under the microscope at Lord's were Alan Smith, the Warwickshire amateur, and Keith Andrew.

Players, Lord's 1962
(left to right) standing: John Edrich, Phil Sharpe, Norman Gifford,
Peter Walker, Micky Stewart, Peter Parfitt   seated: Fred Titmus,
Derek Shackleton, Fred Trueman, Tom Graveney, Keith Andrew

"It was the most special match of my life. To be a professional cricketer and to be chosen to represent all your fellow professionals, it was the greatest feeling. And I really thought I might be going to Australia again. I was 32 and, as a keeper, I was at my best."

It was to be the last such fixture at Lord's, with amateur status abolished that winter, and there was controversy over the Gentlemen side. Jim Laker had long been critical of 'shamateurism', his disgruntlement coming to a head on the previous Australian tour when he discovered that some of the amateurs were receiving more in compensation for lost earnings than he was being paid as a professional. His request to turn amateur, on the grounds that he would be paid more, was not well received, and he became a cricketing pariah when in 1960 Surrey County Cricket Club banned him from The Oval as a result of remarks made in his autobiography.

In 1962 he re-emerged as an amateur, playing at Essex with Trevor Bailey, but this was not quite acceptable to the authorities. For off-spin in the Gentlemen side, they preferred the young Rhodesian David Pithey, a decision that disappointed *The Times*: 'Laker's presence to reinforce a weak amateur attack would have added greatly to the value of the match, as an aid to the selectors and a guide to A.C. Smith's capabilities as a wicket-keeper.'

In the event Alan Smith had sufficient problems with Bob Barber's spin – 'He found the language of the leg-break difficult to understand.' – and *The Times* speculated that the selectors would turn their attentions elsewhere: 'As A.C. Smith had a rather worrying match for the Gentlemen, Millman may just get the vote here.'

In the *Daily Telegraph*, however, E.W. Swanton preferred to advocate Smith 'in view of his ability with the bat', and the selectors shared this view. Their choice for Australia was John Murray and Alan Smith.

'The selectors could surprise us no longer in this direction,' Gordon Ross wrote in *Playfair Cricket Monthly*. 'All the time various combinations of selectors have vacillated on the issue of wicket-keepers, the players up and down the country have, of one accord, hailed Andrew as the best of them all.'

'Smith is a great tryer, who really enjoys his cricket,' Swanton enthused when the party was announced, and *The Times* correspondent wrote in similar vein: 'Murray's position was never in doubt; Smith's can be attributed as much to his character as a man and his usefulness as a bat as to his dexterity behind the stumps.'

Forty years on, it is hard for Keith to read these words as anything other than a prejudice in favour of the amateur. "What are they saying about my character, my enjoyment of cricket, or any of the other professionals? They're astonishing remarks to put into print. In fact, those sentences say more about English cricket than any I've ever read."

Then he returns to a familiar theme.

"With great respect there have never been many writers who know about the skills of wicket-keeping, not compared with the other skills of the game. When I read good writers summarising, they come out with a standard comment about it. You won't find anything about weight distribution or the position of the hands."

Another Test opportunity had passed for Keith, but by now his heart was in captaining Northamptonshire. On a Wednesday afternoon in August, he led his men onto the field at Old Trafford to do battle with Lancashire, the county of his birth.

The morning had been lost to rain, but the sun had come out and the drying pitch proved awkward for the batsmen. The bowling attack was led by county cricket's most unlikely pairing: the out-and-out speed of the six foot seven David Larter and the nagging medium-pace of the five foot five Brian Crump.

Within minutes they had each induced an edge to the keeper, and Lancashire were three for two. Half an hour later Larter struck twice more, both times having his victim caught behind, and the scorecards around the ground, recording fourth wicket down at 36, had 'caught Andrew' written on them four times.

An lbw and a slip catch, both off Mick Allen, broke the sequence but, at 111 for six, Larter returned and claimed two quick wickets, both with 'caught Andrew' in the How Out column. Statham and Hilton hit out but, in the words of the *Daily Telegraph*, 'such things could not be allowed to last long' and, when the 150 was passed, 'Hilton satisfied the itch in Andrew's palms.'

Nine wickets were down, and seven of them had been caught by the keeper. Keith had equalled Fred Price's record for all first-class cricket in England, with just one more catch wanted to equal the world record of eight, held by Wally Grout for Queensland.

'The catches were of varying types,' the *Daily Telegraph* reported, 'including the dive, the leap and the smoothness of reception that speaks of exquisite watchfulness and timing as well as sure-handedness.'

"They were all different," Keith remembers. "There was one that went miles up in the air. Mind you, I always liked playing at Old Trafford."

Larter took the ball for his twentieth over, and he prepared to bowl to the Lancashire number eleven, Ken Howard. He had six wickets already and was looking for seven for the first time in a career that had brought him in two years from the Northamptonshire second eleven to selection for the winter tour of Australia. He was young, he was fast and people were already speculating that he might emulate his county predecessor, Frank Tyson.

He bowled to Howard, the first ball of the over, and Keith can still describe the joy that followed. "Ken nicked it, and it came straight into my gloves. It was my eighth catch, I'd got the world record."

It was not a moment for unobtrusive quietness. "I threw the ball up in the air. Then somebody noticed that the bail was off. He'd edged the ball, but it had clipped the stump on the way through."

So 'Howard, bowled Larter' was the scorebook entry, and 'ANDREW EQUALS ENGLAND RECORD' was the final headline. The telegram from Fred Price congratulated him only on equalling his feat.

*

David Larter was a disappointment in Australia, failing to make the Test team, but there was also a general view that the English fielding was weaker than that of the Australians, with neither Alan Smith nor John Murray, who struggled with injury, securing their position for the longer term.

Since Keith had played his one Test at Brisbane nearly nine years earlier, a succession of keepers had been preferred to him: McIntyre, Spooner, Taylor, Swetman, Parks, Murray, Millman and Smith. He was 33 years old, and he no longer retained any hope of selection.

In any case the summer of 1963 began disastrously for him. The county had hired the services of a local football trainer, 'Mac', and he was keen to impress them with new fitness routines.

"He had us running up and down this tarmac, which hadn't been laid long. We were running as fast as we could backwards, then he'd call 'Change' and we had to turn and run forward. Well, the soles of my plimsolls were sponge rubber and, when I tried to turn, they stuck to the tarmac. My hamstring went like the branch of a tree cracking. You could hear it all over the ground."

"He used to be an army man," Dennis Brookes adds. "All he said was, 'Put him on one side. It's only a hamstring.' He didn't treat it seriously at all, and it put Keith out for quite a while."

For the first six matches of the summer Laurie Johnson replaced Keith. Surrey-born, he had been the number three keeper at The Oval, behind McIntyre and Swetman, moving to Northampton in 1958 in the expectation that a vacancy would occur there within three or four years.

"He was a bit silly to join us," Dennis Brookes says.

"There was a rumour that I was going to retire," Keith says. "And I would have done if I hadn't had the captaincy."

There were even some on the circuit who wondered if, given first-team experience, Laurie Johnson could not become the England keeper.

"He was probably the best taker of the ball in the country," Keith says. "He had huge hands. But he played so many years of second team cricket, and he tended to lose concentration."

Dennis Brookes confirms this. "I heard one or two umpires who said, 'We think Johnson's a better keeper than Andrew.' I said, 'That's nonsense.' Laurie was a very good wicket-keeper, but he wasn't up to Keith's standard. He had a habit like Godfrey of chatting too much, and you can't do that."

"It got too easy for him," Malcolm Scott, their slow left-arm bowler, says. "He had this Cockney sense of humour, and he was always joking. You'd walk down the street with him, and some old chap would go by with a limp. 'There he is,' he'd say. 'Used to bowl left-arm for Northampton.'"

Keith's presence condemned him to nine years in the second team, so he turned his attention to golf where he had less difficulty finding a place in the county side.

For the third game of the 1963 season, still without Keith, they travelled by coach to Worthing, and there Laurie Johnson – like Keith at Old Trafford the previous August – entered the record books, equalling the world record of ten catches in a match. In fact, he could have set a new record of eleven, had he held on to 'a skier which swirled away awkwardly in the wind'.

Again David Larter was the main beneficiary, taking eight for 41 in the second innings, but the England captain Ted Dexter had another Northants player on his mind.

"Laurie Johnson had ten victims in the match," Dennis Brookes recalls, "but Dexter wanted to know about Keith. 'He's done his hamstring,' I said. 'Well, tell him to get fit.'"

Keith smiles. "Later, when he was chairman of selectors, Ted said to me, 'I know nothing about wicket-keeping.' It's the sort of thing Ted would say. So apparently, after the Australian tour, the selectors went to Billy Griffith, the secretary of MCC. He was a keeper himself, and he'd always been a bit of a fan of mine. 'Keith Andrew is the best keeper in England,' he told them."

It was May the twenty-fifth when Keith's hamstring was sufficiently healed for him to return to first-class cricket. Seven days later, the selectors sat down and put his name on the team sheet for the first Test against the West Indies.

"I had the shock of my life. 'Who, me?' I said. That was the headline in the paper. WHO, ME?"

All the newspapers acknowledged his pre-eminence as a specialist keeper. He was 'the best technician in the business' in *The Times,* 'the best available wicket-keeper' in the *Daily Telegraph,* while in the *Guardian* his selection was 'so right in one sense as to be puzzling.'

'He has been England's best wicket-keeper technically for so long,' Denys Rowbotham continued, 'that only doubts about his temperament for big occasions could surely have explained his repeated omission.'

Perhaps it is too easy to jump to these conclusions about 'his character as a man'. He had shown no lack of temperament as a 19-year-old keeping to George Tribe in the Oldham Centenary Match, nor when 18,000 spectators packed the county ground at Northampton for the visit of the 1953 Australians.

But his debut in Brisbane had been marked down as a failure, his tour of the West Indies had not worked out, and now he was in a quandary.

It had long been his ambition to appear in a Test in England. Old Trafford was a favourite ground, and he was confident that he was at the peak of his game. But hamstrings are slow to heal, and he turned to Dennis Brookes for advice.

"What shall I do? I'm not fully fit."

"If you don't play now," came the reply, "you'll never get another chance."

So he reported to Old Trafford, and he said nothing. His room mate in the hotel was Tom Cartwright, who had been called up for the first time, and he can only remember Keith lying on the bed, explaining at great length the plot of the James Bond novel he was reading. It is certainly Tom's memory that it was he who had big match nerves, not Keith.

"I wasn't desperate to play for England by then," Keith explains. "I wouldn't have minded being the captain. That would have been interesting. But I could never see myself fitting into Ted's way of thinking."

On a sunny morning in Manchester Frank Worrell won the toss and decided to bat. Tom Cartwright was made twelfth man, and Keith took the field – not wearing the MCC touring cap he had worn in Brisbane but, for the first time, a full England one. "I got a real kick out of that."

As at Brisbane the England fielding was poor. Brian Statham at mid-on shocked his home crowd by dropping Carew, the surprise occasioning the *Times* correspondent to liken the event to 'spotting a great-crested grebe in the middle of Manchester'. Then, with Statham himself bowling, Conrad Hunte 'snicked the ball between wicket-keeper and first slip, not a chance but it was definitely a mistake by the batsman.'

Not a chance? Keith cannot accept the verdict that he should have caught Morris's inside edge at Brisbane, and ironically he does not accept the consensus on this edge by Conrad Hunte, either.

"I should have caught it. I was wrong-footed, and I didn't go for it. And, although nobody said anything, Brian noticed. He gave me a hard look."

Statham stared at Keith, but he was not one to dwell on his misfortunes. Unlike the 'chance' off Alec Bedser at Brisbane, nothing more was said.

Soon afterwards Keith caught Carew, 'speculating outside the off stump'.

Carew, caught Andrew, bowled Trueman, 16
'Andrew picked it up without any theatrical attempt to reveal
what a difficult catch it really was.' – Ian Wooldridge

But that was the only wicket to fall during the morning. Kanhai was at his brilliant best, Hunte was watchful and patient, and the England fielders climbed the pavilion steps through the Lancashire crowd with slightly heavy hearts – though none will have been as heavy as Keith's when he glanced among the faces around him and alighted on a familiar one.

"I just got to the steps where the bell is, and there in the crowd I saw my father. He didn't speak to me, but I suddenly felt very sad."

Twenty-five years had passed since his father had gone to work in Barrow. As a small boy Keith had clung with pride to the story of his father being on board when the submarine Thetis was re-launched. But he had long had to make his way in the world without him.

"I got upstairs, and I sat down. 'Crumbs,' I thought, 'it's a funny old world.'"

His father would live nearly twenty years more and, although Keith saw him in hospital not long before he died, there was no great reconciliation. He had left Keith and his mother in 1938.

By the afternoon his concentration was back. He ran out Kanhai for 90, but Hunte – profiting from Keith's unspotted lapse – batted through the day. 'He reached his century in four hours, forty minutes,' Wisden recorded, 'his only chance being to Trueman at short leg when he was 66.'

West Indies were 244 for three when bad light brought an early end to proceedings, the day's weather reflecting the spirits of England's supporters: 'From luncheon time onwards the cloud built up. A shining morning deteriorated into a dismal evening.'

The next day Hunte went on to 182, Worrell rolled back the years with a graceful 74 not out – 'never a hurried movement or an ungainly gesture, it was like seeing some film of him in his prime' – and, with Close spilling two chances, England's catching continued to be 'expensively unreliable'. The declaration came at 501 for six, and as at Brisbane Keith left the field, knowing that he had not lived up to his captain's expectations.

"I liked Ted. We used to go to the dogs together when we were in Brighton. And he was a very talented man in every respect, a great striker of the ball. But we were never on a wavelength on the field. He came on to bowl on the first day, and he was all over the place, a lot down the leg side. Colin Cowdrey was at slip. 'He's giving you a rough time, isn't he?' he said. So I said to Ted, 'Shall I stand back?' 'No, stand up,' he said. Everybody else stood back to him, he could be quite quick, but I think he'd got it in his mind, 'They say this fellow's a good wicket-keeper; let's see how good he is.' That's how I felt, anyway. When he stopped bowling, Colin said, 'I bet you're glad that's over, aren't you?' I wasn't at my easiest in the situation, and I think I knew by halfway through the first day that I hadn't made a good impression."

Had his hamstring been a factor?

"It didn't affect me much, but I was a bit conscious of it. But I don't want to make excuses. I know I didn't keep that well."

On the Saturday England lost early wickets, but Dexter and Close led a spirited recovery. At 181 for four the game was almost back in balance, but Close failed to clear the fielder on the long-off boundary and the England lower order subsided to 205 all out.

'First-class cricketers the length and breadth of the country would have blushed to see it,' *The Times* wrote under the headline 'TUMBLE-DOWN BATTING PITIFUL TO SEE'. Titmus, Allen, Trueman and Statham fell in quick succession, managing just ten runs between them, and Keith was left with a not out score of three.

John Edrich and Micky Stewart restored pride when England followed on, batting with determination against the pace of Hall and Griffith and the spin of Gibbs and Sobers. The fifty partnership was clapped, and the clock moved into the last half hour of play. In the dressing room Ken Barrington, always a worrier, sat anxiously in his pads.

"There were only about three or four of us in there," Keith recalls, "and Barrington looked at us. 'Who's night-watchman?' There was no sign of Ted. 'I don't know,' I said. 'Do you want me to go in?' And he said, 'Yes.'"

At twenty past six a roar went up as Hunte at short leg caught Edrich at the second attempt. Keith set off with his bat "and, as I turned right down the steps outside the dressing room, I saw Ted inside the betting tent. But by then my mind was more on the thousands of Oldhamers who'd be watching on the TV."

Frank Worrell, his old friend from league days, had taken Edrich's wicket, and it was a great relief to Keith when the last over came round and he found himself facing not Wes Hall or Charlie Griffith but his old friend. "He even dropped one down leg that I hit for a four."

The scoreboard read 97 for one – Stewart 44, Andrew 4 – and he could spend the weekend imagining glory with the bat on Monday morning.

When Monday came, Hall and Griffith were fresh and raring to go – but Keith was in no mood to be intimidated. "It was the best hour of my Test match life: batting against Wes and Charlie, proving that I wasn't quite the duffer they made me out to be."

'Though ordinarily a number nine or ten,' *The Times* reported, 'there is nothing he likes more than to get in overnight in one of the higher places. Once there he can take a lot of shifting, and the way in which he and Stewart survived together raised a false sense of hope.'

Twelve years earlier the two of them had played together in army cricket at Aldershot. "He was quite a star batsman back then," Micky remembers. "But in the end he could hardly hit the ball off the square."

After an hour the score was 131 for one – Stewart 67, Andrew 15. Then Sobers came on to bowl and ended Keith's determined innings. He had seen off Hall and Griffith and, when Barrington and Cowdrey departed in quick succession after him, *The Times* even suggested that he 'was almost as much at home as anyone during the morning.'

Micky Stewart made 87, but once more the innings subsided and the West Indian openers were left to score one run for a ten-wicket victory that was completed half an hour before tea.

The journalists were quick to point out the lack of depth in the England batting – 'Worrell's opposite number at number seven,' E.W. Swanton wrote in the *Daily Telegraph*, 'was Titmus, and the innings sagged horribly from the fall of the fifth wicket to the end.'

Somehow it was inevitable that a wicket-keeper with more batting potential would be drafted in. Back, after a three-year absence, came Jim Parks.

'Needless to say,' E.W. Swanton wrote, 'Andrew's demotion, as swift as his belated recognition, came through no fault of his. The batting had to be lengthened and the wicket-keeping risk taken.'

It seems that even without his hamstring problem, even if he had given a faultless display behind the wicket, Keith could not have survived.

Jim Parks was an experienced keeper by this time, and he retained the England gloves for the next four summers – though the great West Indian Sir Learie Constantine, writing in 1964, made one last plea on Keith's behalf:

> I hold the view that a man should be played if he is an outstanding keeper, even if he is no use at all with the bat; but he must really be outstanding for that, and not just a mediocrity.
>
> That is my reason for wanting Keith Andrew in the England side. He is in my view the best keeper in England, with as safe a pair of hands as have been covered by the gloves.

By then, however, Keith was 34 years old. His time had passed.

"I've got no complaints," he says. "I played for England twice, and that's absolutely wonderful."

The gloves that Keith wore at Old Trafford now sit in the Jack Russell Gallery in Chipping Sodbury, along with pairs that once belonged to Australia's Ian Healey and the old Gloucestershire keeper Andy Wilson.

In Australia Keith had been given a new pair of gloves by Bertie Oldfield, the great Australian keeper of the '20s and '30s, and he had worn them and just one replacement pair for the last twelve years of his career.

"When I started at Northampton, I had a pair of Godfrey Evans gloves, with white backs and white cuffs. They were the only signed gloves in England at the time. But I didn't really like them. I felt them a bit of an encumbrance. The Oldfield gloves suited me much better. They weren't so big, and they didn't have as much padding. So I could feel the ball better when I caught it."

What was it Alan Knott said? 'Ideally I'd like to take away all sensation of the ball entering my hands.' Keith's aim was quite the opposite.

"I always wanted the sensation that I was catching the ball with my hands. I wore one pair of shammy leather inner gloves, and with Godfrey's gloves I had to pull out a lot of the stuffing. Then I used to thump the palms with a bat, to make them flexible enough, as near my hands as I could.

"English gloves tend to have more padding because the hands get more bruised in the colder weather. But, as long as I caught the ball in the palm, it didn't seem to worry me. When you're standing right back to a bowler like Tyson, you have a natural give with the ball. It was hardest on the slow wickets because you have to stand closer and take the ball lower. I remember one time at Coventry, keeping to Frank. The ball was only a foot or two off the ground, and I was really sore."

The gloves in the Jack Russell Gallery have almost no rubber covering left on them. Was that from thirty years of decay in his loft?

"No, no, that's how they were at the end. I did replace the rubber once or twice, but I was very desperate when I had to do it. It affected the flexibility of the palm. When they were at their best, they were a bit of a mess. The fingers used to collapse when I held them up."

*

While Keith kept wicket in the Old Trafford Test, his Northants team-mates were playing at Derby where the home side's keeper, the 21-year-old Bob Taylor, kept a keen eye on events at Old Trafford.

Bob had grown up in Staffordshire, learning his cricket at Bignell End where the old Lancashire and England batsman John Ikin had retired to play. At the time every young keeper yearned to be a Godfrey Evans, but Ikin told his young protégé about Keith Andrew and, when Bob saw him in action in a Sunday benefit match at Burslem, his mind was made up:

> He made it look so easy – standing up to the spinning wiles of George Tribe and Jack Manning and anticipating the thunderbolts from Frank Tyson when he stood back. From that day on, I modelled myself on Keith Andrew; I wanted to have that quiet air of confidence, that unhurried quality. Looking back on it now, I suppose that ambition stemmed from the area in which I lived – unpretentious, hardworking and unspectacular – and the sort of person I am.
>
> By the time I was 15 there were no doubts in my mind: I wanted to play county cricket. I wanted to be a poorer version of Keith Andrew.
>
> I followed his career with the devotion of a disciple and felt for him when he was brought back for just one game in 1963. He conceded only three byes in a West Indies total of 501, he stood up to Ted Dexter's erratic, medium-pace swingers, and then he made a brave night-watchman's 15 against Hall and Griffith. His reward was to be dropped for the next Test, to be replaced by a superior batsman in Jim Parks.

Bob was nineteen when he made his Derbyshire debut in 1961 but, by the time his glove work started to attract attention, the younger Alan Knott had established himself as England's first choice. Knott was a fine keeper, in the great Kent tradition established by Ames and Evans. He had a lively personality in the field, and he could bat. Once more it seemed that the other tradition of keeping – the quiet craftsman, calm and unhurried, focusing on his principal skill – was not to be rewarded.

Taylor understudied Knott in Australia in 1970/71, where Ray Illingworth gave him a Test in New Zealand as reward for his cheerful dedication. In E.M. Wellings' view in *Wisden*, there was little to choose between the two keepers: 'Knott's agility gave him a marked advantage when standing back. Taylor looked the more polished standing up.'

Knott was a theorist. Not only did he break the mould by standing back to medium-pace bowlers, he also developed a glove that increased his chance of holding on to the catches, as he explained in 1977:

> I'm looking to make my gloves into a cricketing equivalent of a baseball mitt.
>
> When they're new I spend hours working the space between the thumb, index and middle fingers into a shaped cup. That's where most catches are caught, and if you can form a deep cup then even if you don't quite catch it in the right part of the hand, it'll still stick. I also insist on a strong wide web between thumb and forefinger for this reason.

During that summer of 1977 he defected from the England team to play for Kerry Packer's World Series Cricket, and at the age of 36 his understudy finally became a regular in the Test side. In seventeen years of first-class cricket Bob Taylor had become much more than 'a poorer version of Keith Andrew', but he still adopted the same philosophy: standing up whenever possible, wearing gloves that allowed quick hand movement, concentrating quietly on his craft.

"Keith wore Stokes McGown gloves. They were made in Australia, from kangaroo leather. Bertie Oldfield had given them to him. So that's what I wore. I've still got an original pair in the loft somewhere. Then I wore Gray-Nicolls gloves. And they were in the same style, they didn't have webbing."

As England's first-choice keeper for 1978, he received a telephone call from Mitre Sports: "Now you're playing for England, we'd like to sign you on a contract."

Bob hesitated. He had never been paid by Gray-Nicolls, but he felt he owed them first refusal. "Jock Livingston was their man so I rang him up. 'My budget's exhausted,' he said, 'and we go for batsmen. If you've had an offer from Mitre, go for it.'"

He signed for Mitre, and he asked them to copy his Australian gloves.

"They were really football and rugby specialists, they didn't know much about cricket. I thought they were offering to make me some for my personal use, but they made a thousand pairs for the retail market. And of course, when the reps went out with the gloves, the retailers wouldn't buy them. They'd got no webbing. The thousand pairs are probably still in the warehouse.

"After that, whenever they gave me a new pair, I had to sit down and physically cut out the webbing. I never got used to it."

Whatever the theory behind the webbed gloves, the old-fashioned ones did not prevent Bob Taylor from moving to the top of *Wisden*'s all-time list of wicket-keepers, with 1,649 victims.

"He rode the ball so well when he caught it," Keith explains. "When I was making some coaching films, I got Bob to come and help us with the one on wicket-keeping. He spent two days taking every ball we threw at him, and do you know? In the whole two days he never dropped one ball."

They were kindred spirits, as Bob still acknowledges. "Keith is my number one. If anybody ever said to me, 'You look like Keith Andrew keeping wicket,' I'd treat it as an extreme compliment."

Keith played twice for England, held back by a batting average of only 13.4. Bob was more fortunate, playing 57 times with an average of 16.9 – "but that was mainly because we had Ian Botham as an all-rounder in the team." Now Alec Stewart is preferred to Jack Russell, and we are once more in the age of the batsman-keeper.

"In my book," Bob says, "the wicket-keeper is the second most important member of the team, next to the captain. If you look at it historically, all the successful teams have been good in the field, and a good fielding side is based around a good keeper. Look at Ian Healey of Australia. He was a wonderful keeper to Shane Warne, bowling round the wicket into the rough. He had a lot of skill and a lot of courage. It was Ian Healey who made Shane Warne into arguably the best leg-spinner of all time."

He echoes the words of Harry Altham fifty years ago: "Whenever I would pick a side, I would always go for the number one keeper, irrespective of his batting."

Bob Taylor played for England till he was 42, taking part in twice as many victories as defeats, but he does not think that he would ever be picked in today's game. "Sadly, with so much one-day cricket, everybody's got to contribute with the bat. And if Jack Russell can't retain his place, I'm sure I couldn't. Jack's batting average was 27, mine was 17."

The years have passed, with the webbing between thumb and forefinger mushrooming into a large pouch that the Laws of Cricket (2000 code) attempted, not wholly successfully, to reduce in size.

"I don't think we should allow webbing at all," Bob says. "I've seen boys perfecting the catching of the ball in the webbing. And I find that sad. You're supposed to catch the ball in your palm."

Keith agrees, looking at the problem through the eyes of an engineer.

"The catching area of the present-day gloves is far bigger than what I had. So wicket-keeping is reduced to baseball catching. And, of course, the gloves are heavier so they slow the hand movements. They're designed for a slip fielder who catches, that's all. Anybody who can catch a ball can be a wicket-keeper. They're taking the art out of it. And the people who watch cricket are losing something.

"They have all these laws about the size of the bat and the weight of the ball. They went mad when Dennis Lillee wanted to play with an aluminium bat. Yet here we are, altering the whole art of wicket-keeping and, because the average administrator knows nothing about keeping, nothing gets done."

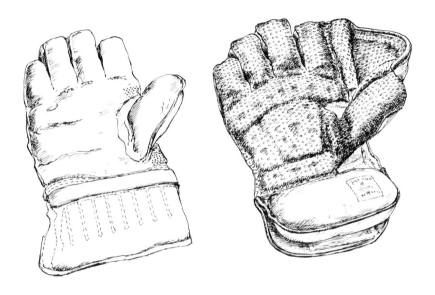

Keith's glove alongside a modern glove

If the wicket-keeper wears gloves, they shall have no webbing between fingers
except that a single piece of flat non-stretch material may be inserted
between index finger and thumb solely as a means of support.
This insert may not form a pouch when the hand is extended.
Section 2 of Law 40 of The Laws of Cricket (2000 Code) – never enforced

"They're astonishing," Keith says. "I think I might be able to play again if I
had a pair of these."

He stops. The habit of a lifetime of unobtrusive quietness gets the better of him.

"You will tell me if I'm going on too much, won't you?"

"No, no, Keith, it's fine. You need to say these things."

"So many things in life have changed for the better, but I do fear for the future of cricket. There won't be a game in this country if we carry on as we're going."

ENGLAND v WEST INDIES – FIRST TEST

Old Trafford. 6, 7, 8 & 10 June 1963

WEST INDIES WON BY 10 WICKETS

WEST INDIES

C.C. Hunte	c Titmus b Allen	182	*not out*	1
M.C. Carew	c Andrew b Trueman	16	*not out*	0
R.B. Kanhai	run out	90		
B.F. Butcher	lbw b Trueman	22		
G.S. Sobers	c Edrich b Allen	64		
J.S. Solomon	lbw b Titmus	35		
F.M. Worrell *	*not out*	74		
D.L. Murray +	*not out*	7		
W.W. Hall				
C.C. Griffith				
L.R. Gibbs				
Extras	b 3, lb 7, nb 1	11		
	(6 wkts, dec)	**501**	(no wkt)	**1**

1-37, 2-188, 3-239, 4-359, 5-398, 6-479

Trueman	40	7	95	2				
Statham	37	6	121	0				
Titmus	40	13	105	1				
Close	10	2	31	0				
Allen	57	22	122	2	0.1	0	1	0
Dexter	12	4	16	0				

ENGLAND

M.J. Stewart	c Murray b Gibbs	37		c Murray b Gibbs	87
J.H. Edrich	c Murray b Hall	20		c Hunte b Worrell	38
K.F. Barrington	c Murray b Hall	16	(4)	b Gibbs	8
M.C. Cowdrey	b Hall	4	(5)	c Hunte b Gibbs	12
E.R. Dexter *	c Worrell b Sobers	73	(6)	c Murray b Gibbs	35
D.B. Close	c Hunte b Gibbs	30	(7)	c Sobers b Gibbs	32
F.J. Titmus	c Sobers b Gibbs	0	(8)	b Sobers	17
D.A. Allen	c Sobers b Gibbs	5	(9)	b Gibbs	1
F.S. Trueman	c Worrell b Sobers	5	(10)	*not out*	29
K.V. Andrew +	*not out*	3	(3)	c Murray b Sobers	15
J.B. Statham	b Gibbs	0		b Griffith	7
Extras	b 2, lb 7, nb 3	12		b 10,, lb 4, nb 1	15
		205			**296**

1-34, 2-61, 3-67, 4-108, 5-181, 6-190, 7-192, 8-202, 9-202, 10-205
1-93, 2-131, 3-160, 4-165, 5-186, 6-231, 7-254, 8-256, 9-268, 10-296

Hall	17	4	51	3	14	0	39	0
Griffith	21	4	37	0	8.5	4	11	1
Gibbs	29.3	9	59	5	46	16	98	6
Sobers	22	11	34	2	37	4	122	2
Worrell	1	0	12	0	4	2	11	1

Umpires: C.S. Elliott and John Langridge

CHAPTER 9

A WINNING FORMULA

1961-1965

On the evening of Tuesday the 22nd of August 1961 the Northampton coach travelled nearly 200 miles from the county ground to Swansea. For the final half hour of their match at Northampton they had struggled in vain to take the last three Warwickshire wickets, and the resulting draw left them firmly rooted to the foot of the championship table.

CHAMPIONSHIP TABLE – 22 AUGUST 1961

		Played	Won	Drawn	Lost	Points
15	Surrey	25	4	11	10	96
16	Nottinghamshire	27	4	4	19	76
17	Northamptonshire	26	3	10	13	56

Only victories at Swansea and Dover, and a Notts defeat against Hampshire, would lift them out of last place. In thirteen years, it seemed, they had come full circle. Runners-up in 1957, they were back where they had spent most summers in the '30s and '40s.

Raman Subba Row was the county captain. He was in his fourth and final year in charge, and in that time he had matured into one of the most successful batsmen in England. He was not a classical player like Dennis Brookes nor an exciting hitter like Jock Livingston but he placed the ball effectively, and his less eye-catching technique was good enough to take him to the top of the national averages in 1960 and to score two Test centuries against the '61 Australians.

But his years of captaincy had not been easy ones. The great names of the '50s – Tribe, Brookes, Tyson, Manning, Livingston – had all retired, and by 1961 he was leading a young and inexperienced side. The only survivors from the 1957 team were Keith and the doughty opener Brian Reynolds.

There were grounds for optimism. With the football pools generating sufficient income for a playing staff of 29, the second eleven, under the wise guidance of Dennis Brookes, won their championship in 1960, and from their ranks emerged some promising youngsters, notably Colin Milburn, David Larter and Brian Crump.

"I only spend the odd afternoon at the County Ground these days," Keith says. "I go with my friend Peter Bason and, when we leave and the sun is dropping in the sky, I often look up at the balcony of the old pavilion. And always I see in my mind's eye Ken Turner and Dennis Brookes, sitting there, deep in conversation, assessing the merits of their latest signing. They were the two great sages of Northamptonshire cricket."

Brian Crump was the son of Stan, the Staffordshire cricketer who had held his own as a professional in the Central Lancashire League in the company of Worrell, Livingston and Tribe, a pit engineer who – if it had not been for the war and for the lack of economic security in cricket – would have been a good county all-rounder, perhaps even an England one. Deprived of the opportunity himself, he wanted nothing more than to see his boy Brian succeed.

A 16-year-old Brian Crump, with his father Stan,
on the occasion of his first appearance for Staffordshire

"I grew up at the back of the Chell ground," Brian recalls, "where Dad was the professional. As a boy, I'd sit at the window, doing my homework, with the players going by. And after a bit Dad would say, 'Oh go on then, get up there.' The North Staffordshire League had so many fine players at that time: John Ikin, Sonny Ramadhin, Frank Worrell. What a place, to go out and bowl to people like Frank Worrell. A magnificent gentleman. It was a pleasure just to bowl a ball at him."

Taking a break from his apprenticeship in the print trade, Brian took lodgings in Northampton in Spring 1960. Having missed out on National Service because of conjunctivitis and acne – "I pretended to be deaf, but that didn't work." – he was away from home for the first time. "I was a bit lonely. I lodged with Laurie Johnson. We were with this woman who went spare if she came back and found us with the television on. Laurie met a girl and got married straightaway. I tended to go out, even when I didn't want to. Playing cricket with the kids in the park, drinking milk out of the milk machines."

"When I met him," his wife Lynn tells, "I think he knew where every milk machine was in Northampton."

"I've never enjoyed beer. At the end of a match, when the tray of drinks came in, mine was always a pint of milk."

By June Brian was in the first eleven, making fifties in his first two matches. Then at the end of the month, with the county without a win and bottom of the table, he encountered for the first time the full might of Yorkshire, the county champions.

"It's one of my best memories. I came in at 118 for four in the second innings, and we wanted 287 to win." He is not a man for statistics, but these figures have never been forgotten. "Subba Row was in. I got on great with him. He was a gentleman, and I never failed to get runs when I batted with him. He talked you through an innings. 'We've just got to try and save the game,' he said, and we batted and batted."

They came together needing 169 in less than an hour and three quarters, most of the batting was gone, and the youngster's innings was punctuated by good fortune.

"I gave a catch to Freddie Trueman at backward short leg, off I went, and the umpire Eddie Phillipson said, 'Not out, it bounced.' Then I went for a quick single off Closey, and there was a direct hit at his end. I was well out, I just kept running towards the old pavilion, and Eddie Phillipson said, 'Not out, I couldn't see whether he broke the wicket. He's blocking my view.' Closey was frothing at the mouth."

Somehow, as always with Subba Row, the runs crept up almost invisibly on the scoreboard. "'We could win this,' he said to me. 'If you and me stay together, we could win this game.'"

With three overs to go, there were 23 runs needed for victory. Then it was four wanted off the last over, Trueman to bowl and Brian on strike.

"He came thundering in, and I ducked. And the next three were exactly the same, and I ducked them all. I wasn't a hooker, I'd been hit on the nose in a second team game, but Raman came down the wicket. 'You've got to take him on,' he said. So I hooked the fifth ball, and it flew away for four. It was fantastic.

"I'll give Fred his due. He came straight up and put his arm round me. 'Well played, lad,' he said. All Closey could do was mumble about Vic Wilson: 'What a bloody useless skipper we've got.'"

The following day another of that summer's newcomers, the six foot seven David Larter, out-bowled the ageing Frank Tyson, taking six wickets for 26 as Worcestershire, too, were defeated. A new generation was tasting its first successes.

"We were all the same sort of age," Brian says, "and we were all hungry to play cricket."

Brian completed one thousand runs in his last innings of the season, took 43 wickets with his off-breaks and, when the following summer he hit his first two hundreds, Northants received an enquiry from MCC about his availability for the winter tour of India. "I wasn't very keen," he admits. "My stomach's never been that good, and I had fears that I would be ill, like Johnny Ikin had been. I played with him at Staffordshire, and I heard how he'd come home in a terrible state and had to have operations. But of course you can't refuse to go."

"Brian's dad Stan was a real tough nut," Keith says, "but Brian was different. When he was in digs in Northampton, it was like the inside of a chemist's shop."

"When I wasn't picked, I was sad – but I also felt relief."

Colin Milburn, the 19-year-old from County Durham, joined him in the first team in 1961, but the 17-stone batsman's swashbuckling style brought him only limited success. Malcolm Scott and the Watts brothers, Jim and Peter, also stepped up from the second eleven, but they were finding their feet at a new level and, with Subba Row often absent at Test matches, the team reached Swansea with just one narrow victory to show for their last 13 weeks of effort.

Subba Row pulled a groin muscle in the fifth Test, and the struggling, young Northants side was left in the hands of their senior professional Keith Andrew for those final matches at Swansea and Dover.

"When I think back to those two games at the end of 1961," Keith says, "I realise that they were the most important matches of my whole career. Without them I would never have been given the captaincy, and it was the captaincy that was my most special time in cricket."

The pavilion at the St Helen's ground, Swansea, stands at the top of a flight of 72 steps, and there in the visitors' dressing room on that Wednesday morning the acting Northants captain prepared for the toss. The weather was unsettled, but he was clear that the advantage would lie with the team which batted first.

"Ossie Wheatley was the Glamorgan captain so in the dressing room I grabbed hold of Peter Watts. 'Come on, Peter,' I said. 'You're going to be Ossie Wheatley. You're going to throw six consecutive tails and, when you've done that, I'll go out and call heads.'" With Peter Watts turning up his collar to look like the Glamorgan skipper, they set to work.

"It was just a bit of fun," Keith says now. "I suppose it helped to relieve the tension."

The probability of a tail is one in two. The probability of six tails is one in sixty-four. A lengthy calculation reveals that it should take an average of 126 throws to achieve a sequence of six tails. But Keith's mind was set on the day ahead.

"Believe it or not, after a while, Peter did throw six tails. So I did exactly as I said. I went straight out to find Ossie, called heads, and it came down tails again."

Then came the unexpected break that made the whole ritual redundant. "I couldn't believe my luck. He put us in."

Down the steps came the two Northants openers: Mick Norman and Brian Reynolds. Mick was a stylish player, at his best against quick bowling, while Brian Reynolds was a gutsy battler, not pretty to watch but always hard to prise out.

Norman pushed the first ball from Brian Evans into the ever-safe hands of Peter Walker at short leg and departed back up the 72 steps. The same fate would befall him in 1964, caught Walker bowled Wheatley to the first ball of the match. Only on that occasion he went out to bat again before close of play on the first day, and he was out to the first ball of the second innings as well. Two golden ducks, both to the first ball of an innings and both on the same day, has cricket ever thrown up a more ignominious day for a batsman – and with the Swansea staircase to negotiate each time? "I reckon I knew every one of those steps by the end of the day," he says.

Brian Reynolds held the innings steady with a determined 86, but the best batting came on the Thursday when Milburn made a career-best 80. 'He put his 17½ stone behind two huge sixes,' the *Chronicle* reported, 'one, a terrific drive, landing on the roof of the rugby football stand.'

When Glamorgan batted, Keith was in his element, marshalling his slow bowlers on the turning wicket and picking up two catches and two stumpings. He could not call on George Tribe, Jack Manning or Mick Allen to bowl slow left-arm, but their successor Malcolm Scott captured seven first innings wickets and, when Glamorgan chased 203 on the last afternoon, he took another five to pull off an exciting victory ten minutes from time, thus 'reviving the faint hope of their escape from the bottom of the table.'

Malcolm Scott was from South Shields, a professional footballer who had played for a Newcastle United side that tried to live up to the triumphs of their predecessors: Jackie Milburn, Jimmy Scoular and Bobby Mitchell. The situation at Northampton had some similarities for him. "KV had kept to George Tribe," he reflects, "and now he was keeping to a pretty ordinary left-arm spinner. But it wasn't so much pressure as at Newcastle. There's very little patience in football crowds."

CHAMPIONSHIP TABLE – 25 AUGUST 1961

	Played	Won	Drawn	Lost	Points
15 Surrey	26	4	11	11	96
16 Nottinghamshire	28	4	4	20	76
17 Northamptonshire	27	4	10	13	68

They needed to win at Dover, and they clambered into the coach in high spirits. With no Severn Bridge, a journey of 300 miles lay ahead of them and, by midnight, they were all dozing.

Colin Milburn in the doorway of the coach, Albert Lightfoot in the front seat

"I remember one journey home from Glamorgan," Keith says, "when Frank Tyson was still playing. We had a bet, who could run the faster, and we finished up, stopping the coach and racing between two telegraph poles. Dennis was captain, and he played old Harry with us. 'What would have happened if you'd pulled a muscle?' 'I daren't think,' I said.

"The coach was the best thing we ever did. It created a great team spirit."

"It kept the team together," Brian Crump agrees. "But I do remember that journey from Swansea. I couldn't travel on a coach unless I sat on the front seat, I suffered from travel sickness, so I used to sit next to Jack Jennings, the masseur. We got into Dover about two o'clock and, being in the front, I was the one to report to the desk in the hotel. 'Northamptonshire CCC,' I said, 'we're here for four nights.' 'We've got no booking for you tonight. ... We've got you booked in next week.' Ken Turner had sent them the wrong dates.

"Eventually they found us a place in Folkestone, and even then four or five of us had to sleep with blankets on a stage. We got to bed at four o'clock."

"The coach journeys were hard," Malcolm Scott says, "especially if you'd been in the field all afternoon, trying to stop the runs. I don't know if it was at Dover, but I remember arriving in the middle of the night at one hotel, and this dog appeared and peed all over my bags."

The next morning, Keith was too tired to play at tossing coins. He went out, called heads and, according to the *Chronicle*, 'brought back bad news to the pavilion. With Kent taking first strike, he faced the prospect of a full day in the field.'

"We'd had about three hours' sleep," Brian recalls, "and it was blazing hot. And the ground at Dover is in a bowl – and is it hot!"

Two years earlier they had lost in a day and a half on this ground, bowled out for 80 and 86 by Kent's David Halfyard. It seemed that Keith's mini-spell of captaincy was set to end in exhaustion and disappointment.

"Everybody knew what the score was," Keith says and, determined to do their best for their quiet keeper, they bowled out Kent for 164. Then, thanks to some positive batting by Mick Norman and Albert Lightfoot, they raced into a first innings lead before close of play.

Meanwhile, according to Brian, "the rest of us got on the side of the bank behind the pavilion and lay asleep on the grass."

After the weekend Kent fought back, and a Peter Richardson century left the visitors 192 for victory. "Look at Brian Crump's figures," Keith says, inspecting the page in *Wisden*. "48 overs, seven for 129."

At lunch on the final day Northants looked in command at 77 for one. But wickets started to fall in the heat of the afternoon, including Milburn who drove three fours in an over, then swung at Halfyard and was bowled. At 140 for five, Brian Crump stepped out to join Brian Reynolds, who was playing a 'cut, thrust and parry innings, with judicious application of the leg sweep.'

"You could see Brian buckling down when the chips were down," Keith says. "He wasn't going to play for England, but he gave his all to Northamptonshire. And when he was trying, everybody could see it. His face was all flushed. 'Get past this,' he seemed to say. He was a very intense chap, trying his heart out, and that sort of attitude spreads. It wasn't just the runs he scored, it was the manner in which he scored them.

"At Dover the wicket was doing a bit, and Dave Halfyard was a fine bowler."

Brian Crump was out with 23 still to win, and Keith Andrew decided to join Brian Reynolds. He had had his best season with the bat – 669 runs at an average of 23.89, with only Parks (32.17) and Murray (26.63) of the wicket-keepers above him – and he dreamt of ending the season in glory.

"That was a bit of a mistake," he jokes now, but at least he did stay – 'he propped up one end while Reynolds made the runs' – and his failure to score allowed his partner to reach a century with a cut for four. Then, with an hour to spare, the ball ran away for four byes, and their four-wicket victory had lifted them to sixteenth position in the final table.

Brian Reynolds

CHAMPIONSHIP TABLE – 29 AUGUST 1961

		Played	Won	Drawn	Lost	Points
15	Surrey	27	4	11	12	100
16	Northamptonshire	28	5	10	13	82
17	Nottinghamshire	28	4	4	20	76

"I'll never forget the coach journey back after that match. We were celebrating as if we'd won the championship."

He looks again at the two scorecards: a determined century from Reynolds, 105 overs in the week from Crump, 18 wickets for Scott, important runs from Norman, Lightfoot and Milburn. "It was such a good team effort," he reflects. "That's what was so heartening."

Back in Northampton in the weeks that followed, there were many discussions about the captaincy, but the crucial one was between Ken Turner and Dennis Brookes.

"I was Ken's sounding board," Dennis says. "He said to me, 'Who are we going to have as captain?' I said, 'Keith Andrew.' He said, 'The committee want to appoint Prideaux.' The old school tie, you see. I said, 'Well, I don't. I think Keith's the man for the job.' Ken was a forceful character, and he won the day."

"That was probably the most exciting thing that ever happened to me," Keith says. "I was besotted by cricket. I never really thought I was, but it was always on my mind. And the captaincy was a real exercise of the mind – a three-day game, with so many facets to consider. Being captain was such a fascinating thing to take on."

The committee appointed the professional engineer, and he immediately surprised them by requesting an incentive bonus. "They weren't offering me that much so I suggested that I could be paid according to the position we finished in the table. I don't think they expected us to do as well as we did so I did quite well out of it. But they did well, too. That next summer, when we went up the table, they recruited an extra 600 members."

The county was not wealthy, and it did not pay its cricketers well, preferring to spend what money it had on maintaining a large playing staff: as many as 29 in 1959. They did not want to go back to the 1930s, when there had been no reserve side.

"That was Ken Turner's policy," Keith says, "and I agreed entirely with it. The young lads were all getting a good grounding in the second team under Vince Broderick and Dennis Brookes. They even won the second eleven championship. They were getting paid peanuts, I know, but I'd much rather see a county spend its money developing young cricketers than employing all these overseas players."

"It was two to a peg in the second eleven dressing room," Malcolm Scott remembers. "There were so many of us that you could score a fifty and find that you weren't playing in the next match. They'd got some lad coming from Bedfordshire."

"Where do cricketers come from?" Ken Turner asked himself. "Where do you start looking for them?" Noticing that Jack Hobbs grew up in Cambridge and Sydney Barnes in Staffordshire, the Secretary took down the old *Wisdens* and researched the roots of every England cricketer since 1900. He found that about half of them came originally from minor counties.

So that is where the county looked, finding among others Milburn and Scott in Durham, Crump and Steele in Staffordshire, Larter in Suffolk and the Watts brothers in Bedfordshire.

"We came from everywhere," Malcolm Scott says. "You should have heard all the dialects and accents in the dressing room."

*

The summer of 1962 was the last in which English cricket attempted to make a distinction between amateurs and professionals. The amateurs were no longer able or willing to play without financial reward, while the younger professionals, infected by the spirit of the age, were less inclined to accept the subservience of previous generations.

The Prime Minister Harold Macmillan had won the 1959 election with the slogan 'You've never had it so good', but this new affluence – with its spread of motor cars, television sets, foreign holidays – was generating a new culture, one in which the youthful American President John F. Kennedy was a more inspiring figurehead than the elderly Etonian Macmillan.

Nevertheless, most county cricket clubs still preferred to appoint an amateur as captain, and Keith in 1962 was one of only four professionals entrusted with leadership. The other three – Somerset's Harold Stephenson, Yorkshire's Vic Wilson and Worcestershire's Don Kenyon – were all older men, drawing authority from their long years of experience, whereas Keith was just 32.

He was Northamptonshire's second professional captain and, even before his term of office began, there were some – like John Arlott in *Wisden Cricket Monthly* – who assumed that, like Dennis Brookes before him, he would have to give way in due course to a waiting amateur:

> If Northants intend that Roger Prideaux should eventually take over, they are fortunate in having a man of Andrew's quality to keep the position warm. He is so retiring that he would no doubt revert to the post of senior professional in his usual courteous and unobtrusive fashion.

But Keith was not only a professional in the formal arrangements made for his payment, he was also a professional in his attitude towards the captaincy.

"I approached it like a technical exercise, how to win cricket matches. I was a professional captain, with professional players, and I had a professional attitude to winning matches. I'd been in the Nottinghamshire dressing room once when they'd just lost seven matches on the trot, and it was like a fun fair. They were all as happy as sand-boys, laughing and joking, as though they were on their holidays, and I thought to myself, 'It's an easy attitude to develop.'

"So, when I became captain, I said, 'We're going to play like Yorkshire, not like Nottinghamshire. I want us to expect to win.' But of course we weren't a winning side. We'd only just avoided finishing at the bottom of the table the previous year so I thought, I don't want to lose the first two or three matches, make silly declarations as the leading teams do. They could risk losing, it wouldn't affect them, but we needed to build up confidence. And you can't build up confidence if you're losing all the time."

Twenty years later he explained this approach to Mike Brearley, who summarised it as follows in *'The Art of Captaincy'*:

> Keith Andrew was a marvellous, unobtrusive wicket-keeper for Northants who played twice for England. His captaincy approach,

with a poor county side, was to try to give his team the experience of *not* losing – which often meant playing for a draw.

"I was disappointed with what Mike put in his book. It's one of my great regrets that I never had more to do with him. But he misinterpreted what I said. We didn't play not to lose. It was simply a first step, getting the players out of a losing mentality. And it worked a treat."

In mid-June they had won two and lost one of the first eleven fixtures. Rain had ruined three finishes, but *Wisden* was critical of 'pedestrian' batting at The Oval, a 'sluggish' lack of purpose at Kettering and 'unspectacular' progress against Lancashire. Then they beat Yorkshire at Northampton, and two more victories in the next four matches took them to fifth in the table.

"I remember very distinctly noticing one morning in the dressing room that some of the team were looking in the paper to see where we were in the table. And I thought, 'That's exactly what I want.' They hadn't been doing that before then. Now they were winning, they were looking forward at the start of each day. Once we'd got to that stage, we could afford to lose."

When they travelled to Buxton in late July, they had won five times and lost only once, their 13 draws the highest in the table. To many it looked like negative cricket, the consequence of letting a professional take charge. It was certainly a contrast with Hampshire's approach the previous summer. Under the cavalier Old Etonian Colin Ingleby-Mackenzie the South Coast county had won the championship with 19 wins, 7 losses and only 6 draws in their 32-match programme.

Yet, whatever Mike Brearley might have understood Keith to have said, the facts bear out a very different story. From their arrival in Buxton in late July 1962 to Keith's retirement at the end of 1966, Northamptonshire failed to reach a positive result – win, tie or lose – in only 46 matches. No county in the country could boast a lower figure, not even Yorkshire (54), certainly not Hampshire (74). Once more, the quiet engineer had been under-estimated.

The game against Derbyshire at Buxton brought their second defeat of the season but, more importantly in Keith's memory, it was the setting for the greatest innings he ever saw, an innings that marked the emergence of the most special talent of his years as captain.

On the second afternoon Colin Milburn, a hefty 20-year-old with big brown eyes and an ever-cheerful smile, stepped out to face Derbyshire's veteran fast bowler Les Jackson. The Northants first innings total of 90 had left them with a deficit of 147, and they were already four wickets down for only 23 runs, all four falling to the relentless Jackson.

"Les was a rough diamond. He was conscious of his background as a miner, and his language wasn't exactly the King's English. But he was such a strong man, with strong shoulders, and he got tremendous whip and deviation off the pitch. He was a great bowler."

All Jackson's contemporaries testify to this greatness, but he played just twice for England, in 1949 and 1961. They say that Gubby Allen disapproved of his round-arm, slingy action. Certainly, the selectors' preference for the Middlesex amateur John Warr for the 1950/51 tour of Australia still occasions disbelief.

"English cricket is wonderful, and John Warr is a lovely man in every sense, but to compare him as a bowler with Les Jackson is nothing short of blasphemy. To take John Warr to Australia in front of Les Jackson, it's not even silly, it's farcical."

At Buxton that day Jackson found himself bowling to another man from a working class background whose unorthodox appearance would count against him in selection meetings.

Milburn had come to the notice of Northants when, at the age of 17, he had hit a century for Durham against the 1959 Indians, and he liked to tell the story of his debut the following summer for the Northamptonshire second eleven.

> I stood two paces inside the dressing-room, looking an out-and-out misfit if ever there was one. Hair unkempt. Shirt unpressed, with the collar edge grey from the perspiration of another day's cricket. My flannels bore that second-hand, seedy look that flannels get when they've been tossed in and out of a cricket bag without seeing a dry cleaner's for months. Worst of all, the objects disfiguring my feet were almost as dirty as a Durham coal-miner's boots, with one of the soles threatening to divorce itself from the main body and with a hole in the other playing havoc with the coarse socks inside.
>
> The skipper was Dennis Brookes. He was distinguished, with greying hair. Erect, composed and dressed without a fault. 'This *is* county cricket, you know, young man,' he said. 'We do have extra boots. We do have another pair of flannels. We do like to look the part. So why not be one of us?'

Though his appearance improved, his outsize body never looked wholly at ease in his clothes. Nevertheless, by July 1962, he was established in the first eleven, and he went out to face Les Jackson with the same positive spirit he always brought to his batting.

"The wicket was green and seaming," Brian Crump remembers, "and Les Jackson was making the ball go off at right angles. He hit you on the inside of the leg, and he didn't just hit you. It went right through the leg. The batsmen were black and blue. Then Colin went in, and he played the most fantastic innings I've ever seen."

"He was a genius," Keith says. "Dexter had a touch of genius, but Milburn was one. After he'd been in a while, I said to the chaps, 'Look out there. You're seeing one of the greatest players you'll ever see.'"

"That was the innings that gave me more satisfaction than any other," Milburn wrote. "I joined Mick Norman, and we put on 152 to save a collapse. We were the only two Northants players to reach double figures, and I was on my way to a century when Mick walked down the wicket and asked me, 'How are you picking up the line so well when there are no sightscreens at Jacko's end?' It was only then that I realised there weren't any."

"The ground at Buxton is on a bit of a plateau," Derek Morgan, one of Derbyshire's bowlers, recalls. "On the edge it dips away into trees, and Milburn hit the ball so hard, it kept disappearing."

His 102, with eighteen fours, came out of a partnership of 152 and, with his dismissal the following morning, the last six wickets fell for seven runs.

"It was nearly dark when he got his hundred," Keith says. "It must be one of the greatest knocks of all time. And the lad didn't play Test cricket till 1966. Can you believe it?"

*

Milburn at number six added dash to a top five who were all near the peak of their games. Reynolds, Norman, Lightfoot and Jim Watts were not names on the selectors' lips, none ever scored 2,000 runs in a season, but in the summer of 1962 each of them topped 1,750, newcomer Roger Prideaux passed 1,650 and, when needed, there were contributions from Brian Crump and Jim Watts' brother Peter.

Even Malcolm Scott at number nine had been good enough as a 20-year-old to hit two fifties for the Minor Counties against the 1956 Australians, though he never developed his promise at Northampton. "You get in at nine or ten," he says, "and your batting goes."

"That's how I felt," Keith says. "By the time number ten goes in, you're usually looking to get into the field. That's where you win most matches. I was a fool, really. I lost interest in my batting. My wicket-keeping took me over."

The county's bowling took shape more slowly. The 22-year-old Larter captured 100 wickets for the first time, winning his first England cap and taking nine Pakistani wickets in his debut match at The Oval. But his partner with the new ball only emerged at Kettering in June.

"I used to bowl off-cutters," Brian Crump tells. "Quite quick, with the odd seamer. During the match at Kettering David Larter went down injured, and Keith asked if anybody could bowl seamers. So Mick Norman said, 'Brian used to bowl them in the league.' I got four wickets, and from then on I started bowling seamers all the time. KV would stick me on and forget me. 'Oh you're still bowling, are you, Brian?' he'd say. I'd bowl 30 or 40 overs an innings."

"Crumpy was always complaining of aches and pains," Keith remembers, "but it never stopped him bowling. I remember him bowling Tom Graveney with one of the best deliveries I've ever seen, and all he could say was, 'Oh, I'll have to go and see the doctor before the next match.'"

"I roomed with Brian," Malcolm Scott says. "Even in the second eleven he used to strap himself up and put on all this embrocation. And he used to see a doctor in Stoke who treated Stanley Matthews. I thought, 'This little fellah's never going to make it in county cricket.' But how wrong can you be!"

His bowling was just as misleading.

"He was like Derek Shackleton," Malcolm says. "From the ring, you'd think, 'This bloke looks innocuous.' But from 22 yards away, it was a different story. If there was anything in the pitch, he'd find it. He'd cut the ball, move it about and he'd watch the batsman's feet. And of course Keith would stand up to him."

David Larter – 'Fred', as they called him – was a different story. A shy man, capable of bowling at great pace, he was not steeped in cricket like Brian Crump.

"He wasn't really a ball-player at all," Malcolm says. "If Peter Watts was bowling leg-spinners and the batsman swept him to fine leg, you or I – if we were fielding down there – we'd make allowance for the spin. Not David! The ball would hit the boards, and the crowd would shout 'Boards! Take him off!'"

"I'd got to look after Larter," Keith says, "treat him with kid gloves. He was a good bowler. In fact, he was probably a better bowler for Northampton than Frank Tyson. But getting him on the field was the problem."

Better than Tyson?

"At his best he was lethal. One of the best I've ever kept to. He swung the ball more than Frank did. Frank used to think he was swinging it – 'Did you see that one go?' he'd say, and I'd always agree. 'My God, yes, Frank.' – and he'd motion with his fingers as if he'd just bowled a leg-cutter. But really with Frank it was purely pace."

The Northamptonshire records of the two fast men support Keith's point:

	Matches	Wickets	Average
Frank Tyson	170	525	20.95
David Larter	134	511	18.19

"I never attacked much with Crumpy. He was a ploy to stop them scoring so that they would try to hit Larter. I had a little mathematical formula. I thought, if I can keep Larter on his feet for six or seven hundred overs, he'll get 100 wickets or thereabouts – and Crumpy will get the same, bowling a thousand overs. I think Brian got Larter a lot of his wickets."

"Yes, well," Brian says, "David got me a lot of my wickets as well."

Then there was Malcolm Scott's slow left-arm bowling. "Malcolm was extremely accurate, and he had a lovely loop to his flight. He wasn't as good a bowler as Tufnell, but he was certainly better than Giles. His trouble was that he didn't have a positive enough attitude. He wasn't aggressive.

"I never appealed unless I thought the man was out. The umpires all knew that. But Malcolm never appealed at all. I used to say to him, 'For God's sake, appeal, Malcolm. I can't keep appealing on my own.' Jack Jennings said to me one day, 'I'll give him a couple of aspirins, tell him they're pep pills.' But they had no effect."

The team was a patchwork of differing personalities, as cricketing teams so often are. There were the ones with grit – Brian Reynolds, Brian Crump, Jim Watts – and the ones who frustrated by seeming to offer so much more.

David Larter. "He was strangely erratic. You never knew what to expect. He'd come into the dressing room in the morning, and I'd throw a ball at him. If he threw it straight back, I knew we might have a good day. But I never got at him in any way. I would get him to bowl a bouncer sometimes. He would hardly ever bowl one, and a bouncer can be a valuable ball. But on the whole I tried not to put too much in his mind when he was bowling."

David Larter

Peter Watts. "He had twice the talent of his brother, but he was always trying too many things: playing shots that weren't on, bowling too many different balls. I liked his attitude, but I think perhaps he thought he was better than he was. And he ended up not making as much of his talent as he could have done."

"Every time he came on to bowl," Brian Crump remembers, "he'd try every variety in his first over: leg-spinner, flipper, googly, quick one. He had to show Keith his full armoury. The crowd used to shout when he came on. 'Boards, here we come.' And Keith would say, 'Thank you very much, Peter. Have a rest. We've seen it all.'"

And Albert Lightfoot, the Shropshire lad. "If he'd had the temperament of Brian Reynolds, he'd have played for England," Keith thinks. "He played the most exquisite shots, and he could swing the ball both ways. But he was such an easy-going chap. He'd come lolloping up to bowl. I used to say to him, 'If I could bowl like you, Albert, I'd be at least twenty miles an hour quicker.' But you couldn't really say anything. You'd call him all the names under the sun, and he'd just look at you."

"His game oozed a rural upbringing," Frank Tyson has written. "With the get-up-and-go of an Allan Lamb, he could have been a Test player."

Albert Lightfoot

The 1961 match against the touring Australians underlines their verdict. Facing an attack that included Davidson, McKenzie and Benaud, Lightfoot batted freely for not out scores of 80 and 57. Then, when Davidson bowled the last ball of the match and Northants needed just one scampered single for a famous victory, he stood rooted to the non-striker's crease as Malcolm Scott ran down the pitch in vain.

"Albert would float off when we were batting," Malcolm remembers. "He'd be next man in, and Keith would be sitting there. 'Where is he? I don't suppose he'll be prepared.' And when we tracked him down, he'd smack his open palm against his forehead. 'Oh baa,' he'd say, 'I've clean forgotten.'"

Keith smiles at the memory. "I can just see him doing it. He'd bowl a wide, and he'd hit his forehead with his palm."

Keith was their quiet master of ceremonies, and his first summer in charge saw the young team finish a promising eighth in the championship table. Furthermore, in May, they won the first one-day tournament to be held in England. At the instigation of the Leicestershire secretary Mike Turner, four Midlands counties – Leicestershire, Northants, Notts and Derbyshire – competed in a knock-out competition with 65 overs a side, all bowled between eleven in the morning and 7.30. In the semi-finals there was an experimental limitation of 15 overs per bowler, but this did not apply in the final.

In their first game at Trent Bridge, scores were low as the slow bowling of Malcolm Scott won the day. 15 overs, five wickets for 23 runs.

"And you were the top scorer in the Northants innings, Keith."

"Was I? Oh my God."

"You made 38 not out. It was 103 for seven when you came in."

"Heavens. It gets better."

Then in the final at Leicester they chased 218 and, thanks to Brian Crump and Jim Watts, won with six overs to spare. The games had provided entertainment on two successive Fridays in early May, and the Northants players were presented with souvenir ashtrays. But little can they have imagined how within a few years the experiment would have mushroomed and transformed the skills and the atmosphere of their cricket.

The Northamptonshire team with the Midlands Knock-Out trophy.

With ITV filming the semi-final at Leicester and nobody needing to be put up in hotels, there was enough cash for Leicestershire's Secretary Mike Turner to buy a second-hand cup and have it replated and polished by a local silversmith

These eleven players – Reynolds, Norman, Prideaux, Lightfoot, Jim Watts, Milburn, Peter Watts, Crump, Andrew, Scott, Larter – would stay together through the next three summers, supplemented by the Trinidadian Don Ramsamooj, the Somerset off-spinner Haydn Sully and Brian Crump's young Staffordshire cousin David Steele. Together they would grow in skill and confidence: seventh in 1963, third in 1964, top at the end of July 1965. Looking at the table in the newspaper was no longer a rare occurrence in the dressing room.

"I look at Keith as the most successful captain Northamptonshire have ever had," Dennis Brookes says. "He moulded a side out of comparatively inexperienced players. My side had much more experience."

"I loved playing with KV," Brian Crump says. "He'd got no edge on him. He was a normal sort of person, and he got the best out of players. He knew how to treat people, and that's the secret of captaincy, isn't it?"

"He was a greatly under-rated captain," Colin Milburn reckoned. "He had a way with every member of the side, and he could read a match as well as any skipper I played under."

"If you bowled badly," Malcolm Scott says, "some of the captains would be at you, and it would make you worse. But Keith would come up quietly. 'Malcolm, take your sweater, have a rest. I'm going to try Fred.' You didn't feel rubbished. He managed everybody superbly."

"You didn't know he was captain, like you did with Raman," Brian says. "He just spoke to people nice and quiet, and everybody got on. People had their moans and groans, but Keith would switch off. If Peter Watts was moaning because he wasn't bowling, Keith would just ignore him."

David Steele likes to tell the story of how, bowling slow left-arm, he took eight for 29 against Lancashire and hardly had an over for several weeks afterwards. Then one day Keith turned rather absently to him. "Steely, you haven't had a bowl for a while, have you?" The youngster's only explanation was that his skipper was a Walter Mitty figure, living in a dream world, but Keith, for all his forgetfulness, knows otherwise.

"Steely was a good all-round cricketer, a real winner," he says, "but we had better slow bowlers. He thought I was being serious, I know, but I was only trying to stop him being so intense. He was so keen to bowl that sometimes he'd mark out his run-up and, if he didn't feel quite right, he wouldn't start. He just stood there, swaying backwards and forwards, for ages. I remember him doing it to John Murray once, and JT turned round to me, 'Who's this? Mister Magoo?' So that's what we called him. Mister Magoo."

Don Ramsamooj was a different character. A Trinidadian he came to Northampton in 1957, spending three years qualifying. He marked his championship debut with a sparkling century against Derbyshire, but in another 115 championship innings he only hit two more, the last – also against Derbyshire – in Keith's benefit match in 1963.

"He was a great stroke player," Keith says. "His first hundred against Derbyshire, he cut and carved them all over the place. But he was a West Indian batsman, playing on wickets that weren't quite West Indian.

"He was a brilliant fielder. The crowd in the West Stand used to clap Donald when he threw the ball in after the batsman had scored a boundary."

Years later, at Lord's, Freddie Titmus reported to Keith a conversation he'd had with Don Ramsamooj.

"I've called my son after you," Don told him.

"What, Freddie Ramsamooj?"

"No," he replied. "Titmus Ramsamooj."

He left the staff at the end of 1964, not to be part of the team that pressed for the county's first championship title in August 1965. By contrast, that was the month when the off-spinner Haydn Sully emerged from the shadows of the second eleven, taking 27 wickets in three vital matches in the run-in to the title.

The most significant newcomer of those years, however, was the young Pakistani Test batsman Mushtaq Mohammad. At the age of 18 he had toured England in the summer of 1962, topping the batting averages and becoming one of *Wisden*'s five cricketers of the year. But Northamptonshire's interest was stimulated the following summer when he returned with a young Pakistan Eaglets side, scoring a classy century against them in a low-scoring match on a green, seamers' wicket at Peterborough.

"It was a masterful display. He was a lovely player to watch. His batting was magical. It wasn't blunt, brute force; he caressed the ball. And he played all the shots. He was an artist. Watching him bat was a joy."

On the third day, with the home team on the verge of defeat, rain washed the game away, and the players gathered in the pavilion to be entertained by Jack Mercer.

"The doorways were full in the dressing room, people were standing on things to see him. He had a big card that got smaller and smaller. Then, when he'd got it down to an inch, he blew at his palm and it was gone. All the time he had this patter, playing up his deafness and wiping his eyes. And he was such a great palmer of the cards. 'Pick a card,' he'd say. Then he'd put it on top of the pack. 'Now just check it.' And of course wasn't the same card. And he'd find it in one of the Pakistani lads' trouser pockets. 'There it is,' he'd say. 'There it is.' They were spell-bound. You should have seen them. I think, if they could have, they'd have carried him off to Karachi.

"It wasn't just the magic tricks, it was the stories he told. He'd tell how he'd been on a boat to the West Indies, doing his tricks, and the captain's parrot had been standing on a perch nearby, giving away all his secrets. 'It's up his sleeve. ... It's in his pocket.' Then one day there was this tremendous storm, and they were all ship-wrecked. And they finished up out on the briny in a lifeboat, just a few passengers, the parrot and Jack. And, after a couple of days, the parrot turned to him. 'Okay, you win,' it said. 'Where have you put the ship then?'"

The following November Keith was in Pakistan with a Commonwealth eleven managed by the veteran Surrey bowler Alf Gover. "Alf could have been a Prime Minister. The Pakistanis all called him Mr Goer. He was so charming to everybody, it made the tour." Keith arrived in Karachi with instructions from Ken Turner to see if he could sign up Mushtaq.

"He'd scored about 150 when I caught him and he didn't walk. Then, when he got to 178, he gave himself out lbw. They had all these balloons at the start of the day, all with Mushtaq on them, and there were prizes for different feats. His 178 was the highest score a Pakistani Railways batsman had ever got at Karachi. In the same match he bowled me with a flipper, and I rang Ken Turner. 'Ken,' I said. 'He's a bloody good bowler, too. He bowls a flipper.' I don't think Ken knew what I was talking about.

"I signed him at the local bazaar. I've got a picture of a snake charmer there."

They played 23 days of cricket, and over half a million people watched them. Tom Graveney averaged 100 in the three representative matches – "the best player of spin bowling I ever saw. George Tribe used to give him one to get him off strike." – while the fearsome West Indian fast bowler Charlie Griffith excited the local crowds.

"At Karachi he bowled his quicker ball to Imtiaz, who went to hook and got an inside edge onto his ear. Down he went, there was blood all over the place, and all round the ground the outfield became covered in oranges. And to his eternal credit Imtiaz got up and shook hands with Charlie. And everybody settled down again."

So was Charlie Griffith as aggressive off the field?

"No, quite the contrary. He was a nice, amiable chap, quite a shy fellow. I got to like him. I thought he needed a friend."

The harder men in the party were the drinkers: Rohan Kanhai, Basil d'Oliveira, Bill Alley. "We went to this night club. They had a Chinese acrobatics team, the Far Eastern Fantasy Group, about to perform, and Rohan asked for some whisky. Well, being Karachi, it didn't look as if we were going to get it, and the atmosphere was becoming a bit unpleasant. I thought, 'There's going to be trouble here.' So I said to the waiter, 'If you get some whisky for Mr Kanhai, I'll stick this postage stamp on the ceiling for you.' The ceiling was way up, fifteen foot in the air, but it was something I'd learned from Jack Mercer.

"The whole audience came to see what was going on. I got quite nervous. I thought to myself, 'I hope this is going to stick.' It was a whitish-red stamp. The trick was to lick it, then put it on a coin you'd concealed in your palm. I used to do it with a half crown. If you threw the coin very hard, the stamp would stick and you'd catch the coin while they were still looking up at the ceiling. And it did stick. The place was in uproar. The Far Eastern Fantasy Group couldn't get on for ages, and of course the bottles of whisky appeared."

Jack Mercer's magic had cast its spell. For the next two summers Mushtaq was scoring his runs for the Northants second eleven.

For Keith, a happy team spirit was vital, and Jack Mercer as scorer was an essential part of that, as was Jack Jennings the masseur.

"We called him Zatopek. He used to wear a white surgeon's jacket and, if anybody was injured, he'd dash out. 'Have a couple of aspirins and run it off,' he'd say. He used to put all our bruises in molten candle wax."

Brian Crump was a regular on the treatment table. "About all the equipment he had," Brian says, "was a heat lamp and Fiery Jack. He was treating me one day for a torn hamstring. He was a great racing enthusiast and, while the lamp was on the leg, he was reading the Sporting Life. I thought, 'I can't feel any heat' and, of course, the light was coming down on the Sporting Life. Then, while he was still reading, he started rubbing the wrong leg."

"We made him the President of our Push Ha'penny League," Keith recalls. "When it was raining, the noise was tremendous. And that helped, too. If you've got a happy team in the dressing room, you're going to get one on the field. It takes away a bit of the anxiety. If, on a rainy day, you're thinking about winning the push-ha'penny competition, you're not going to be sitting by yourself, wondering how you're going to bat against Freddie Trueman.

"I knew early on that 'fellahs' that made you laugh, like Jack Jennings and Jack Mercer, helped to create an atmosphere. If a lad failed, they'd soon bring him out of himself. We won matches because we were a closely-knit bunch of lads. We didn't have any prima donnas. Everybody was trying."

"They were the happiest years of my cricketing life," Brian Crump says. "I used to wake up every morning, and I'd near enough cry if it was raining."

And the greyhound they owned? Lady Be Good?

"It was called The Cosmo Kid," Brian insists. "We had a syndicate. We'd put about fifty pounds on it."

Did it win?

"It was usually slow out of the trap. It came second five or six times."

Second. That was where Northamptonshire finished in 1912 and again in 1957. It was also where they were in the table in July 1965, when Keith was completing his world record of 2,132 runs without conceding a bye.

KENT v NORTHAMPTONSHIRE

Dover. 26, 28 & 29 August 1961

NORTHAMPTONSHIRE WON BY FOUR WICKETS

KENT

P.E. Richardson	c Norman b Crump	25	c Scott b Crump	132
J. Prodger	c Crump b Scott	16	b Crump	3
R.C. Wilson	c Crump b Scott	25	b Crump	4
A.H. Phebey *	run out	0	c Reynolds b Scott	75
D. Constant	c Lightfoot b Scott	1	c Lightfoot b Scott	0
P.H. Jones	c Andrew b Wild	31	not out	87
A.L. Dixon	b Crump	1	b Crump	7
D.G. Ufton +	b Crump	43	c Reynolds b Crump	11
D.J. Halfyard	c Ramsamooj b Scott	0	b Crump	0
A. Brown	c Larter b Wild	15	b Crump	4
D. Baker	not out	1	b Larter	4
Extras	b 1, lb 4, w 1	6	lb 6, w 5	11
		164		**338**

1-43, 2-45, 3-45, 4-58, 5-81, 6-88, 7-105, 8-108, 9-137, 10-164
1-47, 2-53, 3-197, 4-212, 5-223, 6-251, 7-299, 8-311, 9-311, 10-338

Larter	4	0	19	0	6.3	0	9	1
Dilley	4	0	15	0	3	2	11	0
Crump	13.5	2	53	3	48	19	129	7
Scott	19	7	46	4	27	7	86	2
Wild	9	4	25	2	24	5	85	0
Lightfoot					4	0	7	0

NORTHAMPTONSHIRE

B.L. Reynolds	c Richardson b Halfyard	21	not out	102
M. Norman	c Prodger b Brown	77	c Prodger b Baker	24
A. Lightfoot	c Richardson b Baker	90	b Dixon	9
D. Ramsamooj	lbw b Dixon	4	b Halfyard	5
C. Milburn	st Ufton b Baker	28	b Halfyard	19
K.V. Andrew *+	b Halfyard	35	not out	0
B. Crump	c Richardson b Jones	1	c Brown b Dixon	18
M.E. Scott	b Halfyard	13		
J. Wild	c Brown b Halfyard	25		
M.R. Dilley	b Halfyard	0	b Halfyard	0
J.D.F. Larter	not out	0		
Extras	b 14, lb 3	17	b 2, lb 15	17
		311	(6 wkts)	**194**

1-37, 2-186, 3-195, 4-204, 5-243, 6-244, 7-277, 8-278, 9-292, 10-311
1-48, 2-85, 3-108, 4-140, 5-140, 6-169

Brown	16	6	42	1				
Halfyard	17.4	4	55	5	24	3	61	3
Dixon	31	10	80	2	17	4	48	2
Jones	21	8	46	1	15	7	38	0
Baker	23	5	71	1	8.3	1	30	1

Umpires: C.S. Elliott and J.S. Buller

CHAPTER 10

LET'S BE MORE IMAGINATIVE

Into the future

Keith is an engineer. He likes to solve problems. That is his training. He works out what he is trying to achieve, he looks at the materials at his disposal, and he sits at his drawing board until he has created a structure that will meet his requirements.

"What do we want from cricket?" he asks.

"There is a tendency to keep redesigning the game to make it more exciting, and we must be careful with that. Are we creating genuine excitement, based on real skills, or are we just producing gimmicks to get people through the gates, false excitement that will do nothing to preserve the skills of the game? If we're only making entertainment for entertainment's sake, people will eventually get fed up with it."

They are words that could have been spoken by his mother – or, for that matter, by Joyce's mother Edith. "They were two of a kind, true Lancastrian ladies. I remember, whenever Edith came to stay with us, we'd watch television on Saturday evening, then we'd talk about it over Sunday lunch. 'It's all got up to be exciting,' she'd say, 'and that's a fact.'"

Got up to be exciting? The words sound like a cry against the over-commercialisation of the game, the dominance of sponsors and television money.

"No, Ian MacLaurin has done a fine job. He's marketed cricket as never before, and the coffers are bulging. But the danger is that he's sold a game that's not always interesting to watch. And there's something false about that."

So what would make it more interesting?

"We've put so much emphasis on the excitement of the result. We try to manufacture that in a short time through limited overs cricket. And there is a role for that. It has added something to the game. But cricket is about more than just the excitement of the occasion. It's about going home and carrying the memories with you, both that night and in years to come."

The first time I met Keith was in January 1998, and we soon found ourselves reliving the conclusion to the Oval Test the previous August.

Australia needed 124 for victory, and they struggled against the wily flight of Philip Tufnell. The pitch was taking turn, and the tension for the incoming batsmen rose with each wicket that fell. At 88 for five Australia were winning. At 92 for seven the balance had swung to England. Maidens were bowled, singles were eked out, and the last wicket went down at 104. An Ashes Test had been won by an England spinner, and we were glowing with it five months later.

"As a spectacle of pure cricket," Keith said, "that game was fantastic. It had skill, and it had a real contest between bat and ball. One-day cricket tries to manufacture that. And it can't."

'Skill'. The word is never far away when Keith is thinking about the future of cricket.

"We have to look after the skills. In soccer the skills are getting better and better, they're phenomenal, but in English cricket we're not maintaining all the skills of the game. We're certainly not matching the levels of performance achieved by our traditional opponents, particularly Australia.

"In England we seem to be losing all the variety of the game. Spin bowling has played a huge part in our cricket, for the players and for the spectators. For us to dismiss spin, and to lose it from the game as a whole in this country, is not helping us to get anybody to go and watch. It's not as if we are producing many quick bowlers, either. You get this parade of medium-pacers, bowling their overs at a ridiculously slow rate. And I just wonder, is there another formula, another way that might keep the traditional skills of cricket in being?"

As an engineer his first instinct is to look at the materials available.

"We have a ball, a bat and a stretch of turf – and the most important of the three is the turf. If the ball doesn't bounce on the turf, we can't have a game of cricket. End of story.

"The millions of pounds we spend on coaching are ludicrous, compared with the money we spend on researching groundsmanship. The surface on which we play, it doesn't seem to be a factor in the planning of cricket at the highest level. Groundsmen, who are they? They're probably the lowest paid people in the game.

"We've got these inspectors of pitches. What are they supposed to be judging? If the wickets turn too much, that's not good enough. But there is no pace in the wickets, anyway. You see very few wickets where the ball is bouncing. And bounce is everything. Without it we can't produce the more exciting skills of cricket.

"It starts with youngsters. I watched a lot of schools cricket in the mid-'90s, and in nine matches out of ten I hardly saw a genuine stroke off the back foot. The pitches were low and slow, the bowlers were mostly medium-pace, and the batsmen were just plunging forward all the time. Then, when a pitch did have some pace and bounce, I could see the lack of skills.

"The batsmen hadn't developed the confidence to play a wider range of attacking shots. There were no fast bowlers or wrist-spinners. And the wicket-keeping was almost non-existent.

"The fast bowler needs pace and bounce but so, too, does the spinner. When the wickets were uncovered, the ball used to bounce more, and we produced great spin bowlers: Laker, Lock, Wardle, Appleyard, Underwood. But now we just produce military medium, what Jack Manning used to call 'pie throwers'. Shane Warne, had he been born in England, we'd never have heard of him.

"If the ball is bouncing, we're going to get a good contest between bat and ball. And more importantly, it will be a contest between a variety of different types of bowling and different types of batsmen. And the skills of the wicket-keeper will be needed.

"We need BOUNCE," he emphasises. "That will encourage the real skills, and the skills will bring back the excitement."

The paper on the drawing board is blank, but he has picked up the pencil.

"Let's be more imaginative. The ball has got to bounce, and there are only two factors in that: the turf and a round bit of leather. As far as the turf is concerned, if we can't have uncovered wickets, well maybe we should play on artificial ones."

He produces a leaflet from a company manufacturing non-turf pitches. 'PUT MORE BOUNCE INTO ENGLISH CRICKET,' it reads, with a quote from the former West Indian captain Clive Lloyd: 'Low, slow pitches are spoiling English cricket.'

He moves on to the ball.

"The seam has been gradually increased, and that only helps the medium-pace trundler, who is a menace to cricket. We play on green wickets, with a damn great seam on the ball. The ball zooms about off the wicket so that the average bowler can get the best players out, almost by accident. You get ordinary medium-pacers who can bowl virtual leg-breaks. I don't rate seam bowling as a skill at all, and it's ludicrous for providing an entertaining game.

"The television is tremendous. It exposes the excellence. You get Simon Hughes analysing Shane Warne, and it's really gripping to watch. But, when all they say is 'The ball's seamed again,' that's not interesting at all.

"We should play cricket with a ball with a minimum seam. Then we would get back the skills of swing and spin."

He pauses briefly to look at the bat: "They have become too heavy. The lighter the bat, the easier it is to play the bottom-handed strokes, the wristy shots like the cut and the pull. The heavy bats are fine for the vertical bat shots but, if we want the variety of strokes, we need lighter bats that can be manipulated more quickly. That way we'd bring more artistry back into the game."

He summarises once more his thoughts on the wicket-keeping gloves: "If we're going to bring back spin bowlers, then we've got to have proper wicket-keepers. And the gloves have to reward the keeper with good, quick hands. Not great baseball mitts for a slip fielder but smaller ones that reward the skilful keeper."

The sheet on the drawing board is filling up. We want a pitch with bounce, a ball with a less pronounced seam, a lighter bat and smaller wicket-keeping gloves. But the engineer has not finished.

This is not a Roller End Grinding Machine for a textile mill. It is a blueprint for a game that has caught the imagination of millions all over the world, a sporting contest designed to spread friendship, a way of life.

"What a fantastic thing it would be if somebody got a nick in a Test match and walked! What a message it would send out!

"Peter Parfitt once walked at Lord's, and I hadn't appealed. What a game we could sell if cricket was like that! We'd be saying to people, 'That's how we play cricket.' And I think a lot of people would look up to us. Being successful is one thing, but we want to enjoy our lives as well – and part of that enjoyment is friendship between sportsmen.

"If people are cheating, they don't respect one another, and the feeling for the game disappears. You don't go home at night feeling half so well."

It sounds like the words of a generation who will soon be gone, men who lived their lives in less cynical, less money-driven times. The world is not like that any more, the opinion-formers say – but, as Keith is quick to point out, there are other sports which achieve higher standards.

"Take golf. The last Ryder Cup match at The Belfry was a wonderful example of sportsmanship at the highest level. By jingo, we'd have something to offer if we could play cricket like that."

Not just play but write and commentate, too.

"The press quote the television all the time. 'Well, we haven't really lost, because he wasn't really out.' And once you've got that conflict, nobody's ever satisfied. It's not helping cricket. It becomes the talking point, rather than the quality of the play. Is it the cricket the television wants to film, or is it the argument? I wonder why they're going down that road. It's all detracting from the game.

"Cricket is a game," he says. "You play to win. You play to be top of the pile. But that's not *why* you play cricket."

I repeat the words to myself. There are times when Keith can say things with an unusual clarity.

You play to win, but that's not why you play.

"I wish we could put a greater warmth into it. Ian MacLaurin is to be congratulated for the money he has raised, but I don't see him as a font of knowledge about how the game should be played. I don't want us to buy cricket, to buy an England team if you want to put it like that. You can jazz up the television, and it's good up to a point. But I don't think the Australian cricket team has been produced by a commercial approach. They've always played the way they do now, particularly because of the conditions in which they play and learn the game.

"We have to play cricket and to foster its playing everywhere. And we have to look after what is special about it, what makes people love it."

He sits silently for a while.

"Maybe one day it will happen – but only if those of us who believe keep standing up."

What was it Douglas Jardine said to him that night in Oxford?

"Young man, always speak and believe as you do now. Speak with conviction and honesty."

CHAPTER 11
A MONTH TO REMEMBER
August 1965

A great deal had changed in Britain in the eleven years since the television panellists had guessed Keith's story in August 1954. Now, with three channels, there was no break in broadcasting on Sunday evenings, and a survey discovered that the previous Sunday only 10% of the population had been at church – while 79% watched television. The county cricket clubs, sensing a new market, were planning to introduce Sunday play into selected matches the following summer.

After thirteen years of Conservative rule the Labour Party, headed by Harold Wilson, was back in power, promising to forge a more dynamic country 'in the white heat of a scientific revolution'. The Post Office Tower became Britain's tallest building, a new supersonic aircraft Concorde was under construction, and contraceptive pills began to revolutionise the lifestyle of a more affluent generation of young people. The Beatles were awarded MBEs, a woman judge was appointed to the High Court, and the Conservative Party, sensing the mood, turned for the first time to a grammar school-educated man, Edward Heath, to lead them.

In the words of the touring American folk singer Bob Dylan,
The order is rapidly fadin'.
The first one now will later be last,
For the times they are a'changin'.

The old market town of Northampton, based for so long on the manufacture of boots and shoes, was turning itself into a new town, with an Expansion Committee overseeing a planned 50% growth in population. New housing estates, for London's overspill population, were under construction while fresh industries maintained full employment. Supermarkets and bingo halls appeared, along with road-widening schemes and multi-storey car parks. Meanwhile the M1, which had stopped at Rugby five years earlier, now ran to Leicester, with plans to extend it to Nottingham and, by 1969, to Leeds. The local paper was full of enthusiastic optimism: 'Northampton, like the spinning spider sitting in the centre of its web, is linked closer to all corners of the country.'

Nowhere was this optimism more dramatically reflected than in the cricket and football clubs that nestled among the older red-brick houses on the eastern side of the town. From July the 16th the county cricketers sat proudly at the head of the championship table, while the footballers, who five years earlier had been preparing for another season in Division Four, with visits to Aldershot and Workington, now anticipated their first season in the top flight, playing at Highbury and Old Trafford.

It was a fairy tale, and it was Keith Andrew's responsibility to bring the cricketing half of it to a happy ending.

Northamptonshire 1965
(left to right) Jack Jennings, Ray Bailey, Roy Wills, Jim Watts, David Larter,
Peter Watts, Malcolm Scott, Colin Milburn, David Steele   seated: Albert
Lightfoot, Roger Prideaux, Keith Andrew, Brian Reynolds, Brian Crump
Roy Wills? "Roy didn't play many first-class matches," Brian Crump says,
"but he always seemed to get himself in the photographs."

On Tuesday the 27th of July, eleven years to the day after he and Frank Tyson had celebrated the radio announcement that took them to Australia, he stepped out to bat at the County Ground. Needing only 110 to beat Derbyshire, his team had struggled amid mounting tension to 99 for eight, the only substantial partnership ending when the Watts brothers, going for a quick single, collided in mid-pitch. Edwin Smith, the off-spinner, was turning the ball prodigiously, and Harold Rhodes, at his quickest, was extracting nasty lift from the pitch.

"I said to myself," Keith recalls, "'I'm not going to play defensively.' We managed a few singles, all edges. Then Harold pitched one up, and I drove it straight past him for four. Right off the middle of the bat. It was the best straight drive of my life."

'It was a shot which breathed defiance,' the county yearbook recorded, 'and the day was won.'

"Ken Turner got so excited, he nearly fell off the balcony. Apparently he'd had a bet that I'd finish the match that over."

The Cosmo Kid might be slow out of the trap, never finishing better than second, but its owners were now at the front of the race.

CHAMPIONSHIP TABLE – 27 JULY 1965

		Played	Won	Drawn	Lost	Points
1	Northamptonshire	20	8	9	3	86
2	Glamorgan	18	7	8	3	78
2	Somerset	19	7	7	5	78
4	Middlesex	18	6	9	3	72

Each county plays 28 matches
10 points for a win, 2 points for first innings lead in a match drawn or lost

They stayed at the County Ground for the next match, but it held no such excitements on the last day. Middlesex were the visitors and, according to *The Times*, the first two days were full of 'busy and positive cricket': 'Both sides have been prepared to play through all but the heaviest rain, and a sense of urgency has kept the match in top gear.'

The rain had left both second innings to be played on the final day, and the home team needed quick runs for a declaration. The likeliest providers – Norman, Reynolds, Prideaux and Milburn – had all gone by the time the score reached 50 and, with Middlesex sensing victory by bowling out Northants, the crowd was treated to an innings of typical doggedness from David Steele.

"David was always so intense," his cousin Brian Crump says. "He hated getting out. When he was out, he'd sit in the corner with his head down for about three hours."

At lunch the lead was 86, and Keith debated the mathematics with his senior professional. "Brian Reynolds made my job so much easier. He was a great steadying influence on me. I'd say to him, 'Okay, Waddy, how many do you think I should leave them?' And, if he said '85 an hour', I'd know straightaway that we'd got to make it 75."

With Middlesex fellow title contenders, however, they could not get the sums to add up to a declaration that gave them any real hope of victory. Even after 37 years, the memory of the game still irritates Keith.

"Freddie Titmus seemed to think that it was his right to have a declaration, but there wasn't enough time left for us to take ten wickets, not on that pitch. They were near to us in the table, and they could have walked the match."

Eventually Keith left Middlesex to score 158 in eighty minutes, and the batsmen made their feelings clear by crawling to 40 for four off 27 overs. Their earlier meeting at Lord's had reached a similarly frustrating conclusion.

These two Middlesex matches were the only Northamptonshire games that summer to wither away in such acrimony and, by an unfortunate stroke of fate, present on both occasions was the man whom history would entrust with the most widely-read judgement on Keith's captaincy. "Michael Brearley wasn't too thrilled, and it gave me a bad reputation in his eyes."

'Keith Andrew's approach,' Brearley wrote, 'was to try to give his team the experience of *not* losing – which often meant playing for a draw.'

In the three-day game, when rain shortened the playing time, the last day declarations were critical, and the next game at Clacton provided a very different approach. At lunch on the final day Trevor Bailey's Essex were 127 for six in their first innings, still 175 behind, and, in the words of *The Times*, 'the afternoon's proceedings seemed likely to be reduced to drab routine.'

Did Keith and Trevor come to an understanding in the 40-minute break? The reporter from the *Northampton Chronicle* certainly thought so: 'During lunch the captains worked out the time factors giving either side an equal chance to win.' Such collaboration might be frowned on by some, but it was not forbidden – and, in any case, as Keith recalls, it could be achieved without the formality of such a discussion.

"I knew we couldn't win if they didn't declare so I threw the ball to Micky Norman. 'Come and have a bowl, Micky,' I said. 'They might get a few runs, and who knows what might happen?' Trevor was batting. He was a very astute cricketer, and he heard me. He knew what I was up to. And of course he knew that they weren't going to get any points if they didn't declare."

In 2½ overs Essex saved the follow-on and came off, Keith declared the Northants second innings closed after just one ball, and suddenly Essex were chasing a target of 146 at a run a minute. It seemed a generous declaration, the batsmen started boldly, but the sun came out and gradually the pitch responded to the spin of Malcolm Scott. By a quarter past four, it was all over, with Essex out for 88. 'Such is the glorious uncertainty of cricket,' wrote *The Times*, 'though perhaps there will be some who will question its validity under terms such as this.'

In the championship Northamptonshire had opened up a ten-point lead – though Glamorgan, their nearest rivals, had three matches in hand.

CHAMPIONSHIP TABLE – 3 AUGUST 1965

		Played	Won	Drawn	Lost	Points
1	Northamptonshire	22	9	10	3	98
2	Glamorgan	19	8	8	3	88
3	Middlesex	20	7	10	3	82
4	Somerset	21	7	8	6	78
5	Worcestershire	20	6	10	4	74

Northamptonshire had played more matches because their season had to finish early, a consequence of sharing many of their facilities with the football club, whose first home match against Arsenal would be on the evening after the cricketers packed away their kit in the next door field. At that point the other counties would have two or three matches still to play.

"Sections of wooden terracing had to be erected right across the outfield, about twenty yards in from the boundary. It made the fielding a bit rough for the first match or two, where the boards had been."

But the Northampton ground was not known for the quality of its facilities. "The dressing room floor was all wood," Malcolm Scott says. "You had to tiptoe through in case you got splinters in your feet. And if the opposition team came off first and went in the showers, they'd use all the hot water and yours would be cold."

As the 'Barclay's World of Cricket' put it, 'The pavilion has merit more in historical association than in modern amenity.'

TO GLORY ON A SHOESTRING, was the excited *Chronicle* headline for their preview of the football season. With £20,000 being spent on re-roofing the stand, enlarging the press box and laying down more duckboards on the cricket field, 'builders, electricians and groundsmen are working frantically.'

To accommodate them, the cricketers played without a break from the 5th of May to the 24th of August. So, with victory achieved against Essex, their coach pulled out of Clacton on its 220-mile journey to Cardiff. It would be the game of the season, a top-of-the-table clash such as the little county of Northamptonshire had never experienced in their undistinguished history.

David Larter left them, off to the Test at Trent Bridge, but the others settled into their usual routines. There was Brian Crump avoiding travel sickness in the front seat, next to Jack Jennings. "One year the Wellingborough Supporters' Club gave Jack an ultra-sound, and I had to carry it around for him everywhere he went."

There was Jack Mercer holding court at the card table. "Of course I coached Valentine in Jamaica, from the age of fourteen. His age, not mine. With Ramadhin he bowled England out, as you know. Ramadhin bowled the googly. He signalled to the wicket-keeper when he was going to bowl it. Our batsmen soon sorted that out so they changed the signal day by day."

One who rarely joined the card tables was Malcolm Scott. "I'd seen the card games when I was a professional footballer. The journeys were long from the North-East, and a lot of money changed hands – ten pounds sometimes, when people were only earning fifteen or eighteen a week. And there'd be accusations of cheating, a lot of friction. I know the cricketers only did it to pass the time. It was pence, not pounds. But I preferred to read a book."

Brian Reynolds was the sergeant-major who kept everybody in order, the perfect foil for Keith's more abstract mind. "He was on a different wavelength, more down-to-earth. Sometimes, I think, I gave people a bit more credit than they deserved, where he read people as they were. I treasured him more than anybody."

"He was a hard cricketer," Brian Crump says, "with lots of guts. If he got hit, he just stood there. We called him The Cube. Mick Norman at the other end was like a rake; he never looked as though he fancied facing the quicks. Brian got hit once at Leicester, it split his eye, and there was blood everywhere. They rushed on with water, and he waved it away. 'No, it's all right,' he said. 'Give it to Mick.'"

Mick was a quiet passenger on the coach, a natural cricketer with a deep religious faith. "In London," Brian says, "he used to take me to dances at the

Catholic Club. Then in Gloucestershire one time we finished up having lunch in a monastery." They even tell of the morning Mick appeared after breakfast on the steps of the next door hotel. He had been out to mass and returned to eat in the wrong establishment.

They might joke that he did not fancy quick bowling, but he played it well enough and the previous winter he had shown his bravery by rescuing an elderly lady from a fire and finishing with hot fat from a chip pan all over his hands. The burns were severe enough to leave him in Stoke Mandeville Hospital for several weeks.

A prolific run-scorer in the early '60s, he was having a bad spell, and it was not passing unnoticed. "We were watching the game one day," Brian recalls, "and Jim Watts turned to Mick. 'You're not having a very good season, are you, Mick? You're only averaging 17.99' He knew everybody's average to two decimal places. It used to annoy me. I've always hated averages."

"Micky was a great team man," Keith says. "A brilliant fielder, and he wasn't a bad batsman. But he didn't believe in himself as much as he should have."

Colin Milburn was not so quiet, not so riddled with self-doubt, but he too was not scoring many runs that summer. Critics were starting to suggest that he should rein in some of his more ambitious shots – 'Aggression is his forte, impetuosity his fault,' was one journalist's judgement – but Keith did not share that view. 'I spent years in the world of coaching, and the one thing I will take credit for is that I never, ever gave Colin Milburn any real advice. I knew I had a genius on my hands, and I wasn't going to tell him how to quell that genius. It would have been a sin.

"I used to get angry when people went on about his weight," Keith says. "He was as good a short leg catcher as I ever saw. In fact, he holds the county record for most catches in a season. His only problem was that he would try to get too close to the bat. Dangerously so. I was always pushing him back. Then, when he played for England, they had him running around in the outfield. There were people criticising him who weren't fit to lace his boots."

Reynolds and Norman. Prideaux, Milburn and Steele. The Watts brothers. Crump, Lightfoot, Scott and Andrew. Their total of Test caps was the two won by Keith, yet they arrived late in the evening in Cardiff at the head of the championship table, eager and determined to widen their lead.

Jack Jennings and Jack Mercer were vital members of the group, even the coach driver. "We selected him as well," Keith says. "Not that he was interested in the cricket. He always disappeared during the game. We suspected we knew where he went, but we never asked."

"I shared rooms with him a few times," Brian Crump recalls. "He used to snore all night."

"We had another driver in later years," Malcolm Scott adds. "He was interested in cricket. He used to get all stroppy if we didn't win."

The anticipation of the Northamptonshire team was matched, according to the *Times* correspondent, by a rising excitement in Glamorgan. 'Cricket fever in Wales is beginning to approach the temperature of seventeen years ago. None of the 1948 champions remains in the side, but there is no lack of them around the ground, wistfully ready to take the field again if the call came. The crucial meeting of the two leading sides in this year's championship attracted a big patriotic crowd to the unlovely Cardiff Arms Park ground.'

"Our Colin. That's how I always remember him."

Ossie Wheatley was the Glamorgan captain, as he had been four years previously when Keith had had Peter Watts trying to throw six consecutive tails in the Swansea dressing room. But in the championship run-in of 1965 he had no need to work on his luck. "Heads," Keith called as the Glamorgan skipper flipped the coin, and heads it was. He had won his eighth toss in a row. The chance of that was one in 256 and, with uncovered wickets and a wet summer, it gave him a crucial advantage in this tightest of championship races.

"Luck plays its part in cricket," he reflects, "and we did have our share of good luck that summer."

On a soft pitch the decision to bat seemed ill-fated when Norman, Reynolds and Milburn were all out with only 29 on the board, but by close of play the game had evened up. Northamptonshire 186, Glamorgan 90 for three.

In the evening Keith was off for dinner with Ossie Wheatley, Colin Milburn was at the heart of life in the bar, while the non-drinkers slipped away to eat in peace. "We'd go for a meal," Brian Crump says. "David Steele, Jack Jennings, Jack Mercer and me, occasionally Jim Watts. We'd talk cricket all evening and, of course, Jack Mercer would do his tricks at the table, like making the salt cellar disappear."

On Thursday morning six thousand spectators crowded into the ground, Glamorgan's largest gate for ten years, and the television highlights of the day's play are preserved on black-and-white BBC film that Keith loads into his video recorder. The tape contains just eight deliveries, the only commentary provided by Keith and Joyce as they travel backwards almost forty years.

Brian Crump bowls the first ball to the tall, angular figure of Peter Walker, who glances to leg and raises his bat. The camera pans to the applauding crowd, and the bare, white scoreboard reveals his fifty. It is 146 for seven. They are only 40 runs behind the Northants score.

Malcolm Scott flights the second ball up to Don Shepherd. With a belligerent heave the batsman sends it high over wide mid-off, and the umpire signals four. In the background Keith advances two or three paces towards the bowler. "Oh dear," Joyce says, "Things are getting serious. You've got your hands on your hips." Now the scoreboard reads 189 for nine – Shepherd 22, Wheatley 10 – and Glamorgan have taken a first innings lead.

A different batsman attempts to lap the third ball round to leg, slipping and spooning a catch to mid-wicket. In an instant he is walking back to the pavilion. "That's Brian Reynolds. So typical of him, bat under his arm and away. He didn't mess about when he was out." Northamptonshire are 19 for three.

Then David Steele is beaten by Don Shepherd's flight and bowled.

The fifth, sixth and seventh deliveries are all bowled by Hamish Miller to Roger Prideaux. The first two are chipped back to the bowler, only to be dropped. The third sees him clean bowled. Slip and the keeper give a little clap, and the players nonchalantly stroll into the middle of the pitch. The scoreboard shows 19 for five. With Glamorgan's three-run lead, Northants are only 16 in front.

The eighth and final ball has Peter Watts caught behind off Don Shepherd. Now it is 32 for six.

The pitch was lethal. The *Times* correspondent reported of Watts' innings that 'he just got his bat to a ball that shot through low; the next rose at least two feet higher and took an edge.'

"We were dead and buried," Brian Crump says. "While I was waiting to go in, we got on the phone and cancelled the hotel for the night."

Lightfoot was next man in, playing his first game for six weeks, and his captain was watching with less than usual calm. 'Was my hunch of playing Albert going to come off?' he wrote in his column in the *Northamptonshire Evening Telegraph*. 'I'll tell you, Samson couldn't have uncrossed my fingers at that moment.'

Was the easy-going Albert the man for a crisis?

"At Trent Bridge one day," Keith says, "he put his hand up to stop the bowler as he was running in. 'Has anybody in your side got a pair of scissors?' he asked. 'I just want to snip off that blade of grass that's on a length.' Reg Simpson was their captain, a rather autocratic character. You should have seen the look on his face."

At Cardiff Keith's crossed fingers brought better fortune for a while. Jim Watts and Lightfoot survived to take tea at 49 for six, then continued their 'stout-hearted partnership' till the score reached 78, when a ball from Don Shepherd popped up and Albert was caught at short leg.

On an awkward pitch they were seven wickets down, just 75 runs in front, with their last realistic hopes resting on the same two men, Brian Crump and Jim Watts, who had bowled unchanged all morning to keep them in the match.

"There are winners and losers in life," Keith says, "and those two were winners."

Brian opted for counter-attack, striking sixes off both Shepherd and Pressdee and helping to add 53 runs in only 45 minutes. Jim Watts completed a 'determined 51' and, with a final total of 141 leaving Glamorgan 139 for victory, the day ended with the home side playing out a maiden over, the wicket-keeper David Evans sent out as night-watchman.

The two captains spoke to the local radio station, and Keith remembers the gist of what he said. "The pitch has eased out now so we're certainly far from favourites – unless there's a rain storm and the pitch becomes a lot more difficult again." The interviewer smiled. "Well, I'm sorry to tell you, Keith, the forecast is very good."

Victory for Glamorgan would bring the two teams level once more in the championship, with the Welsh county enjoying three matches in hand.

In the midst of the collapse Colin Milburn had been caught first ball at slip, and Glamorgan's Tony Lewis recalls that the big man was in no mood to settle for an early night.

Morning came and, with Milburn presumably still sleeping off his evening out, his captain prepared for the day.

"I was in my room, shaving," Keith remembers. "It was very dark, and I switched the light on. I thought it was going to be a beautiful sunny day, but dark clouds had come over. It rained for about half an hour in the middle of all this sunshine. It was unbelievable."

Don Shepherd confirms this. "I was staying with friends in the outer parts of the city, and it didn't rain there. But, when we came into the ground, the Arms Park was sodden."

Keith, for all his appearance of absent-mindedness, is not an easy man to hoodwink. "I remember, whenever we played Yorkshire, Brian Close would come out for the toss, and he'd never give me his team. And he'd have all these extra players in the pavilion. I said, 'Come on, Brian, you must think I was born yesterday.' And he'd say, 'Oh yes, I'm sorry, I forgot.'"

Here in Cardiff the joker in the pack was not Brian Close but the indomitable Wilf Wooller, the former Glamorgan captain who now masterminded the county from his secretary's office.

"I hurried down to the ground and, believe me, you've never seen anything like it. There must have been every roller that was available within miles of the ground, rolling the outfield till it looked like glass. They were making it as fast as possible. It was typical Wilf Wooller. I liked him immensely, he was a great sportsman, but he was up to every trick. But I liked playing against men like that. You knew you had a game on. I said, 'Come on, Wilf.' And he said, 'We're going to get the runs, anyway.'"

Their efforts did not solve the problem of the pitch which, once the sun and wind set to work, became 'as awkward as at any time in the match'. The night-watchman Evans survived for 55 minutes, taking the score to 22, but in quick succession he was joined back in the pavilion by Hedges, Jones and Pressdee, all out to 'lifters', and Walker, to a 'creeper'. It was 57 for five and, according to Rex Alston in the *Daily Telegraph*, 'the batsmen were all on tenterhooks.'

Tony Lewis and Alan Rees added 20 slow and careful runs – "We were worried about Tony Lewis, he was looking a bit of a threat." – but, on the stroke of lunch, Albert Lightfoot got a ball to pop up and Lewis fell to a diving catch at short leg by a bleary-eyed Milburn. According to Keith in the *Evening Telegraph*, 'he moved like a ballet dancer and caught the edged shot in the region of silly mid-on, inches from the ground.'

'It was a stunning catch,' Tony Lewis says, his mind running back to their drinking session the previous night. "How he saw the ball, let alone caught it, I'll never know."

It was 77 for six, 62 more runs were wanted, and a crowd of four thousand ate their sandwiches in anxious expectation. It was not a sparkling run feast, but the difficult conditions were making for a game that would long stay in the memory.

"More often than not, if you went to Glamorgan, the wicket did something," Keith says. "I thought that was good. It made for a much more interesting game. Some of these bland wickets, where people like me can go in and get fifty, are no good to anybody."

"It was a fantastic game of cricket," Brian Crump agrees, and nobody played a greater part in it than the diminutive bowler. He sent down 42 overs in the first innings, scored a vital 31 on the second afternoon and was now working his way through another 35 consecutive overs. "About every ten overs, KV would pass by. 'Oh, you're still bowling, are you?' he'd say."

"Now that was a game when it was vital to have the keeper standing up," Keith says. "If I'd have stood back to Brian Crump, it would have been a different game. I stood up, I kept the batsmen in the crease, and Crumpy could hit a spot where the ball was lifting. I've never been so bruised."

Immediately after the interval Crump threw down the stumps to run out Euros Lewis, then Miller edged a ball onto Keith's pad and it rebounded for a catch by David Steele. Eight wickets were down for 86, and there were 53 runs wanted for victory.

'Three quarters of an hour of swelling tension followed as the ninth wicket pair, Rees and Shepherd, took the score past 100 and onward. Defensive strokes were clapped, singles acclaimed and, when Rees suddenly hooked Crump into the crowd, their rapture knew no bounds.'

Then Malcolm Scott replaced Crump, and Don Shepherd launched into a big hit. The ball hung in the air long enough for the crowd to make 'discouraging shouts' as Roger Prideaux circled underneath it. "It went up miles," Keith says, "and I'll never forget Roger. He went three sheets of white, and everybody was backing the ball. But to his eternal credit he caught it."

Crump returned to take the final wicket, and Northamptonshire had won. "I was shattered," Brian says. "They had to carry me off the ground."

The captain broke away from his jubilant team. "There used to be a telephone box just outside the pavilion. I went straight into it and phoned Ken Turner. 'Get the flag up, Ken,' I said. 'We've won the championship.'"

News came through that Middlesex were losing at Canterbury, and the journey home was jubilant.

CHAMPIONSHIP TABLE – 6 AUGUST 1965

		Played	Won	Drawn	Lost	Points
1	Northamptonshire	23	10	10	3	108
2	Glamorgan	20	8	8	4	90
3	Somerset	22	8	8	6	88
4	Middlesex	21	7	10	4	82
5	Worcestershire	21	6	11	4	74

The pretty school ground of Wellingborough was the setting for their next challenge, and at the start Keith's team posed for the *Chronicle* photographer in front of the thatched pavilion. At their feet lay the inscribed stone brought back from W.G. Grace's house in Bristol by one of the school's masters, with its inscription, 'Not for an age but for all time'.

For the ninth successive time Keith won the toss – probability, one in 512 – and chose to field. But, an hour into the final morning, 'nothing seemed more certain than that this match would peter out into a tame draw.' Norman Hill and Brian Bolus 'were in no discernible difficulty', the bowlers were 'Sully, an inexperienced off-spinner, and Watts, an occasional leg-spinner', and the Nottinghamshire second innings had reached 95 for no wicket, a lead of 31.

There then followed 'twelve minutes of fantastic cricket', during which six wickets fell in the space of sixteen balls without addition to the total. 'The batting was woefully feeble', the remaining men added only a further 26 and, with ominous black clouds scudding across the sky, Reynolds and Milburn knocked off the 58 required runs in just 45 minutes.

Rex Alston's report ended with two paragraphs of tribute to the man at the centre of this triumph:

> How much Northamptonshire will owe to their captain Andrew should they pull off the championship does not appear on the scorecard or in the record books.
>
> His thoughtful, almost meticulous placing of the field, his shrewd bowling changes, his classical wicket-keeping, and his quiet yet firm leadership, have turned Northamptonshire into a team who believe in themselves, and their ability, weather permitting, to win their remaining games.

Back at the County Ground, they entertained Kent in the next fixture. The pitch had bounce and turn, 'the sort of pitch that should guarantee a finish', and the press box was crowded with leading writers, sensing the destination of the championship. The *Times* correspondent, in particular, was full of praise for what he was witnessing:

> Even if it meant feeling a little less happy every time the aeroplane took off, it would be good, one of these days, to see Milburn on tour. He is a cricketer deserving of every encouragement. ... Crump rather personifies this Northamptonshire side, who are having such a heartening season. They are mostly more experienced and versatile than one realises. ... Prideaux looked an England player, his defence being sound and his strokeplay convincing. ... What Northamptonshire lack in colour, they make up for in a good general level of competence. They are also well-equipped with all-rounders, the backbone of many successful sides, and unlike some of their rivals have four spinners of various kinds.

Luck seemed to desert them. The toss was lost, and David Larter, whose pace and bounce had done so much to take them into contention for the title, broke down with a pulled hamstring after just one over. 'A specialist was seeing him today,' the *Chronicle* reported, 'and, if the diagnosis was that he had pulled the leg muscle, he was likely to be out of cricket for the rest of the season.'

The misfortune did not, however, prevent their winning the match. On a pitch that became 'a barren waste', Larter's absence was little felt as once more it was Haydn Sully, a willowy figure with long, spinning fingers, who did most to secure a fourth successive victory. 'It was a bad wicket,' John

Thicknesse thought in the *Daily Telegraph*, 'but before anyone points an accusing finger, let it be said that the victory it helped Northants to achieve was only their third in ten games at their county headquarters.'

Now the championship was nearing its denouement.

CHAMPIONSHIP TABLE – 13 AUGUST 1965

		Played	Won	Drawn	Lost	Points
1	Northamptonshire	25	12	10	3	128
2	Glamorgan	22	10	8	4	110
3	Worcestershire	23	8	11	4	94
4	Somerset	24	8	8	8	88
5	Middlesex	22	7	10	5	82

History was in the making, and the *Times* correspondent started to speculate about the scenes that might accompany the completion of Northamptonshire's final match:

> The last time a speech was made from the balcony of the pavilion at the County Ground was on Whit Monday 1939, when Northamptonshire gained their first victory in a championship match since the May of 1935. The next time may be a more notable occasion – after the match with Gloucestershire, ten days from now.

At Old Trafford another coin came down as a head but, with a crowd of five thousand cheering the inspirational bowling effort of their captain Statham, the Northamptonshire score was soon 30 for four, and the decision to bat looked questionable. The Old Trafford groundsman, according to the *Daily Telegraph*, had been under instruction all summer to prepare 'interesting wickets' and it was some achievement for Jim Watts to survive till lunch, alongside an unusually restrained Milburn. When they both fell after the break it was 85 for six, and once more the lower order all-rounders, this time Lightfoot and Crump, had the work to do.

"That was the best innings I saw Colin play," Brian Crump says. "He only got 30-something, but Brian Statham and Ken Higgs bowled magnificently and the wicket was very difficult for the first hour and a half. Albert got 64, I got 73, but it was Colin who set it up for us. If he'd gone early, there's no way we'd have got any runs."

Returning on the Monday, Northamptonshire's total of 231 suddenly seemed mountainous as again Haydn Sully found both turn and bounce. He took eleven wickets in the day, with Lancashire managing just 80 and 179, and victory came within the extra half hour. 'Sully achieved his success,' *The Times* considered, 'by the old-fashioned but still important principle of keeping a good length and bowling steadily to well-set fields, admirably controlled by Andrew, a wicket-keeper captain who is not afraid to make bowling changes or fielding experiments.'

Denys Rowbotham in the *Guardian* took up this theme with even greater enthusiasm:

> Andrew planned with refreshing imaginativeness. He varied off-spin with Crump's seam, off-spin with leg-spin and left-arm spin, and cleverly interchanged his two left-arm spinners, Scott and Steele. Never for long did he allow a batsman the same pace, spin, arc of flight, or angle of approach. Best of all, he placed deep fields in anticipation of drives and never surrendered in the process a close attacking position. His impeccable wicket-keeping (four catches and a stumping) completed an exemplary performance.

"KV had fantastic ideas," Brian Crump says. "One match he decided he was going to bowl everybody for one over. Six or seven bowlers."

"Cec Pepper was umpiring," David Steele adds. "When it was my turn, and I gave him my sweater, he turned to me, 'What's going on here? Have I got BO or something?'"

The day after Northamptonshire's triumph at Old Trafford, Glamorgan were left one wicket short of victory at Leyton, and the championship table now showed Keith's men 28 points in the clear. A celebratory dinner was already under discussion.

CHAMPIONSHIP TABLE – 17 AUGUST 1965

		Played	Won	Drawn	Lost	Points
1	Northamptonshire	26	13	10	3	138
2	Glamorgan	23	10	9	4	110
3	Worcestershire	24	9	11	4	104
4	Middlesex	23	8	10	5	92

Worcester was the next destination for the Northamptonshire coach. They were the reigning champions. Like Northants they had won six of their last seven matches. But their run of success was being built on a stuttering May and June, and their slim mathematical chance of retaining the title would be gone if they could not win during the next three days.

Once more the playing surface drew comment from the press box. 'The pitch has been prepared, or rather under-prepared, to ensure a finish,' *The Times* suggested, 'the ball coming through at uneven heights and moving for a while off the seam.'

Before play had started, Keith had told the *Evening Telegraph* that it looked 'rough and fast', adding 'I hope that no batsman is injured in any way.'

Three weeks earlier a *Daily Telegraph* survey on pitches had been conducted among journalists and county captains and, amid much general concern, two grounds were singled out for especial condemnation: Old Trafford and Worcester, 'both grounds where historically the turf has always made good wickets.' The majority of respondents thought that this was primarily the result of deliberate policy.

"What about Northampton?" Keith asks when I tell him about the article.

"No, it's just Old Trafford and Worcester," I reply. "In fact, somebody's mentioned Northampton as a good wicket."

"Really?"

The Worcester pitch was 'bone hard' and, when the coin again came down head up, Keith opted to put runs on the board first. It was not an easy decision, but then nor had been the selection of his team.

David Larter had recovered from his hamstring injury, having had an extensive run-out in the nets at Old Trafford under the supervision of Jack Jennings. He was their one fast bowler, the pitch was quick and uneven, and he had had a glorious summer, high in the national averages and now an established member of the England side. "I had to pick Larter. There was no question about that."

But whom should he have dropped? The choice seemed to lie between Albert Lightfoot, Malcolm Scott and Haydn Sully. Lightfoot was a useful seamer who had scored a vital 64 at Old Trafford, Scott was the number one slow bowler, a fixture in the side all summer, while the young Sully was euphoric with his first taste of real success, 27 wickets in the last three matches.

Three times in the previous four games they had found themselves six wickets down for not many – 85 at Old Trafford, 106 at Northampton, just 32 at Cardiff – and each time the later batsmen had rescued them. On that basis Albert Lightfoot was a reassuring presence. With Peter Watts and David Steele both capable spinners, and the pitch looking quick, the choice came down to Scott or Sully. Once Keith's thinking had reached this point, there was no doubting the outcome. Sully might be the man of the moment, but Scott was still the better bowler, dependable and experienced. "Haydn was a good bowler, especially on a turning wicket, but he wasn't as accurate as Malcolm. His short legs would be down at deep mid-wicket some days."

To gasps of surprise in the press box the tannoy announced that Larter was replacing Sully in the Northamptonshire side. He had taken eleven wickets at Old Trafford, and now he would be carrying the drinks.

"It was the right decision," Keith still insists.

Jack Flavell, the veteran Worcester fast bowler, was 'full of steam', taking four wickets on the lively pitch and leaving the visitors at lunch in a familiar crisis, 81 for six. The extra batsman Lightfoot had gone for just two runs, but in the afternoon Jim Watts and Brian Crump came once more to the rescue. They added 87 together, Scott contributed a patient 20 and even Keith stayed an hour for four. "The pitch was turning," he recalls, "but it was slow turn. Dougie Slade was bowling, and he wasn't difficult to play out."

The final total of 211 seemed no more than adequate when they came off but, after Larter's first over, it looked better than that. Running in from the river end, he extracted pace and lift from the wicket. "I took his first ball," Keith remembers, "and I thought, 'Christ!'" Later in the over Larter caught the edge of Don Kenyon's bat, and the ball flew to Brian Reynolds at slip. "It nearly took his hands off. Brian was a brave chap, with such strong hands, but the ball came through so fast, it almost knocked him over." It was nought for one wicket.

There was an hour to play, and the evening crowd knew that the match was entering a vital phase.

Larter was the key to Northamptonshire's success. He was not a 100 per cent man like Crump or Jim Watts.

"There were times when he didn't have the heart for it," Brian Crump reflects. "He went to Australia, and he spent all the time on the beach."

"If he wasn't bowling his quickest," Colin Milburn wrote, "Keith would rile him by moving nearer the stumps. Then he would really zip them down."

At Worcester, however, he was clearly in the mood. By the third over, the *Daily Telegraph* reported, 'Larter had worked up a pretty fast speed.'

Then came the moment that Keith has never forgotten, the moment when the luck of all those tossed coins went into reverse. Larter ran in again, and he pulled up lame.

His hamstring had gone. There was no question that he was not trying. But the grittier of his team-mates, knowing the importance of the game, were not immediately inclined to sympathy.

"I was so upset," Keith says, normally such a quiet and unobtrusive figure, "that I kicked the new ball almost into the pavilion."

Keith asked Larter if he could bowl off a shorter run and, according to the *Chronicle*, his reply was "I'll give it a go." 'He bowled off three walking paces and a two-stride shuffle and stood in the gully between overs.' With Worcestershire 51 for two at the close, Larter's condition meant that the home team, according to Henry Blofeld in the *Guardian*, held 'a slight advantage'.

It did not last on the second day. Though Larter bowled several ineffectual overs off his short run, it was Malcolm Scott who achieved most on 'a wretched pitch, on which the batsmen have not known what to expect next.' He took five wickets, Larter one, and the home team were 183 for eight when Jack Flavell came out to bat. Though a fast bowler himself, Flavell had no reputation for bravery against pace and Keith backed Larter, even at reduced speed, and Crump to remove him.

"I thought David ought to be able to frighten him, and Crumpy kept missing the edge. We had no luck at all, but then we'd had our share of luck in the previous matches – at Clacton, for example, and with all the tosses."

'Flavell generally takes more wickets in a season than he scores runs,' the *Daily Telegraph* reported, 'but now he gave a highly dramatic and rustic performance with the bat.'

The two points for first innings lead went to Worcestershire, and the visitors batted again, six runs behind. 'Northamptonshire must have bitterly regretted leaving Sully in the pavilion,' Henry Blofeld thought.

Malcolm Scott

Under grey skies the reigning champions took the field. It might have been a Thursday afternoon in mid-August, a working day, but there was a 'splendid' crowd, with 'all the old faces back who enjoyed such agonies of suspense a year ago.' The destination of the county championship pennant, flying above the pavilion, was at stake. There were no easy runs to be had, none of the artificial entertainment of the limited overs game. They were watching a contest between bat and ball, on an awkward wicket, and it mattered.

Carter bowled Milburn for ten, Flavell completed Prideaux's second pair in a month, Steele and Peter Watts fell to Gifford's spin, and the score was 39 for four.

In the modern game a coach would be waiting to analyse the batsmen's technical deficiencies, but only one of this Northamptonshire team ever had advice on hand.

"Mrs Prideaux was an England ladies cricketer," Malcolm Scott remembers. "In the bar she'd be telling Roger what he was doing wrong. 'Your bat's coming down from third man. By the time you're getting round, the ball's past you.'"

The evening light at Worcester was murky, the spinners were in tandem, and another recovery was required, this time from Brian Reynolds and Jim Watts.

They took the score to 94, but in the final minutes Reynolds was caught at slip and the *Daily Telegraph* headline declared that 'KEY TO TITLE MAY BE HELD BY P.J. WATTS'.

"I was having a drink later with Don Kenyon," Keith says. "We were looking out of the pavilion, and I saw Jack Flavell limping past. His shoe was cut away, and he'd got a blood-stained bandage on his foot. I said to Don, 'That doesn't look so good.' But he just sipped his pint. 'Don't you worry about that, KV,' he said. 'He'll be running down that end tomorrow morning.'"

Larter and Flavell. Two fast bowlers, two different personalities.

Jim Watts completed his fifty, but for once he found no support down the order. Lightfoot, 0. Crump, 2. Scott, 10. Larter, 0. Andrew, 5 not out. They managed only 130 – "We batted very badly in that second innings." – and Worcestershire had most of the day to score 125.

At Lord's, where 'all day long messages were coming in from Worcester, much as in Shakespeare's historical plays', the other title contenders, Middlesex and Glamorgan, were locked in a gripping struggle, but Northamptonshire could not increase the pressure on them. Kenyon and Ormrod were back in the pavilion with only 16 runs on the board, but that only brought Tom Graveney to the wicket. 'Once he had begun to play with the air of infallibility that makes batting look the easiest thing in the world, Worcestershire's victory was never in doubt.'

Scott and Steele bowled slow left-arm in tandem, and the *Daily Telegraph* once more returned to the team selection on Wednesday morning: 'How Andrew must have regretted the decision not to play off-spinner Sully.'

"The committee tried to tell me after the match that it was a turning wicket. Well, it was. It turned later, but it only turned slowly. And there's a world of difference between a ball turning quickly and one turning slowly. A lot of non-cricketers don't realise that.

"In any case, the game was all over by then. And they had Tom Graveney. Tom was the best player of spin bowling that's ever lived. No, we lost it with our batting – we needed runs from one of Milburn or Prideaux – and, of course, with David Larter breaking down."

He remains unrepentant. "The better team won."

He also defends the pitch, as he and Don Kenyon did in a joint statement after the match:

> In a game that has seen much good cricket with the result always in the balance, we should like to make it clear that, in our opinions, the wicket on which we have played was an ideal cricket wicket for the game. We should be more than happy if all our matches were played on pitches such as this.

Their winning sequence had been brought to an end, but it was not a disaster. Glamorgan's match at Lord's had finished as a draw so that only Worcestershire had gained ground on them – and their chances of the title, according to *The Times*, were 'more theoretical than practical'.

CHAMPIONSHIP TABLE – 20 AUGUST 1965

		Played	Won	Drawn	Lost	Points
1	Northamptonshire	27	13	10	4	138
2	Worcestershire	25	10	11	4	114
3	Glamorgan	24	10	10	4	110

Saturday the 21st of August was another ill-fated day for the dreams of Northampton's sporting folk. The football team lost 5-2 at Everton – 'Their performance was workmanlike and no more,' Eric Todd summed up in the *Guardian* – while the cricketers, back at the County Ground, were repeatedly frustrated by the rain. Each time they agreed to start, a further downpour seemed to arrive, and at close – with Keith winning his twelfth toss in thirteen – they had reached just 75 for one against Gloucestershire.

It was a bad day for Northampton, made worse when the football club complained that the cars of the cricket supporters had left a rutted track of tyre impressions in their penalty box. The cricket club countered that heavy vehicles had similarly churned up the cricket outfield.

Meanwhile, thirty miles to the north, Glamorgan had made better progress between the showers, reducing Leicestershire to 64 for six, while in Worcester a fuller day's play had seen Surrey skittled out for 94, the home side reaching 72 for two in reply. With the forecasters promising more unsettled weather, Northamptonshire needed some urgent cricket to redeem the lost time.

And who better than Colin Milburn to provide it?

In two hours on Monday morning he took his overnight score of 47 to 152. It was his first century of the summer, the highest score yet in his career, and his seven sixes included three that cleared the trees and landed in neighbouring gardens, one narrowly missing a greenhouse.

'I doubt if an innings has been played in the championship all the summer better attuned to his side's need of the moment,' Jim Swanton wrote with due formality in the *Daily Telegraph*. His colleagues were less stiff: 'It was an innings of muscular shoulders,' Christopher Ford wrote in the *Guardian*, 'one that could as easily have been described in the heavyweight language of the boxing ring.' In *The Times*, 'His innings would have brought the house down at Melbourne or Bridgetown. One day, I hope, he will play like this often enough to encourage the selectors to give him a run for England. First, maybe, he will have to count the calories more carefully than he does at present. At the moment he makes Cowdrey look positively emaciated.'

"I used to tell Colin," Keith says, "if he wanted to play for England, he'd have to score more hundreds and he'd have to lose weight. 'Why don't you drink halves instead of pints?' I said, and all he'd reply was, 'My father Jack drank pints, and I'm going to drink pints.'"

"Colin's father might have had a drink at the cricket club," Malcolm Scott explains, "but his mother was a strong Methodist, a tee-totaller."

"That day at Northampton," Keith says, "he came in at lunch, and I said to him, 'What are you having then, Colin?' He said, 'Two halves, please, guv.'"

Keith smiles with pleasure as his eyes drift momentarily away. "It was worth playing just to know and see Colin at his best."

Milburn's 152 had come out of a total of 227 for five and, after a lunch-time declaration, Gloucestershire collapsed to 33 for four before being rescued by a patient 86 by Arthur Milton. At Leicester and Worcester the other two contenders for the championship were establishing winning positions, but here at Northampton a result still seemed a long way off.

And so it was to be. Glamorgan and Worcestershire completed innings victories, but rain dogged the day at Northampton. When play finally got under way, Gloucestershire declared, Milburn hit two more sixes – 'as high as they were long' – and the visitors were set a target of 181 in 2½ hours.

At 53 Malcolm Scott's arm ball bowled Nicholls, but once more the exemplary technique of Arthur Milton thwarted further progress. It was not a pitch such as they had played on at Cardiff, Old Trafford and Worcester – 'It played well to the end,' was Jim Swanton's verdict – and the prospect of victory was remote.

"I said to Ken Turner," Keith recalls, "'I thought we'd get at least a bit of turn.' He said, 'We couldn't do that. Everybody's watching.'"

In the end the point became academic as more black clouds swept over the ground, the drizzle turned into a downpour, and the players ran for shelter.

'As skipper Keith Andrew faced television cameras in the murky light and damping rain, his men sang in the dressing-room showers – the season over and their work done.'

There were no triumphant speeches from the balcony, and attention quickly passed to the football ground where reserve team players and ground staff started to lay out the duckboards for the arrival of Arsenal the next evening.

According to the *Evening Telegraph*, 'The last damp overs were played out to a backing of frantic activity on the adjoining Cobblers' pitch as builders strove to finish off the ground improvements in time.'

The match would be a one-all draw, and Northampton would achieve the same score on the Saturday when Denis Law would lead out the Manchester United team.

CHAMPIONSHIP TABLE – 24 AUGUST 1965

		Played	Won	Drawn	Lost	Points
1	Northamptonshire	28	13	11	4	140
2	Worcestershire	26	11	11	4	124
3	Glamorgan	25	11	10	4	120

The *Times* correspondent summed up the position. 'WEEK OF IDLE SUSPENSE FOR THE COUNTY LEADERS', read its headline.

It is to Northamptonshire's advantage that they have their points already on the chart. It is to Glamorgan's advantage to be playing their last three matches in Wales. It is to Worcestershire's advantage that their opponents are two of the weaker counties, on present form.

The weather stayed unsettled, and Keith spent Friday on the Northampton Golf Club course with Laurie Johnson. "I'd got a radio, and I tuned into the lunch-time cricket scoreboard."

On an awkward wicket at Cardiff Derbyshire's Harold Rhodes had put in a spell of fiery fast bowling that had destroyed the Glamorgan batting so, even with victories in their final two matches, the Welshmen could only draw level with Northamptonshire.

At Bournemouth, meanwhile, rain had meant that the game was less advanced. 'Worcestershire, 363 for nine, declared. Hampshire, 217 for six,' the announcer read, and Keith turned to his golfing companion. "That means Hampshire have saved the follow on. A draw's the only result now." And a draw, as they both knew, would end Worcestershire's title ambitions.

'Northamptonshire can almost begin to celebrate,' the early edition of the *Worcester Evening News* proclaimed. 'They seem assured of at least sharing the title.'

Just imagine it. The little county of Northamptonshire, with a team of honest tryers, stood on the verge of the first championship in its history. Keith, who had passed up a place at Manchester University, had stayed in cricket to lead the county who had given him so many years of pleasure, and now he could repay his debt by delivering the trophy that had been for so many years beyond their wildest dreams.

"I want us to play our cricket like Yorkshire," he had told his young side at the start of 1962. "I want us to expect to win."

On the coach home from Dover at the end of 1961 they had been celebrating their sixteenth place as if they had won the championship. Now, four happy years on, they were to find out what the real thing was like – with the town council planning a civic reception.

Keith had adopted 'a scientific attitude to winning matches'. He was not a cavalier, not in the mould of Raman Subba Row, giving away advantage in the quest for brighter cricket. But neither was he a captain who sought to inhibit the natural ability of Milburn and Prideaux, the raw pace of Larter, the attacking leg-spin of Peter Watts.

"Keith had a way with everybody," Colin Milburn wrote. "He never gave me the rollocking that I might have expected from other captains. If he had interfered with me, tried to change me for the immediate benefit of the side, I might never have stayed in county cricket. It is something for which I shall be grateful to him for ever."

Norman Yardley, the former Yorkshire and England captain, selected Keith – 'that gentle, quiet character of cricket' – as one of his cricketers of the year:

As captain of Northants I think he has done a magnificent job. Not only this season when he has held them at the top for so long but for quite a few years. Few people ever thought that his quiet, gentle ways would fit him for leadership. But, when he was given his chance, these were exactly the qualities that blended the useful, rather than spectacular, players Northants had into such a fine fighting unit.

Keith is one of the best advertisements for England's band of top cricket professionals. The old cliché of "a player and a gentleman" fits him well.

Under Keith's calm and perceptive captaincy, Northamptonshire were set to win the county championship of 1965 – and that Friday lunch-time, when they heard the cricket scoreboard, still survives in all their memories.

Then, down at Dean Park, Bournemouth, Colin Ingleby-Mackenzie, cricket's greatest cavalier, captaining Hampshire in front of their home crowd for the last time, changed everything.

He declared the Hampshire innings closed.

He did what Trevor Bailey had done at Clacton, and Don Kenyon replied as Keith had done by closing his innings, too, after one ball. A dead game was back alive, with Hampshire needing 147 to win in 2 hours 40 minutes.

A feeling of foreboding started to well up around Northampton.

Worcestershire's Roy Booth recalls well the events at Bournemouth. "Ingleby misread the situation completely. Just before lunch it was wet, but the sun had come out, not brilliant but it was hot. We came in for lunch, and Ingleby had declared. We were in a tent, and it was getting hotter and hotter, and the pitch was literally steaming. The ball was coming right up. Roy Marshall was fairly wild about Ingleby declaring. He had a great whack at it, and it went up in the air. They were all out for 30-something. It was really nasty.'

The newspaper reports confirm the story. According to Henry Blofeld in the *Guardian,* 'The sun made a crust on the wet surface of a wicket which was hard underneath, and for the 65 minutes of the innings Flavell and Coldwell were downright dangerous.' For Rex Alston in the *Telegraph*, 'The sun shone in all its glory from two o'clock, turning a normal wicket into a batsman's nightmare.' Meanwhile, in *The Times*, 'It would have taken a batsman of the highest class and courage to have made many runs on the wicket as it was yesterday afternoon. Marshall, having taken a body blow from Flavell in the opening over, was out to an airy-fairy shot in Flavell's second over.'

Flavell took five for nine, Coldwell five for 22, as Hampshire were dismissed for 31.

'Ossie Wheatley and Keith Andrew will probably want me hanged from every flagpole in the country,' Ingleby-Mackenzie said, 'but I can assure them that we wanted to win as much as Worcester.'

After that it was somehow inevitable that Worcestershire would travel along to Hove and win, though even here the result was still in doubt on the last afternoon.

'I was standing on the sixth tee of the Northampton Golf Club,' Keith wrote in the *Evening Telegraph*, 'when I heard the news on our portable radio that Worcester were 54 for four, wanting 132 to win. For what seemed like the hundredth time in the last week, my heart leapt in hope.'

Brian Crump was back working as a printer, with the radio commentary of the Oval Test in the background. "John Arlott was commentating. They'd just had a terrific thunderstorm, and he said, 'I wonder if this rain will reach Hove before they finish there.' And of course it didn't. But within half an hour of Worcestershire winning, the ground at Hove was flooded. It was all very disappointing. We didn't even have a meet-up in the winter."

The civic reception was forgotten, though Malcolm Scott still possesses the gift from the Northamptonshire committee that marked their second place. An unremarkable ball-point pen, with the inscription, 'M.E. SCOTT 1965'.

Worcestershire had won ten of their last eleven matches. For the first time in the history of the competition, a county had become champions without ever having held first place during the season.

FINAL CHAMPIONSHIP TABLE

		Played	Won	Drawn	Lost	Points
1	Worcestershire	28	13	11	4	144
2	Northamptonshire	28	13	11	4	140
3	Glamorgan	28	12	10	6	132

The passing of thirty-seven years have made Brian philosophical. "We hadn't got to win it, had we?"

Keith accepted his defeat gracefully in a statement. 'We lost to a great team. I think we had a bit of luck during the season, but I also think the saints looked down kindly on Worcester as well. There is no doubt about it. They are a great cricketing side.'

Among those who felt the sadness of Northamptonshire's failure was Colin Cowdrey, who wrote in *The Cricketer*:

> I spent the last ten days of the season imagining myself in Keith Andrew's shoes. I compared each bulletin of scores. I shared the excitement and was saddened by the disappointments. I was discouraged by the rain against Gloucestershire, I was excited by the bad weather Worcestershire were having at Bournemouth. I sang the praises of Derbyshire's Harold Rhodes who put an end to Glamorgan's hopes at Cardiff. But then .... At the last I sat staring into oblivion. I came to, trying to acknowledge with all the chivalry I could muster, that Worcestershire were the better side and took what pleasure and pride I could out of Andrew's near miss.
>
> I toured Australia with Keith in 1954/55. He is a quiet, modest but extremely confident cricketer and, behind the stumps, a true artist. He is a thoughtful captain and deserves the respect he earns from his team. He has given himself to the task, almost a dedication, of leading Northamptonshire to their first title. He enjoys every moment of it.

"I was terribly disappointed," Keith admits, "and I wasn't very pleased with how the game at Bournemouth had gone, particularly as the championship was at stake. But, once the dust had settled, I knew that we had a lot to be pleased about. We'd done a great deal better than people had expected. We were a good team, we were used to winning and, with Mushtaq qualified to play, I thought we had a chance to win it the next year."

'He will be disappointed,' Colin Cowdrey concluded in *The Cricketer*, 'but not the least deterred. He will be back again next year with the same combination plus Mushtaq, and next August, unless I am very much mistaken, he will be in the top three again. It just depends upon "that little bit of luck".'

'We were third last year,' Keith told the *Chronicle*. 'We are second this, so who can tell what might happen next season?'

'What a year of pride for local sports followers!' proclaimed the paper. 'First Division football for the first time in Northampton, the Saints supreme again as the cream of English rugby, and the county cricketers within a rainstorm of becoming champions for the first time. Make no mistake about it. Northamptonshire will WIN the county championship next year – rain or shine.'

GLAMORGAN v NORTHAMPTONSHIRE

Cardiff. 4, 5 & 6 August 1965

NORTHAMPTONSHIRE WON BY 18 RUNS

NORTHAMPTONSHIRE

M. Norman	lbw b Wheatley	4	b Miller		3
B.L. Reynolds	c & b Wheatley	9	c Miller b Shepherd		14
C. Milburn	c E. Lewis b Shepherd	16	c Pressdee b Miller		0
R.M. Prideaux	c Walker b Shepherd	40	b Miller		2
D.S. Steele	lbw b E. Lewis	55	b Shepherd		0
P.J. Watts	b Shepherd	26	c Walker b Shepherd		51
B. Crump	c Hedges b Shepherd	5	lbw b Pressdee		31
P.D. Watts	c & b Wheatley	25	c Evans b Shepherd		10
A. Lightfoot	c E Lewis b Shepherd	0	c Walker b Shepherd		17
M.E. Scott	c Walker b Shepherd	1	c Walker b Pressdee		3
K.V. Andrew *+	not out	0	not out		0
Extras	lb 3, nb 2	5	b 4, lb 6		10
		186			**141**

1-8, 2-15, 3-29, 4-115, 5-139, 6-144, 7-164, 8-166, 9-186, 10-186
1-13, 2-13, 3-19, 4-19, 5-19, 6-32, 7-78, 8-131, 9-139, 10-141

Wheatley	16.3	9	16	3	9	6	23	0
Miller	15	5	45	0	12	4	21	3
Shepherd	34	20	32	6	31	15	51	5
Pressdee	10	3	20	0	11.3	5	14	2
E. Lewis	24	8	68	1	8	3	22	0

GLAMORGAN

B. Hedges	lbw b Steele	47	c P.D. Watts b Crump		12
A. Jones	st Andrew b Scott	21	c Andrew b P.J. Watts		13
P.M. Walker	c & b P.J. Watts	55	lbw b Lightfoot		10
H. Miller	c Steele b Crump	1	c Steele b Lightfoot		1
A.R. Lewis	c Reynolds b P.J. Watts	20	c Milburn b Lightfoot		15
J. Pressdee	c Steele b P.J. Watts	0	c Steele b Crump		2
A. Rees	c P.D. Watts b Crump	2	lbw b Crump		37
E. Lewis	c Steele b P.J. Watts	0	run out		2
D.L. Evans +	lbw b Crump	3	lbw b Crump		9
D.J. Shepherd	not out	22	c Prideaux b Scott		9
O.S. Wheatley *	b Crump	10	not out		0
Extras	lb 6, nb 2	8	b 4, lb 6		10
		189			**120**

1-27, 2-83, 3-84, 4-129, 5-133, 6-138, 7-143, 8-150, 9-158, 10-189
1-22, 2-26, 3-36, 4-54, 5-57, 6-77, 7-79, 8-86, 9-115, 10-120

Crump	41.2	15	77	4	35.1	11	65	4
P.J. Watts	28	9	43	4	15	4	17	1
Scott	13	5	43	1	1	0	4	1
Steele	10	4	18	1				
Lightfoot					20	8	24	3

Umpires: John Langridge and P.A. Gibb

CHAPTER 12

A WONDERFUL ADVENTURE

There was no glorious final chapter in the story of Keith Andrew's career at Northampton. He captained one last summer, 1966, but the town's great sporting success was on the wane. During the winter the footballers fought valiantly but in vain, relegated only on the final Saturday of the season when they lost at Blackpool.

"They had a good team, especially defensively," Malcolm Scott says, "but the locals didn't really twig. 'No, me ducko, they shouldn't be in this division.' They were used to being in the old third division, and they were quite happy with that."

On that same final Saturday, with the duckboards cleared away and cars once more driving onto the football field, the cricketers were knocked out of the Gillette Cup by Glamorgan. Managing a total of only 67, they had lost long before the final whistle had blown on the footballers' efforts at Blackpool.

The first championship match at the County Ground brought an even more painful defeat. Entertaining Gloucestershire, the team who had thwarted their title bid the previous August, they seemed on the verge of a thrilling victory. Gloucestershire, with nine wickets down, wanted three to win off two balls when their number eleven Barrie Meyer attempted an ambitious single. The newly qualified Mushtaq threw the ball at the bowler's end stumps, it missed by a fraction, and the resulting overthrows brought the batsmen victory. It was not to be Northamptonshire's summer.

Larter broke down in May and, when Scott joined him on the injury list in early July, the team were, in the words of *Wisden*, 'under-equipped to exploit some pitches where their own batsmen struggled.' Despite a thrilling win over the West Indies and a double over the champions Yorkshire, whose cricket Keith had sought to emulate, they could finish only fifth in the final table. 'A creditable performance,' *Wisden* said, 'yet a considerable disappointment.'

Despite all this, county spirits were raised by the Test selection, at long last, of Colin Milburn. Still playing his natural game, as Keith had insisted, he hit five centuries in the first seven weeks: the third, a career-best 171 at Leicester in front of Alec Bedser the chairman of selectors, the fourth at Trent Bridge the fastest of the summer, the fifth at Lord's in only his second Test. He was the first batsman in England to complete 1,000 runs, pipping his fellow Northants opener Roger Prideaux.

At Lord's a group of England supporters, imitating the West Indians who had earlier hoisted in the air their own centurion David Holford, attempted to do the same to Milburn – but, as he was quick to point out, 'There was a subtle difference, adding up to about 7½ stone.'

That was on the Tuesday and, four days later, England's newest star was back at Lord's with his county team-mates, enjoying their captain's last appearance at the home of cricket.

Keith had been bowled for nought there in 1951, for the Combined Services, and he had walked back through the Long Room, past the member with the eye-glass, to run the bath where Bradman had lain.

He had hit the winning runs there in 1956, when he and Bob Clarke, of all people, had put on 49 for the ninth wicket. "It was one of my greatest days with the bat. I remember Don Bennett taking the new ball, and I hit his very first delivery with it past mid-on and ran two to win the game. We had Mr Crosse there, one of our greatest fans. He was the Crosse of Crosse and Blackwell Soup, and he was up with us on the balcony. He used to get so excited, leaning over, that we had to make it one of twelfth man's duties to keep an eye on him."

In 1962 Keith had represented the Players in the last match against the Gentlemen, one of the greatest honours of his career.

Now he was determined to mark his final appearance in style.

"I said, 'I've never hit a six at Lord's. I'll bet anybody I'll hit one today.' Everybody took me up on it. David Steele said, 'I'll bet you five Woodbines.' He was notoriously careful with his money. I'd better not say what Jack Jennings promised to do. And Milburn said, 'I'll take the lot of you to the Ace of Clubs night club, and I'll pay.'

"We were playing at the top end of the square and, when I went out, Ron Hooker was bowling. He dropped one short, and I had a swing at it, got a top edge and it flew away towards Father Time."

"It just popped over the fence," Brian Crump remembers. "I said to him afterwards, 'I bet that six gets further and further every year, Keith. I bet one day it'll be halfway up the Clock Tower."

But no, not with Keith. "It just crept over the boundary," he says. "But I do remind Ron Hooker every year when we meet at the Cricketers' Golf match. He says it's the only reason I invite him to play."

And were the bets all paid up?

"We had the greatest night out of all time. Colin knew everybody at the club. I've never seen so many waiters."

"Keith took us down to Soho in his car," Brian says. "When we came out, he'd forgotten where he'd parked it. He had to go back in the morning to look for it."

"Did I?" Keith says absently, and his mind returns to Colin Milburn.

"They dropped him for the final Test. Can you imagine it? He'd hit a hundred at Lord's, he'd hooked Wes Hall in front of square, and two matches later he'd been dropped."

'We wanted a fielding side,' Alec Bedser said. 'Milburn is unlucky but, if people want to play for England, they have to think about these things.'

"But he was a brilliant fielder close to the wicket," Keith fumes. "Why did they have him running around in the outfield?"

With more runs in the first four Tests than any other English batsman, Milburn went down to Clacton and he fired his riposte.

"When play started, I liked to sit down with a cup of tea and a sandwich," Keith says. "And I'll never forget that day. They hadn't been playing an hour, and there was nobody on the off side in any acknowledged position. There was no mid-off, no cover point, no gully. Barry Knight was bowling, and he had four men on the boundary. They were giving Colin the single, and it was still in the first hour. I was spell-bound. I don't think I'd even touched my sandwich."

"The ball came onto the bat at Clacton," Essex's captain Gordon Barker explains, "and the outfield was very fast. If I'd left a normal field, he'd probably have holed out. But the way he was going, I thought he might have 200 by lunch."

They restricted him to 100 but by tea he had 203. He took 18 off one Acfield over, including a six over the sightscreen, but, with the field back, "I had to run a hell of a lot of singles," he said.

The temperature was near eighty, and in the dressing room he stood red-faced. "It was like he'd got a sweat suit on," Keith recalls, "and there was a great puddle on the floor where he was standing."

He had lost two pounds in weight.

"He had a lovely personality, and he was intelligent, too, a good teacher. There was a lot more to him than people knew. But people took advantage of his nature. Ingleby-Mackenzie and Barry Knight wanted to put him on as a night club turn, and I wrote to them, not a very nice letter. 'You get on with what you're good at, and let Colin get on with what he's good at.'"

The memories of Milburn's innings – at Buxton and Clacton, at Lord's and Adelaide – are still fresh to this day, but he played in only five of England's next nineteen Tests. Then, in the winter of 1968/69, he seemed finally to have triumphed over all the prejudices. Playing for Western Australia under the captaincy of Tony Lock, he was the leading run-maker in the Sheffield Shield, his 'rip-roaring' displays including an innings of 243 at Brisbane, 181 of which came in two hours between lunch and tea. Then, summoned by England to Karachi, he went straight into the final Test and hit a quick-fire 139.

He was the star that English cricket desperately needed, more than the cautious Geoffrey Boycott. 'Boycott was like a gardener tending an allotment,' the *Observer* drama critic Kenneth Tynan wrote of a partnership between the two of them, 'whereas Milburn was opening up the West.'

But tragedy struck. In May he lost an eye in a motoring accident and, though attempted a comeback and tried his hand at broadcasting, nothing really worked out for him again. In a pub car park he died of a heart attack at the age of 48.

"When he was at the height of his fame," Malcolm Scott says, "he had a lot of hangers-on. But none of them were at his funeral."

"It was so sad," Keith says. "I know it sounds sentimental, but I just wish he'd met the girl of his dreams. He'd have made a super father."

*

Keith's last match was at Edgbaston, where he was presented with a silver cigarette box by Roger Prideaux, on behalf of all the team, and he bowled Haydn Sully for fifty overs, so that the off-spinner could complete his 100 wickets for the season. "He was very deserving of 100 wickets, and I somehow knew that he wouldn't do it another year."

Thirteen years earlier his predecessor Freddie Brown, also making his last appearance for Northamptonshire, had been told that Bob Clarke had 97 wickets, and his response was less considerate. "I couldn't care bloody less," he is said to have replied, and so it is that Sully, not Clarke, appears in the list of those who have taken 100 wickets in a summer.

Keith was nearly 37 years old, his children were ten and eight, and he was now employed by an engineering firm in Market Harborough, working on special projects.

"The cricket had been a wonderful adventure, but I had to get on with the rest of my life."

*

The football club fell through the divisions faster than it had climbed them, back at Aldershot and Workington by the winter of 1969/70. By then Milburn had lost an eye, Larter, Scott and Sully had all gone, and the county was back in the lower reaches of the championship table.

While working with Keith on this book, I published John Barclay's account of Sussex's brave attempt to win the title in 1981. Like Northamptonshire they had never previously won, and the margin of their failure, two points, was even narrower than that of Keith's team.

'With the passing of time the disappointment of not winning has grown,' John wrote. 'I can never quite put it to the back of my mind.'

I sit and read the words to Keith, and he smiles a painful smile. "I know exactly how he feels."

Under Mushtaq's captaincy they would rise again to second place in 1976, even winning the Gillette Cup, but by then only David Steele would survive of Keith's 1965 team.

Steele had acquired a reputation as a batsman hard to shift from the crease, both because of his fine defensive technique and because he did not subscribe, as most of Keith's generation did, to the philosophy of walking when you knew you were out.

"His dad didn't play cricket like mine did," his cousin Brian Crump says. "I was brought up always to walk. I still think that's how the game should be played."

But times were changing.

"I was batting with Steely at Old Trafford once," Keith recalls. "He edged this ball from Tommy Greenhough to 'Chimp' Clayton, the keeper, and I turned round and put my bat down. Then, when I turned back, he was still there, halfway up the pitch and prodding away at it. Chimp was having apoplexy. 'Bloody hell, Steely,' I said. 'What's going on? You knocked the cover off that.' 'I didn't, you know,' he said. 'I only got a little nick.'"

With the Australians touring in 1975, spearheaded by the seemingly unstoppable attack of Lillee and Thomson, the new England captain – South African Tony Greig – turned to the hard-to-shift Steele, and by December the 33-year-old 'Mister Magoo' had become the BBC Sports Personality of the Year.

"He was a real grafter," Keith says. "He fought every inch of the way."

Milburn and Steele both made the transition from county to country with ease, but it was not an opportunity offered to many in Keith's team.

"There are a lot of players who would have performed better at a higher level," Brian Crump reckons. "I thought Albert Lightfoot would have done. But then you've got to be there at the right time."

"If I'd been a selector," Keith says, "I'd have had Brian in the England team. He wouldn't have let anybody down."

"KV always says that, if I'd been four inches taller, I'd have played regularly."

But what about Stan, Brian's father, who played his cricket in the leagues?

"He was certainly a better cricketer than me, and a better cricketer than David. But he was a pit engineer, and he couldn't afford to be a county cricketer."

Brian's last summer with the county was 1972, when he was 34. The runs were still coming, a century at Chesterfield in one of his last games, but the wickets had largely dried up.

"I remember bowling at the County Ground to Closey, when he was playing for Somerset. I came running in, and all of a sudden he stopped me. And there was this little lad sitting in front of the sightscreen. And of course it was Neil, my lad. So then there was Lynn creeping across and grabbing him. And Closey said, 'Is that thy lad then? … Now I know how tha gets wickets.'"

Thirty years on Brian is still playing second eleven league cricket in the Potteries – 64 years old and not yet defeated by the aches and pains.

On the last Saturday of the summer of 2002, he went to the wicket with his team 26 for six, with two hours 20 minutes left. His opponents were competing for the championship with his son Neil's club, and he was under strict instructions not to let them win.

"I batted all the overs for 30 not out. We finished up on 98 for eight. And for the last 15 overs I was in with my daughter Julie. I'd talked her into playing, she used to play for the England Ladies' Team, and she stayed with me to the end – for one not out.

"I've told Lynn that I've called it a day," he says. Then he looks with a conspiratorial smile. "But I don't know. I've still got the bug for it. I still love playing."

"How lovely," Keith says. "Brian's a cricketer through and through, and that's what English cricket needs."

Keith turned to golf rather than play to such an age, but he too has cricket in the family. In the 1980s his son Neale, living in Nottingham, rang to say that he was playing for a newly-formed side and could Keith come up one Sunday to give them some coaching.

"They were called The Howdy Boys. They'd been started by a pop group of that name. A real range of characters, from all walks of life. There were Oxbridge graduates, pop musicians, all different races and levels of ability. A great bunch of lads. They prepared this lovely afternoon tea for me, and they made me their President."

Neale is a sculptor, a quiet craftsman who has steadily built up a national reputation that blossomed when two major works came into public view in the summer of 2002. On the banks of the Thames at Marlow, the Queen unveiled his larger-than-life bronze figure of Sir Steven Redgrave. Then in Kirkby in Ashfield the Australian daughter of Harold Larwood unveiled the magnificent image of her father, again in larger-than-life bronze, his glory frozen for all time as he reaches up with his leading arm and prepares to send down another lightning-fast delivery.

But Neale is not one to draw attention to his own achievements – as his father discovered when, sitting one day in his office at Lord's, he received in the post the Nottinghamshire Cricket Association annual for 1994. It was customary for all the county associations to send him their handbooks so he was only browsing its contents with a cursory flick. Then, when he reached page 72, he had the shock of his life.

'Nottinghamshire and District Sunday Cricket League. Neale Andrew (Howdy Boys) won the batting award with an average of 196.50 including not out scores of 114, 107 and 86.'

Neale, Keith, Clare, Joyce

"He'd never mentioned it to me. I had no idea that he was that good."

What was it John Arlott said about Keith?

'Few cricketers of his considerable gifts can have been quite so modest. Had he been more self-assertive, he must have played far more often for England.'

And Clare?

"She follows after her mother. Good-looking, out-going. She qualified as a schoolteacher, but she very soon became involved in childcare. She started out with Dr Barnardo's; now she's in Sussex, a senior officer with OFSTED, inspecting nurseries and the like."

There are three grandchildren. Neale has a young boy Seth while Clare has Sarah and Christopher – and Christopher is already taking wickets a-plenty in his local cricket.

As with Brian Crump, the game is passing down the generations.

*

For Keith there was one last opportunity to redeem his failure to win the championship in 1965.

When Ken Turner finally resigned as Secretary in 1984, Keith was Director of Coaching at the N.C.A. but he applied to Northampton to be Ken Turner's successor. The interviewing committee was chaired by Peter Arnold, his opening partner in his first Club and Ground game, when he had hitched a lift in an ice-cream van. He was duly appointed.

'COUNTY ROLE WON'T STUMP KEITH,' was the *Chronicle* headline, and he was full of excitement in the interview:

> I had to do a bit of heart-searching before I went for the job. My present job is very enjoyable and satisfying. But I feel as though my whole life has been training for the County Ground job. I will be with people I know and respect, and I am immensely proud to be following someone like Ken Turner. At the moment I think I'm walking on air.

With Geoff Cook, Wayne Larkins, Rob Bailey and Allan Lamb, he knew that the batting was good enough, but his master plan involved returning to the sort of cricket he had enjoyed in his own playing days. "I knew the Northampton wicket, and I wanted to employ two of the very best spinners. Derek Underwood was a possibility as he was coming near the end of his career at Kent, and I was optimistic that I could sign a high quality overseas star."

It was not to be. Before long, the newspapers were running a different headline – NORTHANTS UPSET BY ANDREW, in the *Daily Telegraph* – as they reported his shock withdrawal. The county was once more advertising the vacancy.

"If there's one thing in my cricket life that I regret, that was it. I let so many people down, especially Peter Arnold. I'll always appreciate the way he behaved towards me during the controversy that followed."

But what happened to make him change his mind?

"I'll never be able to put it into words. ... I felt I was being given the chance to put the record straight for 1965. ... But the NCA was such a big thing ... I felt dreadfully annoyed with myself for taking the job ... I didn't even get to the point of finding out the salary. ... I lay awake at night ... I feel I was careless in the extreme."

It is almost as if we are back on *Guess My Story*, and I am sitting on the panel, trying to make sense of his answers. What was it he said? "Joyce and Frank were so articulate. I'd gone. They'd never have found out from me. We'd have been there all evening."

I do not press too hard. The pain is still there.

"Then Northamptonshire appointed Steve Coverdale, and he was absolutely right for the job."

"It worked out well in the end," Peter Arnold reckons. "The club didn't suffer too much."

Nearly twenty years have passed. Steve Coverdale is still Chief Executive, and he has overseen many improvements, not least the indoor cricket school that now stands at the old football club end.

British Timken is no longer the club's great benefactor, but Lynn Wilson, whose family firm built the house in Weston Favell where Keith and Joyce lived, has taken their place. "He keeps a low profile," Keith says, "but he's contributed as much to Northamptonshire over the years as anybody."

Despite its small population the county still holds its own, though the entry in the *Playfair Cricket Annual* tells the same story that it has told for more than a quarter of a century.

Northamptonshire
County Champions: 0
Best – 2nd 1912, 1957, 1965, 1976

CHAPTER 13

BACK TO THE GRASS ROOTS

1975-1994

There were no grass roots in Keith's childhood. He played his cricket in the ginnels, in the streets and in the playground. There was no sports field at any school he attended and, even when he was sent to the Oldham Schoolboys trial, the match was on a shale surface.

"It's a myth that cricket was played in state schools from way back," he says. "It was played in grammar schools, but they were only for a small part of the population."

With most Oldham children leaving school at fourteen, it fell to men like Eric Denison, Werneth's professional, to promote interest in cricket, and Keith's first experience of coaching occurred on summer evenings at the club.

"What are we going to do about cricket in the state schools?" Gubby Allen asked in the 1948 MCC committee, and from that plaintive cry stemmed the establishment of Lilleshall and the first group coaching schemes. But through the '50s and '60s, cricket struggled for an income, and the initiatives were limited and poorly funded.

Then in the mid-'60s the incoming Labour Government, with Denis Howell as Britain's first dedicated Minister of Sport, created the Sports Council to inject central revenue into more than fifty sports. MCC, as a private members' club, could not receive this funding so cricket created new structures, among them a National Cricket Association – N.C.A. – whose role was to look after all aspects of youth and recreational cricket.

By this time Keith's playing days were over. He had moved on from engineering, branching out as the Managing Director of a shop-fitting company. With his two children, Clare and Neale, growing up, his life was full without cricket.

Then came disaster. An ambitious project saw him badly let down, and he found himself teaching mathematics and P.E. at Sponne School in Towcester. "I was in a bit of a wilderness," he says, but even at this lowest point in his life he found a few moments that still bring a smile to his face.

"I enjoyed the teaching. They gave me some of the lower classes, and there was this lad, not a bad lad but he hadn't a brain in his head. I tried to encourage him by showing him how to throw the javelin, and he broke the school record with his coat on. Then I took in one of my golf clubs, and he loved it. He didn't always make contact, but his first two real shots finished up somewhere down the Brackley Road."

It was all a far cry from the commercial projects he had been directing a year earlier.

"I just felt sorry for him, and I wanted to give him a bit of a lift."

Keith's own lift came early in the summer of 1975 when the school secretary passed him a telephone message. It was from Freddie Brown.

Twenty-two years had passed since that July day, when 18,000 Northampton folk had crowded into the County Ground to watch their team take on the all-conquering Australians. They cheered Frank Tyson's dramatic first over, and they applauded again when their new wicket-keeper stumped first Harvey, then Craig, the latter off a leg-break bowled by Brown. For Keith it was a golden day and, though he never again played for the county under Freddie Brown's leadership, it established something between the two of them that led first to his selection for the tour of Australia the following year and now to this telephone call.

"We definitely had a bond. I got to know him in later life, and I could sense that he had this feeling for me – like an older brother, maybe, or a father."

Keith was at a low ebb in his life and, when he returned the older man's call at the end of the school day, he found himself picked up.

"Keith," came the familiar voice, brisk but warm. "I want you to do a job."

Freddie Brown had become Chairman of the NCA and, though Keith had not been active in cricket for nine years, he wanted him to take over as their coach for the North of England.

"He didn't offer the job to me. He told me I was going to take it."

It was a big decision. He still had hopes of reviving his engineering career, and he was not sure that he wanted to uproot the family after so many happy years in the Midlands. But Joyce brought his hesitation to an end.

"Go back to the cricket," she told him. "That's where you're happiest."

He attended an interview at Lord's and, by September, they had moved to St Anne's on the Fylde Coast. He set up office at Old Trafford and began to plan the county's first under-16 tournament, to be staged the following summer.

"I put an advert in all the Lancashire papers, calling a meeting for a Saturday afternoon, and the place was packed. I got a grant from the Greater Manchester Corporation. And I went to see Cedric Rhoades, the Lancashire chairman. I said to him, 'I want to borrow Old Trafford for a week in August.' He looked at me. 'What on earth are you on about now?' But I got Tommy Burrows on my side. He'd been the previous chairman, and he was very involved in all the coaching and schools cricket. And we got it through."

The county was divided into eight regions. Coaching sessions were held, with trials to select the squads. Then, with Lancashire travelling up to Blackpool to play Warwickshire, the ground was prepared for the arrival of more than one hundred boys. It was the hottest summer of the century, a young Viv Richards was hitting 291 against England at The Oval, and the tournament lasted five happy days.

The Eastern region were the winners, with their all-rounder Brian Heywood collecting the Cricketer of the Week award, but Keith's eye was caught by a much less likely figure, a little boy of twelve playing for the West.

"They were from Warrington and North Cheshire, the weakest team there. The chap running them was a boozer, and they were a bit of a shambles. They didn't win a match. But they had this lad. His mum and dad came to watch him every day. He was the youngest player in the whole tournament and his pads were far too big, but he had something special. He had timing."

There are cricketers in Keith's career whom he remembers with a special gleam – the graceful Frank Worrell, with the occasional sadness in his eyes, the swashbuckling Colin Milburn, with his carefree smile, the magically artistic Mushtaq – and Neil Fairbrother, the boy from Warrington, is another.

"I saw him years later, and I said to him, 'You scored 21, didn't you?' And quick as a flash he corrected me. '24,' he said.

"I had him in the England Under-19 team, and I said to him, 'You can play for England before you're 21 if you get your act together.' He was a sucker for the long hop, he'd hit it straight up in the air to mid-wicket, but I feel he did settle. After all, he had an average over 40. He was a very special player. But the England selectors were dreadful. They said he was a one-day cricketer. Have you ever heard such nonsense?"

Whether Neil Fairbrother could have been a great Test batsman if he had not been discarded so quickly, we will never know. But certainly the Old Trafford tournament – run on a budget of £1,800 – offered youngsters like him opportunity, coaching and encouragement beyond anything Keith had known at the same age, and it continued for several years.

Some time later Keith went up to the University of Lancaster, where the English Schools Cricket Association was putting on a course for a group of 15-year-old boys.

"I wanted to take a film of fielding, and they had about twelve boys there. They were all good, but one of them was really outstanding. I've never seen anything like it: the pick-up and throw on the turn, it was astonishing. At the end of the session somebody said to me, 'You know who he is?' 'I've no idea,' I said. 'It's Micky Stewart's son, Alec.'"

Then, at a coaching session in Durham, Keith arrived with a video camera and monitor, attracting some sceptical comments. "What the hell are you doing, KV?" These were years when new ideas were being tried, with no thought of what might one day become of them.

For four years Keith kept busy in the North. Then the post of National Director of Coaching was created, to be based at Lord's, and he found himself being interviewed by the NCA's new chairman, Don Robson, a very different man from his predecessor. "Freddie Brown wasn't involved so much in the decisions. He was really a figurehead. He loved life, he had a huge feeling for cricket, and he recognised that, with his personality, he had something to give to the recreational game."

By contrast, Don Robson had been a professional footballer and was now a leading Labour Party man in the North-East. He was not at all someone that Brown and Gubby Allen expected to find in a position of power at Lord's.

"He came down into the cloisters of Lord's, and he was a bit over the top at first. It took Gubby Allen a while to respect him. But he was a real go-getter, a clever man, and with his background he understood what a parlous state the recreational game was in. In my view he's been the biggest single influence on cricket in this country in the last quarter of a century."

Don himself laughs at the suggestion that his Labour Party roots were a handicap in any way. "There are more politics in Lord's," he says, "than there are in Westminster, although they wouldn't think that."

The interview, as Don remembers it, did not bring out the best of Keith.

"He was very nervous. He talked a lot without getting to the crunch, but he was obviously committed."

So began fifteen years at Lord's, the last eight spent as the NCA's Chief Executive. They were not years that brought him into the limelight, but during them most of the structure that now underpins the England and Wales Cricket Board was developed, with the counties assuming a greater responsibility for the club cricket played within their borders.

"That was a major step forward," Don Robson believes. "The first-class game and the recreational game are working together with the same aims and objectives. Previously, the first-class game was organised to protect county cricket and the England team."

The NCA provided a formal umbrella for a multitude of organisations servicing the minor counties, schools (both private and state), several thousand clubs, women's cricket, umpires, coaches, groundsmen, even the Combined Services and the Lord's Taverners. It co-ordinated funding applications, it developed a popular insurance policy for clubs, it produced training films, and it ran festivals and tours for young cricketers.

For both Keith and Don Robson, however, their greatest achievement was the establishment of a national coaching scheme, developed from the Lilleshall awards and aimed

Don Robson

at enabling school teachers and club members throughout the country to introduce boys and girls in groups to cricketing activities.

"Most teachers outside the public schools knew nothing about cricket," Keith says. "So our job was to go out to the schools, to find the teachers who had a sporting inclination and to show them how to coach cricket.

"At first many of the professional cricketers looked down on our courses, they talked about 'our bits of paper', they said coaching was all about being in the nets. But that comes later. You've got to get people organised and interested first."

A comprehensive structure was established. The six national coaches worked with district coaches, they in turn trained club coaches, and the clubs co-operated with schools in initiatives that developed the skills of cricket.

"The traditional choices in England," Don says, "were football in winter and cricket in summer. But young people today have so much more choice – and they also follow music and use computers. So cricket has to shape itself around that. For many years sport was neglected in teacher training so, rather than rely on that, we built up our own system of qualified people. And it was Keith who was the architect of it all."

The nervous man, who 'talked a lot without getting to the crunch', turned out to be a much clearer thinker than Don Robson anticipated.

"He brought a real professionalism to the job. He often appeared as a bit of a joke, he had this light-hearted approach and he could talk sometimes without quite getting to the point, but his reports were superb. He had a very clear mind, and his analysis was usually spot on. NCA provided the first forum for the recreational game, and it started out as a bit of a whinge. But Keith turned it into an analytical forum, and from that it became an achievement forum.

"I was Chairman of the NCA for twenty years, and we had all sorts there. There were poseurs, people who weren't workers, people who were full of their own importance, and Keith was none of those. He was the best."

For Keith the coaching was primarily a way to reach out to youngsters such as he had been. "I played as a boy in the streets and in the park. Now, if they do anything, they'll play football. That's why we need organised schemes."

The technical skills fascinate him – the five bowling positions, the weight distribution for the keeper, he can even get agitated by the inappropriateness of telling a young batsman to 'get your foot to the ball' – but he has always been one to value the natural talent of the individual. "The whole point of the skill analysis we introduced was to improve the young cricketer's natural game, not to force them to play in a particular way."

He did not quell the genius of Colin Milburn, he admired the ungainly Les Jackson, and he played a crucial part in rescuing the career of the under-achieving young Northants opener, Wayne Larkins.

"It was some years after I'd retired. Ken Turner asked me to captain the second eleven at the end of the season. They were going to get rid of Larkins, and they wanted my opinion. He was a bit of a wild boy, but basically he was shy, he'd got no confidence.

"I gave him a bowl. He didn't have the temperament to be an all-rounder, but it kept him in the game. And, when he batted, he got 70-odd on a pig of a wicket."

Within a few years Larkins was batting for England, and Keith was watching the television anxiously with his fingers crossed. He could spot the technical fault, but that was not the intervention he wanted to make.

"When he was nervous, he started moving across his stumps before the ball was bowled. He was playing against the West Indies, Garner was bowling, and of course he was lbw in an over or two. It was all his anxiety. Get rid of that, and he wasn't half a player."

For Keith, for all his technical understanding, the human aspect is the most vital. That was what he looked for when he encouraged people to take up coaching – as he did with the West Indian Test cricketer Reg Scarlett, who went on to produce a string of county cricketers from his cricket school in the London Borough of Haringey.

"He came on one of our courses, and I got him to help me run an event at Loftus Road. He was so good that I talked him into coaching. A big fellah, with a great sense of fun, he was a real star. His school was a great example of what can be done. He could have been the West Indies coach."

Keith becomes as animated talking about good coaching as he does when he remembers the great players. His team of six: Les Lenham 'the best batting coach I've ever seen', Bob Cottam and Bob Carter the bowling specialists, Graham Saville 'a great manager of young men', David Wilson the educationalist hard at work in Scotland and the North's Doug Ferguson, 'the best all-round coach of young people there's ever been.' Behind them was Terry Bates, a development officer who 'made a huge contribution'.

An Advanced Coaching Award Course, on the occasion of a presentation to Gubby Allen to mark 30 years of involvement in coaching schemes
(front row, left to right) Graham Saville, David Wilson, Bob Carter, Jim Lane, Gubby Allen, Keith, Les Lenham, Doug Ferguson

They were not household names, and their efforts received little recognition. "I took them all for a meeting with Peter May when he was chairman of selectors. He had no idea of the work they were doing." But they trained not only the young players and their teachers but also the coaches employed by the first-class game.

"There were only two chaps who came on the advanced course over all the years who achieved distinctions: David Lloyd and Micky Stewart. They were both natural coaches at the highest level. World class."

And their examination?

"Les Lenham had to give David Lloyd a viva at the end, and he said to him, 'Now then, David, you're playing at Northampton on a turning, lifting wicket, the great George Tribe is bowling and you're next in. What would you do?' And David Lloyd said, 'I'd pad up.'"

Beyond them there was Tom Cartwright in Wales, Don Wilson at Lord's and the younger John Barclay bringing children from city streets to learn cricket in the grandeur of the Arundel Castle grounds.

"Surely the best coaches should be teaching the most needy age groups, not wandering around South Africa on a tour. The captain is the main man on tour. He needs to have overall command and respect. He shouldn't have less authority than the coach."

His mind goes back to his winter in Australia.

"Geoffrey Howard was one of the great managers. Being in his presence was a wonderful experience because of his manner, his dedication to his job. George Duckworth was scorer, a great player from the past, and he had something to give. And Len as captain, a hard man, he knew how to play the game. The thought of David Lloyd, or Duncan Fletcher, as coach, telling Len Hutton what to do seems rather bizarre."

By January 1979 Keith was back in Australia, assistant to Freddie Brown on a six-week under-19 tour. Their party included Jonathan Agnew, Norman Cowans and Kim Barnett while the Australians fielded a young David Boon.

"Being in Australia with Freddie Brown was the experience of a lifetime. He'd captained England there in 1950/51 and, wherever we went, people welcomed him. They all remembered the fighting spirit of his team. I'd no idea how popular he was."

England had been second best to Australia in every encounter since the war, but the 40-year-old Brown did not give up. When his team won the final Test at Sydney, the Australian crowd – recognising the unquenchable spirit of the former prisoner-of-war – swarmed in front of the pavilion, crying, 'We want Brown.'

Jack Fingleton called him 'the most popular English captain I can remember'. Ray Robinson wrote that 'his drives seemed to be full of red corpuscles, like the ruddy face above the kerchief knotted at his neck.' And a quay-side vendor in Sydney famously sold his lettuces by calling out, 'Only a shilling and 'earts as big as Freddie Brown's.'

"He was a great mixer," Keith recalls of the 68-year-old Brown. "He could get on with anybody, whatever their walk of life. He had this wonderfully large personality. He could laugh, and he could take success and failure. Nothing ever seemed to bother him.

"I can see us in these two beds in a dormitory in some college in Adelaide. There were mosquitoes everywhere, and he was covered in bites. He wasn't one hundred per cent at the time, but he never gave way.

"I'll never forget the day he left. He had to go early, and he didn't want to. He was visiting his old stamping grounds, and he was with young people he liked. He'd given them all so much attention. When he went out of the dressing room for the last time, he looked so sad."

Freddie Brown, Don Bradman, Nigel Felton (tour captain) and Keith

And the results on the field?

"We didn't do badly. We drew the series, but it was a real eye-opener to see the quality of young Australian cricketers everywhere we went. Our man of the tour was Kim Barnett. He scored lots of runs, and he bowled leg breaks. We met up with George Tribe, and he taught him how to bowl the googly. He should have been encouraged to develop his bowling." He pauses to deliver a familiar line: "And he should have played much more for England."

He has used much the same words about the Derbyshire miner Les Jackson, the Durham-born Colin Milburn, and the little lad from Warrington, Neil Fairbrother. He says it about Matthew Maynard, from Anglesey, and Rob Bailey, who came from Staffordshire to Northants like Brian Crump and David Steele before him. They were all outsiders, cricketers with a potential greatness that he feels the English game has been reluctant to recognise and nurture.

"Rob Bailey was a beautiful striker of the ball. He hit it like Milburn, only straighter, whoosh over mid-off. He averaged over 40, and he scored his runs quickly. He was a class batsman, but he only played four Tests. If he and Neil Fairbrother had had the opportunities that others enjoyed ...."

The passion is there, but he holds himself back from saying too much. "Rob was such an unassuming chap," he says. "He went down after they dropped him, but he was still a very fine player."

Keith has moved in the highest circles of Lord's, with Freddie Brown and Gubby Allen, but he has never forgotten the humbler conditions in which so much cricket is learnt and played.

"Nobody loves Lord's more than I do, but I do feel that it would be good for cricket if we took the meetings out more. The North, with all its support for cricket, all its clubs, does feel a bit left out of it sometimes.

"And the divide in schools cricket is a disaster. The private schools and the state schools. How I wish all the schoolboys could play in one competition. I mean, are we one country or not?"

Even with Don Robson negotiating the politics, these were not changes that the N.C.A., the poor cousin of the MCC and the Test and County Cricket Board, could effect. But there was plenty of other work to be done.

Youth cricket saw the introduction of the National Softball Competition, with a semi-hard ball, Kwik-Cricket, modelled on Kanga Cricket in Australia, and a two-yearly international Youth Festival.

There were Under-13 and Under-15 sides, an England Amateur XI, indoor six-a-side tournaments, regional coaches nurturing cricket in the counties. For the first time cricket was recognising that, if it was to survive in the modern world, it would have to put in place national and local structures that had not seemed necessary fifty years earlier when cricket had been the nation's favourite summer game.

"The NCA must succeed or cricket will fail," Cedric Rhoades, the Lancashire Chairman, said. "The recreational game is the base of the pyramid with Test cricket at the top. The stronger the base, the better the game."

"I feel that the cricket establishment missed out on the NCA," Keith says now. "The three separate bodies – the MCC, the TCCB and the NCA – never came together as they should have done, and we used to have such a battle to get money. I had to put in major plans to get £10,000, and an artificial wicket cost £3,000."

In his last years there he became Chief Executive, the role of Director of Coaching passing to Micky Stewart. The administration at Lord's grew and grew: "I remember Micky saying to me one day, 'There are all these computers in there, and we've got holes in the nets."

He retired officially in 1994, but he was retained as a part-time consultant for another two years, working with the Finance Director Cliff Barker on a possible new structure for a unified English Cricket Board. Much of it came into being – though history barely acknowledges his contribution.

*

Back in the early 1980s Keith was responsible for a set of films on the skills of cricket, sponsored by the National Westminster bank, and the one on spin bowling won a BAFTA award. The split-screen, slow-motion comparisons lack the penetrative camerawork of Channel Four, but they were a great step forward in 1982.

"I could see what made Ian Botham such a great bowler. He bowled his in-swing and his out-swing almost with the same action. On the split screen you can hardly tell the difference."

A half-red, half-white coaching ball was manufactured to provide extra clarity, with the film on spin bowling featuring a split-screen focus on the leg-breaks and googlies of the Pakistani wrist-spinner Abdul Qadir.

The film was made at Southgate Cricket Club on the day after Abdul had helped spin Pakistan to their first victory over England since 1954, and their celebrations looked like getting in the way of Keith's arrangement.

"It was ten o'clock at night before I got hold of him at the hotel. The team was going up to Leicester in the morning, and he had the match off. 'Abdul, there's a taxi coming for you at half past seven.' I had to spell it out. His English wasn't that good at that time. And, as I was leaving, he said, 'I have no kit.' So early in the morning we had to get in through the back of the Lord's shop and dress him up."

Abdul, Keith and the film crew

The film shows clearly his grips for leg break, googly and flipper. "He was so co-operative. He told me everything. I liked him a lot. And later he started to ring Joyce and me from all over the place. 'Mister Andrews, what do you think? They want me to play at Kent.' I advised him not to go. I said, 'If you play for an English county, they'll all learn to read you.' He took my advice, and later on he thanked me. In fact, he wanted me to be his manager."

Keith gave the film to the England captain Bob Willis before their next tour of Pakistan. But the scores from Karachi and Lahore did not suggest that it had been of any benefit. With three five-wicket hauls in the three-match series, Abdul was a major factor in his country's first series victory over England, and the film was eventually returned. "Bob Willis said to me that he didn't show it as he thought it might put our batsmen off. He hadn't even taken it out of its cellophane covering."

The film on batting involved a demonstration by Graham Gooch, and this too created problems.

Gubby Allen was listed on the credits as Special Consultant and, with a house just beyond the gates at Lord's, he became a close confidante of Keith. "I had a wedding to attend once, and I mentioned that I was going to Moss Bros to hire a suit. He insisted on my borrowing one from him. It wasn't really my size and, as I was putting it on, he told me that he'd worn it when he was knighted.

"My predecessor as National Coach, Peter Sutcliffe, had developed this stance with the bat up, and Gubby didn't like it. And of course Gooch had got his bat up in the air in our film. I was going to the final editing, and Gubby said, 'I'd like to come and see it.' And I thought, 'Oh my God, he's going to insist on re-filming it.'"

The former England captain was eighty years old, but he was still as keen on coaching as ever. "I bought him lunch. I remember him asking me about these hamburgers. 'What are these things? ... All right, I'll have one.' I could see he was getting tired and, by the time we were showing the film, he'd nodded off. There were no problems with Gooch's back-lift."

Forty-five years earlier, when Keith had been a seven-year-old boy playing improvised cricket in the poorer streets of Oldham, Gubby Allen of Eton, Cambridge and Middlesex had been captaining England in Australia. The game of cricket had brought them together, sharing the same passion for the development of coaching, and Keith had worn the great man's suit.

"For all his severity, I thought he'd really got something. He came into my office one day and gave me a copy of his book. And he'd dedicated it to me."

The page is opened: 'To Keith, with best wishes and gratitude for your great services to cricket. Gubby Allen.'

"Can you believe it? A chap like me. To be thanked like that by Gubby. One of the greatest men in the history of English cricket. It was a very special moment."

The opening scene of the BAFTA-winning film on spin bowling features a knot of children playing cricket on a rough patch of grass on a housing estate. The script, written by Keith himself, was narrated by Tony Lewis.

'A clear sky, a warm summer sun and no school. Time for the serious business of cricket. Which one of these boys doesn't imagine himself as his own particular hero? A Botham perhaps, a Gower, a Richards or Imran. To them this is no makeshift pitch sandwiched between blocks of flats but Lord's. And who knows what enthusiasm like this might bring? Perhaps one day they *will* play at Lord's – score a century, take a hat-trick, bowl at the speed of sound or with the skill and guile of the masters of spin.'

So much of Keith's life and values are on display in these short films: the fascination with the skills, the romance of the game and the determination to create – through education – paths that lead from rough patches of grass to the smooth, well-tended turf of the Test match grounds.

"I had such fun making those films. It was one of the most fascinating times I've ever had in cricket."

CHAPTER 14

A LUCKY MAN

Keith has told me his story, and I have guessed it as best I can.

He was the boy at the end of the school line who by determination became a graduate of the Institute of Mechanical Engineers, the boy bouncing the tennis ball who became one of the best wicket-keepers of his generation.

On a Thursday afternoon in Oldham he stumped Winston Place off George Tribe, and it led to fourteen happy years as a county cricketer. Then, in front of 18,000 spectators, he stumped Ian Craig off Freddie Brown, and that led not only to a tour of Australia but, later in life, to twenty years working for the National Cricket Association.

He stood in for Raman Subba Row, and two unlikely victories led to five absorbing years as captain of a Northamptonshire side full of talented young cricketers.

The unobtrusive keeper from Oldham, he has known the friendship of Frank Worrell and Colin Milburn. He has worn the suit in which Gubby Allen was knighted, toured Australia alongside Freddie Brown and helped Abdul Qadir.

"I've been a lucky man," he says. "And the best day of my life was when I went to watch that football match at Oldham Athletic and I met Joyce."

*

But it has not all been good fortune. The father who walked away, the disappointing Australian tour, the illness on the boat to the Caribbean, the failure of his business and, of course, the county championship he never won.

At his peak he was for many the greatest wicket-keeper in the world, yet he played only twice for his country, in Tests that were nine years apart. He was a victim of the changing expectations of the wicket-keeper's role – and of that chance that Morris edged past him at Brisbane.

"I was at the Centenary Test at Lord's in 1980," he told me casually one day, "and I found myself sitting next to Arthur Morris on a coach. We started talking about that catch, and he said to me, 'I nicked one before that, and you didn't appeal.' And, when he said it, I had a sort of memory of one that went between his bat and pad – and my thinking that there was something funny about it. But I didn't realise he'd got an edge."

He smiles philosophically. "I don't suppose it would have made any difference. But it is all chance, isn't it?"

There is no trace of bitterness.

"I'm so glad that I've written this book with you," he says. "I feel you've put into words what I want to say about it all."

He breaks into a smile.

"I think we'd better stop now. Or I'll be losing my reputation for having such a bad memory."

KEITH VINCENT ANDREW

Born 15 December 1929

Career record
390 matches

BATTING: 4,230 runs at an average of 13.38

Highest score: 76 versus Yorkshire at Harrogate 1957

BOWLING: 2 wickets

WICKET-KEEPING: 723 catches   181 stumpings

ACKNOWLEDGEMENTS

I wrote this book as a result of many visits to Keith Andrew, and I would like to express my thanks to him and to Joyce for making me so welcome each time. It was a long journey, but my little car was always driven in expectation of an enjoyable day.

I had a long day with Brian and Lynn Crump, and that was a great pleasure, too, as were my trips to see Dennis Brookes and Malcolm Scott. I also spoke on the telephone to Peter Arnold, Doug Ferguson, Don Robson and Bob Taylor. I visited Werneth Cricket Club where I was helped by Jack Roscoe. I drew on interviews I have conducted with other cricketers and cricket people, particularly Gordon Barker, Roy Booth, Vince Broderick, Tom Cartwright, Geoff Edrich, the late Geoffrey Howard, Doug Insole, Derek Morgan, Mick Norman, Don Shepherd, Micky Stewart, Rupert Webb and Bryan 'Bomber' Wells. I would especially like to thank Micky Stewart for his foreword.

I would like to thank Jim Ruston and the Jack Russell Gallery for letting me inspect Keith's wicket-keeping gloves and David Yorath for lending me a modern pair. The drawings of the gloves are by Susanna Kendall.

I would like to thank the following for kindly agreeing to read and comment on the manuscript: Ron Deaton, Humphrey Keenlyside, Douglas Miller, Peter Rear and David Smith of Corsham. I am lucky indeed to be able to call on such high quality support.

Most of the photographs in this book belong to Keith Andrew, though I have also borrowed from Dennis Brookes, Brian Crump and Malcolm Scott. The photograph on page 178 is reproduced with the kind permission of Advertiser Newspapers Limited, Adelaide and the State Library of South Australia. The late Geoffrey Howard gave me the two photographs of Frank Tyson and the speed test in New Zealand, and I have reproduced the pictures of David Larter, Albert Lightfoot and Brian Reynolds from the long-defunct *Playfair Cricket Monthly*. If any photographic source believes that they are theirs, they should contact me to rectify the matter.

I have made regular use of the following reference books:
Wisden Cricketers' Almanack
Playfair Cricket Annual
Bailey, Thorn & Wynne-Thomas, *Who's Who of Cricketers*
    (Newnes Books, 1984)
Robert Brooke, *A History of the County Cricket Championship*
    (Guinness, 1991)
Jim Ledbetter & Peter Wynne-Thomas, *First-Class Cricket, 1930-39*
    (Limlow Books, 10 volumes, 1991-2002)
Swanton, Plumptre & Woodcock, *Barclays World of Cricket* (Collins, 1986)

I have also read and occasionally quoted from the following books:
Ian Addis, Mick Dean & Brian Slough, *Brian Reynolds* (Diametric, 2000)
Keith Andrew, *The Handbook of Cricket* (Pelham Books, 1989)

Keith Andrew, *The Skills of Cricket* (Crowood Press, 1984)
Trevor Bailey, *Wickets, Catches and the Odd Run* (Collins Willow, 1986)
Trevor Bailey & Fred Trueman, *The Spinners' Web* (Willow Books, 1988)
Mike Brearley, *The Art of Captaincy* (Hodder & Stoughton, 1985)
Freddie Brown, *Cricket Musketeer* (N. Kaye, 1954)
Learie Constantine, *The Young Cricketer's Companion* (Souvenir Press, 1964)
Matthew Engel & Andrew Radd, *The History of Northamptonshire C.C.C.*
        (Christopher Helm, 1993)
Simon Hughes, *Jargon-Busting: The Analysts' Guide to Test Cricket*
        (Channel 4, 2001)
Len Hutton, *Fifty Years In Cricket* (Stanley Paul, 1984)
John Kay, *Cricket in the Leagues* (Eyre & Spottiswoode, 1970)
Brian R. Law, *Oldham, Brave Oldham* (Oldham Council, 1999)
David Lemmon, *The Great Wicket-Keepers* (Stanley Paul, 1984)
Michael Marshall, *Gentlemen and Players* (Grafton Books, 1987)
Peter May, *A Game Enjoyed* (Stanley Paul, 1985)
M.C.C. Cricket Coaching Book (Naldrett Press, 1952)
Colin Milburn, *Largely Cricket* (Stanley Paul, 1968)
Patrick Murphy, *The Centurions* (J.M. Dent & Sons, 1983)
Patrick Murphy, *'Tiger' Smith* (Readers Union, 1981)
Michael Parkinson, *Parkinson on Cricket* (Hodder & Stoughton, 2002)
Jim Parks, *Runs in the Sun* (Stanley Paul, 1961)
K.S. Ranjitsinhji, *The Jubilee Book of Cricket* (William Blackwood, 1897)
Alan Ross, *Australia 55* (Michael Joseph, 1955)
Alan Ross, *Through The Caribbean* (Michael Joseph, 1960)
David Steele, *Come In Number 3* (Pelham Books, 1977)
Bob Taylor, *Standing Up, Standing Back* (Willow Books, 1985)
Frank Tyson, *A Typhoon Called Tyson* (William Heinemann, 1961)
Peter Walker, *Cricket Conversations* (Pelham Books, 1978)
Chris Westcott, *Class of '59* (Mainstream Publishing, 2000)
Ian Wooldridge, *Cricket, Lovely Cricket* (Robert Hale, 1963)
Frank Worrell, *Cricket Punch* (Stanley Paul, 1959)

also from the following newspapers:
The Times, Daily Telegraph, Manchester Guardian, Northampton Chronicle & Echo, Northamptonshire Evening Telegraph, Oldham Chronicle, Worcester Evening News

from the following cricket magazines:
The Cricketer, Playfair Cricket Monthly and Wisden Cricket Monthly

and from the yearbooks of Northamptonshire County Cricket Club.

I have also had access to an unpublished memoir by Ken Turner.

Keith and I have had a lot of fun writing this book, and I hope that you, the reader, are able to share that with us.

Stephen Chalke

Bath, April 2003

INDEX

(close family omitted)

Acfield, David 165
Achong, Ellis 52
Agnew, Jonathan 177
Aird, Ronnie 67
Alker, Alf 46-7,49,53,80
Allen, David 105
Allen, Gubby 71-2,122,171,173-4,178,181-2
Allen, Mick 83,100,116
Alley, Bill 55,131
Alston, Rex 147,149,160
Altham, Harry 71-2,88,109
Ames, Les 24,87,89-90,107
Appleyard, Bob 77,135
Arlott, John 15,121,160,169
Arnold, Peter 59,74,169-70
Badcock, Ted 47,51
Bailey, Mr 46
Bailey, Rob 169,178
Bailey, Trevor 21,24,29,40,88-90,
99,141,159
Bakewell, Fred 60-1,79
Barclay, John 166,177
Barker, Cliff 181
Barker, Gordon 165
Barnes, Sydney 15,120
Barnett, Charles 52
Barnett, Kim 177-8
Barrett, Mr 60
Barrick, Des 65,67
Barrington, Ken 93,105
Bason, Peter 112
Bates, Fred 55
Bates, Terry 176
Bedi. Bishen 12
Bedser, Alec 11,23-4,26,40,95,103,163-4
Benaud, Richie 29,127
Bennett, Don 164
Berrill family 31-2,36-7,42,59
Binks, Jimmy 11
Blofeld, Henry 153,160
Bolus, Brian 148
Boon, David 177
Booth, Arthur 51
Booth, Roy 159-60
Botham, Ian 109,179,181
Bowes, Bill 21
Boycott, Geoff 12,165
Bradman, Don 33,55,58,82,164,178
Brearley, Mike 121-2,140-1
Brock, Fred 50,52,69,85
Broderick, Vince 60,63,66-7,75,120
Brookes, Dennis 12,25,33,38,60-7,
77-84,88-9,93-4,101-2,
112,117,120-1,123,129

Brown, Freddie 34-5,38,65-7,69,77-8,
80,82-4,166,172-3,177-8,182
Brown, W.C. 64
Bullimer, Leo 62
Burrows, Tommy 172
Cahn, Julien 62
Cannings, Vic 71
Carew, M.C. 103
Carter, Bob 155,176
Cartwright, Tom 102-3,177
Chappell, Greg 12
Cherry, Helen 18
Childs-Clarke, Arthur 65
Clark, Nobby 31,60,62
Clarke, Bob 34,38-9,67,77-9,164,166
Clayton, Geoff 166-7
Close, Brian 12,57,85,104-5,114,147,167
Coldwell, Colonel 38-9,68,70,73
Coldwell, Len 160
Compton, Denis 21-3,25,28,38,40,66,88,94
Constantine, Learie 47,106
Cook, Geoff 169
Cottam, Bob 176
Coverdale, Steve 170
Cowans, Norman 177
Cowdrey, Colin 20-1,25-6,35,84,94,
98,104-5,157,161
Crabtree, Harry 71
Craig, Ian 35,172,182
Crump, Brian 11-4,16-7,100,112-20,123-9,
132,139-53,155,160-1,164,166-7,169,178
Crump, Julie 167
Crump, Lynn 114,167
Crump, Stan 52,113,115,167
Cullen, Leonard 60
D'Arcy, John 91
Davidson, Alan 127
Davies, Haydn 89
Davis, Eddie 67
Davis, Percy 66-7
De Courcy, Jim 34
Denison, Eric 51,171
Dennis, John 59
Dexter, Ted 93,98,102,104-5,107,123
d'Oliveira, Basil 131
Dooland, Bruce 34,82
Duckworth, George 22-4,56,177
Dyson, Jack 49,52,80
Edrich, Bill 22-3,25,38-9,66
Edrich, Geoff 54,79
Edrich, John 13,105
Edwards, Alec 69
Emmett, George 88

Evans, Brian 116
Evans, David 146-7
Evans, Godfrey 8,11-2,15,22-8,31,35,40,
42,73-4,88-91,95,106-7
Fairbrother, Neil 173,178
Farrimond, Bill 49
Ferguson, Doug 16-7,176
Fiddling, Ken 31,58,79
Fingleton, Jack 177
Fitzmaurice, Des 54
Flavell, Jack 152-3,155,160
Fletcher, Duncan 177
Ford, Christopher 157
Freeman, Tich 87
Gallagher, Hughie 55
Garlick, Gordon 65
Garner, Joel 175
Gavaskar, Sunil 14
Gayson, Eunice 18
Gibbs, Lance 8
Gifford, Norman 155
Giles, Ashley 125
Gonzales, Pancho 22
Gooch, Graham 180-1
Gover, Alf 130-1
Gower, David 12,181
Grace, W.G. 148
Graveney, Tom 12,20,28-9,124,131,155-6
Greenhough, Tommy 94,166
Greig, Tony 167
Grieves, Ken 56
Griffith, Billy 102
Griffith, Charlie 8,105,107,131
Grimshaw, Norman 60
Grout, Wally 100
Gutteridge, Leslie 84
Halfyard, David 118
Hall, Wes 8,105,107,164
Hammond, Wally 51
Harbhajan Singh 97
Harris, Jack 33
Harrison, Leo 40,73
Harvey, Neil 24,27,31,33-5,52,74,172
Hassett, Lindsay 33
Healey, Ian 106, 109
Heath, Edward 138
Hedges, Bernard 147
Heywood, Brian 172
Higgs, Ken 150
Hill, Alan 26
Hill, Norman 148
Hilton, Colin 100
Hilton, Jim 49,52
Hilton, Malcolm 46-7,49,52,80
Hoad, Lew 28

Hobbs, Jack 120
Holding, Michael 12
Holford, David 163
Holt, J.K. 52
Hopkins, Gerard Manley 27-8
Hooker, Ron 164
Horne, Kenneth 35
Howard, Geoffrey 21-3,26,78,80,87,89,177
Howard, Ken 100
Howell, Denis 171
Hughes, Simon 86-7,89,97,136
Hunte, Conrad 103-4
Hutton, Len 22-3,25,28-9,34,40,52,
61,65,73,75,89,177
Hutton, Richard 29
Ikin, Jack 54,113,115
Illingworth, Ray 12,58,85,108
Imran Khan 181
Imtiaz Ahmed 131
Ingleby-McKenzie, Colin 122,159-60,165
Insole, Doug 88
Jackson, Les 40,122-3,178
Jakeman, Freddie 32,67,72-3
James, Ted 91
Jardine, Douglas 84,137
Jennings, Jack 117,125,131-2,142-3,145,164
Johnson, Laurie 101-2,114,158
Jones, Alan 147
Jupp, Vallance 31,60-1,79
Kanhai, Rohan 104,131
Kelleher, Harry 9
Kennedy, John F. 121
Kenyon, Don 121,152,155,159
Kershaw, Les 57
Knight, Barry 165
Knight, Billy 84
Knott, Alan 15,95,106-8
Kumble, Anil 97
Laker, Jim 11,40,77,81,98-9,135
Lamb, Allan 127,169
Langdon, David 18
Langridge, Richard 90-1
Larkins, Wayne 169,175-6
Larter, David 12-3,101,112,115, 124-6,
128,142,149,152-3,155-6,159,166
Larwood, Harold 35,168
Law, Denis 158
Lees, Raymond 52
Lenham, Les 176-7
Levett, Hopper 87
Lewis, Euros 148
Lewis, Tony 146-7,181
Leyland, Maurice 64
Lightfoot, Albert 117-9,123,127-8,
143,146-7,150,152,155,167

Lillee, Dennis 12,110
Lindwall, Ray 26,33
Lister, Lionel 64
Livingston, Jock 34,38,52,54-6,58,65,67, 70,77-8,81-3,108,112
Livingston, Marjorie 82
Lloyd, David 176-7
Loader, Peter 22
Lock, Tony 11,40,77,135,165
McDonald, Colin 34
McIntyre, Arthur 11,40,71,73,101
McKenzie, Graham 127
MacLaurin, Ian 134,137
MacMillan, Harold 121
Mankad, Vinoo 52
Manning, Jack 75,79,82-3,87,107, 112,116,134
Marlar, Robin 90-1,94
Marshall, Roy 160
Matthews, Austin 60-1
Matthews, Stanley 124
May, Peter 25-6,29,84,93-4,176
Maynard, Matthew 178
Menzies, Robert 26
Mercer, Jack 11,14,56,59,70,72,77,79, 129-32,142-3,145
Merritt, Bill 63
Meyer, Barrie 163
Milburn, Colin 10,15,112,115-7,119-20, 122-4,128-9,140,143-7,149-50, 153,155-7,159,163-7,173,175,178
Milburn, Jackie 116
Miller, Hamish 145,148
Miller, Keith 12,33
Millman, Geoff 11,95,101
Mills, Granville 47
Milton, Arthur 157
Mitchell, Bobby 116
Morris, Arthur 23-6,31,33-4,69,73,103,182
Muralitharan, Muttiah 97
Murray, John 90-1,95,98-101,129
Murray-Walker, Peter 65
Mushtaq Mohammad 15,130-1,161,163, 166,173
Nelson, Robert 64
Nicholls, Ron 157
Norman, Mick 116,118-9,123-4,128,139-43
Northway, Reggie 60,79
Nutter, Albert 65,77
Oakman, Alan 91
Oldfield, Bert 86,89,106,108
Oldfield, Buddy 36,65
Ormrod, Alan 155
Packer, Kerry 108
Parfitt, Peter 137
Parkinson, Michael 12
Parks, Jim, jnr 58,90-1,93-5,101,106-7,118

Parks, Jim, snr 55
Partridge, Reg 62
Pascoe, John 31
Pepper, Cec 53,55-6,151
Pertwee, Michael 18
Peters, Jim 18
Phillipson, Eddie 114
Pithey, David 99
Place, Winston 54,57-8,182
Pope, George 52
Prentice, Frank 63
Pressdee, Jim 146-7
Preston, Norman 24-5
Price, Fred 100
Prideaux, Roger 83-5,120-1,124,128,140, 143,145,148-9,155-6,159,163,166
Prideaux, Ruth 155
Pullar, Geoff 52
Qadir, Abdul 179-80,182
Radd, Andrew 10
Ramadhin, Sonny 113,142
Ramsamooj, Donald 128-30
Ranjitsinhji, K.S. 86
Redgrave, Steve 168
Rees, Alan 147-8
Reynolds, Brian 67,83,112,116,118-9,124-5, 127-8,140,142-3,145,149,152-3,155
Rhoades, Cedric 172,179
Rhodes, Harold 139,158,161
Rhodes, Wilfred 70,72
Richards, Viv 172,181
Richardson, Peter 84,117
Robertson, Jack 12,38
Robins, Walter 91,93
Robinson, Ray 177
Robson, Don 173-5,179
Rochford, Peter 11
Rosewall, Ken 28
Ross, Gordon 92,99
Rowbotham, Denys 102,151
Roy, Pankaj 32
Russell, Jack 95-7,106-7,109
Saqlain Mushtaq 97
Saville, Graham 176
Scarlett, Reg 176
Scott, Malcolm 13-4,101,115-6,118-20,124-5, 127-9,140-3,145,152-6,158,161,164,166-7
Scoular, Jimmy 116
Shackleton, Derek 125
Sharp, Harry 38
Shepherd, Don 145-8
Sheppard, David 98
Simpson, Reg 25,146
Slade, Dougie 152
Smith, Alan 98-101
Smith, Colin 57
Smith, Edwin 138

188

Smith, 'Tiger'   15
Snow, C.P.   80
Sobers, Garfield   8,12,94,96,105
Spooner, Dick   40,73,101
Starkie, Syd   67
Statham, Brian   22,100,103,105,150
Steele, David   16,120,128,140,143,
    145,148,151-2,155,164,166-7,178
Stephenson, Harold   11,40,121
Stewart, Alec   95-6,109,173
Stewart, Micky   8-9,58,105-6,173,176,179
Stott, Clifford   47
Subba Row, Raman   83,85,93,112,
                   114,129,159,182
Sully, Haydn 128,130,148-50,152-3,155,166
Sutcliffe, Peter   181
Swanton, E.W.   99,106,157
Swetman, Roy   89-91,93,101
Tallon, Don   79
Taylor, Bob   13-5,95,107-9
Taylor, Brian   73,89,101
Taylor, Ken   29
Tendulkar, Sachin   96
Thicknesse, John   149-50
Thorpe, Graham   96
Thrower, Percy   18
Timms, Jack   62
Titmus, Fred   105,129-30,140
Todd, Eric   156
Train, Jack   18
Tremlett, Maurice   71
Tribe, Dorothy   53,72
Tribe, George   24,34-5,39,41,52-9,65,67,
          72,75,78-84,87,89,95,97,102,
          107,112,116,131,177-8,182
Trueman, Fred   12,40,58,77,103-5,114,132
Tufnell, Philip   125,134
Turner, Ken   59,67-8,112,117,
    120,131,139,148,157,169,175
Turner, Mike   127-8
Tynan, Kenneth   165
Tyson, Frank   16,18-23,25-8,31-2,
    34-6,38-42,59,65,70,72,74-84,100,
    107,112,115,117,125,127,139,170,172
Ufton, Derek   89
Umrigar, Polly   56

Underwood, Derek   135,169
Valentine, Alf   142
Venables, Terry   57
Verity, Hedley   51
Voce, Bill   71
Walcott, Clyde   55
Walford, M.M.   51
Walker, Peter   116,144-5,147
Walmsley, Wally   54
Walsh, Jack   62-3
Wardle, Johnny   77,89,135
Warne, Shane   97,109,135-6
Warr, John   123
Warrener, Turner   49,73
Washbrook, Cyril   53,65,78-9
Watts, Jim   13,115,120,124-5,128,
               139,143,145-6,150,152-3,155
Watts, Peter   13-4,115-6,120,124-6,128-9,
               139,143-5,149,152,155,159
Webb, Rupert   90-1
Weekes, Everton   55-6
Wellings, E.M.   108
Wells, Bomber   58
West, Peter   18-9
Wheatley, Ossie   115,144-5,160
White, Crawford   25
Wild, John   39
Willis, Bob   180
Wills, Roy   139
Wilson, Alan   74
Wilson, Andy   106
Wilson, David   176
Wilson, Don   177
Wilson, Lynn   170
Wilson, Vic   114,121
Wooldridge, Ian   103
Wooller, Wilf   147
Wordsworth, William   27
Worrell, Frank   52-6,96,103-6,113,173,182
Worthington, George   28
Worthington, Stan   56
Wright, Doug   89
Wright, Harry   49
Wright, Hugh   59
Yardley, Norman   159

FAIRFIELD BOOKS

17 George's Road, Fairfield Park, Bath BA1 6EY   **Tel: 01225-335813**

The following books are available **post free** from Fairfield Books.

Runs in the Memory – County Cricket in the 1950s
by **Stephen Chalke**   illustrated by **Ken Taylor**

Twelve county cricket matches brought back to life by the memories of the participants – including Arthur Milton, Tom Cartwright, Martin Horton, Dickie Dodds, Dennis Brookes, Jim Parks, Malcolm Heath, and Ken Biddulph.

Cameos of recall are two-a-penny, ten-a-page in this quite riveting book. Right up my street - any romantic's street, in fact. Unquestionably the book of the year.   **Frank Keating**, The Guardian

Paperback, b&w illustrations, 192pp **£10**   *ISBN: 0953119653*

Caught in the Memory – County Cricket in the 1960s
by **Stephen Chalke**   illustrated by **Ken Taylor**

Another twelve county cricket matches recreated, participants including Peter Walker, Keith Andrew, Robin Hobbs, Alan Oakman and Don Wilson.

I commend it wholeheartedly – and not least for the splendid illustrations by Mr Ken Taylor. He won't remember, but once he trod on my toe in the tea interval at Bramall Lane. He could grind my whole body into the ground without trace if he compels Mr Chalke to produce another volume.

Peter Tinniswood, Wisden Cricketers' Almanack

Hardback, colour illustrations, 224 pp **£16.95**   *ISBN: 0953119610*

Fragments of Idolatry – from 'Crusoe' to Kid Berg
by **David Foot**

Character studies of twelve sportsmen and writers whom the award-winning author has admired in his life: Raymond Robertson-Glasgow, Carwyn James, Patsy Hendren, Alan Gibson, Tom Cartwright, Reg Sinfield, Jack 'Kid' Berg, Maurice Tremlett, Walter Robins, Alec Stock, Alf Dipper, Horace Hazell.

Sports writing on another plane.   **Ian Wooldridge**, Daily Mail

Hardback, b&w illustrations, 176pp **£15**   *ISBN: 0953119637*

One More Run
by **Stephen Chalke**, with **Bryan 'Bomber' Wells**

The uplifting and joyful reminiscences of Gloucestershire off-spinner 'Bomber' Wells, one of cricket's greatest characters, all set in the context of Sam Cook's benefit match against Yorkshire at Cheltenham in 1957.

A blissful remembrance of a time when cricket and the world were different. Bomber Wells – there was a summer's day in his face and laughter in his soul.

Michael Parkinson, Daily Telegraph

Paperback, b&w illustrations, 128pp **£8**   *ISBN: 0953119629*

At the Heart of English Cricket
– The Life and Memories of Geoffrey Howard
by **Stephen Chalke**   foreword by **Scyld Berry**
The reminiscences of the distinguished administrator, who managed the dramatic 1954/5 tour of Australia. The Cricket Society Book of the Year 2001.
There is no ennui, no monotone in the telling of his story. This most nostalgic read is also a prescient commentary on the men and the politics of world cricket over the past half a century.   **Frank Tyson**, Cricket Lore
Hardback, b&w illustrations, 224pp **£16**   *ISBN: 0953119645*

The Appeal of the Championship
– Sussex in the Summer of 1981
by **John Barclay**   foreword by **Rt Rev David Sheppard**
The story of Sussex's quest for their first championship, told by their captain.
The immortal Botham's staggering exploits of that year have inspired several hefty volumes, but none comes near the charm, wit and entertainment of John Barclay's recollections.   **Tim Rice**, Daily Telegraph
Hardback, b&w illustrations, 160pp **£14**   *ISBN: 0953119661*

Harold Gimblett – Tormented Genius of Cricket
by **David Foot**   foreword by the late **John Arlott**
A new edition of one of cricket's classic biographies. The story of the great Somerset batsman who tragically ended his own life.
There is no other book like it in cricket literature; no-one else has ever gone – or honestly attempted to go – down into the pit with a cricketer. Mr Foot deserves the admiration and thanks of all who care for human truth in a game which does not always face facts. **John Arlott,** Wisden Cricketers' Almanack
Hardback, b&w illustrations, 176pp **£15**   *ISBN: 095311967X*

Guess My Story
– The Life and Opinions of Keith Andrew, Cricketer
by **Stephen Chalke**   foreword by **Micky Stewart**
The story of a great wicket-keeper and a superb county captain, a man whose abilities and ideas have not had the recognition they deserve.
Hardback, b&w illustrations, 192pp **£15**   *ISBN: 0953119688*

Books due to be published later in the year 2003 are:

Born to Bowl – The Life and Times of Don Shepherd
by **Douglas Miller**

A Bloody-Minded Yorkshireman
– The Remarkable Story of Bob Appleyard
by **Derek Hodgson & Stephen Chalke**